The Siege of Magdala

The Siege of Magdala

THE BRITISH EMPIRE AGAINST THE EMPEROR OF ETHIOPIA

Volker Matthies

Translated from German by
Steven Rendall

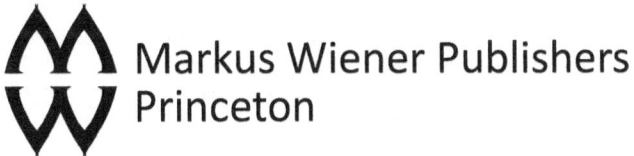
Markus Wiener Publishers
Princeton

Copyright © 2012 by Markus Wiener Publishers, Princeton, New Jersey, for the English edition

Copyright © 2010 by Ch. Links Verlag GmbH, Berlin, for the German edition, entitled *Unternehmen Magdala: Strafexpedition in Äthiopien*, by Volker Matthies

The translation of this work was funded by Geisteswissenschaften International—Translation Funding for Humanities and Social Sciences from Germany, a joint initiative of the Fritz Thyssen Foundation, the German Federal Foreign Office, the collecting society VG WORT, and the Börsenverein des Deutschen Buchhandels (German Publishers & Booksellers Association).

Cover image: Harbor of Zula, from the collection of Volker Matthies.

All rights reserved. No part of this book may be reproduced or transmitted in any form or by any means, whether electronic or mechanical—including photocopying or recording—or through any information storage or retrieval system, without permission of the copyright owners.

For information, write to: Markus Wiener Publishers
231 Nassau Street, Princeton, NJ 08542
www.markuswiener.com

Library of Congress Cataloging-in-Publication Data

Matthies, Volker.
[Unternehmen Magdala. English]
The siege of Magdala : the British Empire against the Emperor of Ethiopia / Volker Matthies ; translated from German by Steven Rendall.
p. cm.
"Copyright [MARC+93] 2010 by Ch. Links Verlag GmbH, Berlin, for the German edition, entitled Unternehmen Magdala: Strafexpedition in Äthiopien, by Volker Matthies."—P. iv.
Includes bibliographical references and index.
ISBN 978-1-55876-551-1 (hardcover : alk. paper)
ISBN 978-1-55876-552-8 (pbk. : alk. paper)
1. Magdala, Battle of, Amba Maryam, Ethiopia, 1868. 2. Ethiopia—History—1490-1889. 3. Amba Maryam (Ethiopia)—History—19th century. 4. Great Britain. Army—History. 5. Ethiopia—Foreign relations—Great Britain. 6. Great Britain—Foreign relations—Ethiopia. I. Rendall, Steven. II. Title.
DT386.3.M38 2012
963'.041—dc23
2011033727

Markus Wiener Publishers books are printed in the United States of America on acid-free paper and meet the guidelines for permanence and durability of the Committee on Production Guidelines for Book Longevity of the Council on Library Resources.

For Bairu Tafla

Contents

List of Maps and Illustrations ix
Foreword to the English Edition, by Richard Pankhurst xv
Introduction: A Curious Campaign xix

CHAPTER 1: Mysterious Ethiopia 1
CHAPTER 2: Tewodros II Defies Queen Victoria 7
CHAPTER 3: The European Hostages 19
CHAPTER 4: The British Empire Prepares for War 27
CHAPTER 5: A Harbor City Built Overnight 53
CHAPTER 6: Embedded Journalists 63
CHAPTER 7: The Long March to Magdala 73
CHAPTER 8: The Aroge Massacre 105
CHAPTER 9: The Assault on the Fortress 115
CHAPTER 10: The Looting of Ethiopian Cultural Treasures 135
CHAPTER 11: Orderly Withdrawal 141
CHAPTER 12: The Victors' Triumphal Return to England 155
CHAPTER 13: Balance Sheet: Military Intervention
     without Colonial Occupation 169

Notes 179
Bibliography 195
Index of Geographical Names 203
Index of Names of Persons 205
About the Authors and Translator 209

Maps and Illustrations

The publisher wishes to thank the following individuals and institutions for granting access to illustrations in their respective collections that have been reproduced in this book: Richard Pankhurst, Volker Matthies, Princeton University Library, and Kassahun Checole of Africa World Press.

Page xviii. Ethiopia today.

Page xx. Map of Magdala expedition.

Page 3. The ox plow was one of the important tools for agriculture in Ethiopia.
> Thomas Holland and Henry Montague Hozier, *Record of the Expedition to Abyssinia, compiled by order of the Secretary of State for War.* London 1870.

Page 4. The fortification of Gondar, which was for two years the capital city of the Ethiopian empire.
> Richard Andree, *Abessinien, das Alpenland unter den Tropen und seine Grenzländer. Schilderungen von Land und Volk vornehmlich unter König Theodoros (1855-1868).* Leipzig 1869.

Page 8. Tewodros setting an example to his men by building a road to transport cannons from Dabra Tabor to Magdala.
> Richard Pankhurst, *Ethiopia Engraved.* London 1988.

Page 10. Emperor Tewodros supervising the crossing of the Blue Nile.
> Hormuzd Rassam, *Narrative of the British Mission to Theodore, King of Abyssinia.* London 1869.

Page 16. The house where Consul Cameron and the Rev. Mr. Stern were first imprisoned.
> Henry Morton Stanley, *Coomassie and Magdala: The Story of Two British Campaigns in Africa.* London 1874.

Page 20. The village of Gafat, near Dabra Tabor, where Tewodros's craftsmen resided and where his cannons and mortars were cast.
> Richard Pankhurst, *Ethiopia Engraved.* London 1988.

Page 24. The British diplomat Hormuzd Rassam, who negotiated between Emperor Tewodros and Queen Victoria.
: Africa World Press, Trenton, NJ.

Page 35. Sir Robert Napier, the commander-in-chief of the British coalition troops in Ethiopia. He was later knighted as the "Lord of Magdala."
: Gerhard Rohlfs, *Im Auftrage Sr. Majestät des Königs von Preussen mit dem Englischen Expeditions-corps in Abessinien.* Bremen 1869.

Page 38. The Port of Massawa on the Red Sea in modern-day Eritrea.
: From the collection of Volker Matthies.

Page 39. The Harbor of Bombay, where elephants were taken on board for the Magdala expedition.
: *The Illustrated London News* (1867-1868).

Page 42. The eccentric Captain Speedy, in one of his typical outfits made of lion skin, with a spear.
: Photograph by Lawrence Lowe.

Page 47. The Swiss adventurer Werner Munzinger, who served as a consultant and translator for the British during the Magdala campaign.
: Richard Andree, *Abessinien, das Alpenland unter den Tropen und seine Grenzländer. Schilderungen von Land und Volk vornehmlich unter König Theodoros (1855-1868).* Leipzig 1869.

Page 51. The British expanded the village of Zula into a major port city as part of their massive logistical campaign during the Magdala expedition.
: *The Illustrated London News* (1867-1868).

Page 56. A bridge for the railroad track built especially for the Magdala campaign by the British.
: Thomas Holland and Henry Montague Hozier, *Record of the Expedition to Abyssinia, compiled by order of the Secretary of State for War.* London 1870.

Page 59. Hindu troops, who were included in the multicultural British invasion army during the Magdala expedition.
: Josef Bechtinger, *Ost-Afrika. Erinnerungen und Miscellen aus dem Abessinischen Feldzuge.* Wien 1870.

Page 64. The *Illustrated London News* with several illustrated reports about the Magdala expedition.
: From the collection of Volker Matthies.

MAPS AND ILLUSTRATIONS   xi

Page 65. The New Pier at Annesley Bay in Abyssinia was primarily used by the British Navy to unload army supplies.
> Painted by William Simpson. In Frederic Alan Sharf, David Northrup, and Richard Pankhurst, *Abyssinia, 1867-1868: Artists on Campaign: Watercolors and Drawings from the British Expedition under Sir Robert Napier.* Hollywood, CA 2003.

Page 70. Sir Henry Morton Stanley.
> Henry Morton Stanley, *Coomassie and Magdala: The Story of Two British Campaigns in Africa.* London 1874.

Page 76. Thirty thousand transport animals were used by the British army to carry supplies.
> From the collection of Volker Matthies.

Page 79. Dragging Tewodros's great mortar "Sebastopol," named after the battle in the Crimean War, from Dabra Tabor to Magdala.
> Richard Pankhurst, *Ethiopia Engraved.* London 1988.

Page 81. Going up to attack Magdala.
> Henry Morton Stanley, *Coomassie and Magdala: The Story of Two British Campaigns in Africa.* London 1874.

Page 91. Maria-Theresia silver dollars were the most commonly used currency in 19th-century Ethiopia.
> Richard Andree, *Abessinien, das Alpenland unter den Tropen und seine Grenzländer. Schilderungen von Land und Volk vornehmlich unter König Theodoros (1855-1868).* Leipzig 1869.

Page 94. Prince Kassai of Tigray, one of the most important allies of the British against the Emperor Tewodros.
> Africa World Press, Trenton, NJ.

Page 101. The meeting between Prince Kassai and Sir Robert Napier in February 1868 near Hawzen.
> From the collection of Volker Matthies.

Page 102. A photo of Prince Kassai and his officials posing with the British officers of the Magdala expedition.
> Africa World Press, Trenton, NJ.

Page 108. Attack plan of the British troops on the way to Magdala. In the center is the plateau of Aroge.
> Thomas Holland and Henry Montague Hozier, *Record of the Expedition to Abyssinia, compiled by order of the Secretary of State for War.* London 1870.

Page 112. A quick-firing Snider-Enfield rifle, which was used for the first time in the battle of Arogé during the Magdala expedition. The breech-loading feature (the gun was loaded in the rear of the weapon instead of in the muzzle) allowed for faster reloading.
> Theodor von Kodolitsch, *Die englische Armee in Abyssinien im Feldzuge 1867-1868*. Vienna 1869.

Page 113. The Battle of Aroge, April 10, 1868. In the foreground, slain Ethiopian warriors.
> Thomas Holland and Henry Montague Hozier, *Record of the Expedition to Abyssinia, compiled by order of the Secretary of State for War*. London 1870.

Page 114. A rocket of the naval brigade, one of the new weapons developed during the Magdala expedition, had disastrous effects on the enemy.
> Theodore von Kodolitsch, *Die englische Armee in Abyssinien im Feldzuge 1867-1868*. Wien 1869.

Page 116. Tewodros with two of his lions. The lion was a symbol of royalty (Massaia VII, 59).
> Richard Pankhurst, *Ethiopia Engraved*. London 1988.

Page 118. Map of Magdala and its surroundings.
> Ferdinand Freiherr von Stumm, *Meine Erlebnisse bei der Englischen Expedition in Abyssinien, Januar bis Juni 1868*. Frankfurt 1868.

Page 127. A drawing of the suicide of Emperor Tewodros on April 13, 1868.
> Richard Andree, *Abessinien, das Alpenland unter den Tropen und seine Grenzländer. Schilderungen von Land und Volk vornehmlich unter König Theodoros (1855-1868)*. Leipzig 1869.

Page 127. The corpse of Emperor Tewodros exhibited in front of the victors.
> Geoffrey Last and Richard Pankhurst, *A History of Ethiopia in Picture*. Oxford 1974.

Page 131. The exit of Emperor Tewodros's defeated army and civilians after the British conquest.
> *The Illustrated London News* (1867-1868).

Page 132. The departure of the freed hostages with their relatives and servants.
> *The Illustrated London News* (1867-1868).

Page 134. List of the principal chiefs liberated from Magdala, showing the length of their imprisonment, and where they went after their release.
> Captain Henry Montague Hozier, *The British Expedition to Abyssinia*. London 1869.

MAPS AND ILLUSTRATIONS   xiii

Page 136. The cross of Emperor Tewodros II of Ethiopia, among the spoils taken by General Napier.
: *Magazine Pittoresque* (1871).

Page 142. Thatched church at Magdala where Tewodros was buried after his suicide on April 13, 1868.
: Richard Pankhurst, *Ethiopia Engraved*. London 1988.

Page 143. Magdala in flames.
: *The Illustrated London News* (1867-1868).

Page 144. British troops retreat to Zula, the starting point of the campaign.
: *The Illustrated London News* (1867-1868).

Page 156. Frontispiece of the *Record of the Expedition to Abyssinia*.
: Thomas Holland and Henry Montague Hozier, *Record of the Expedition to Abyssinia, compiled by order of the Secretary of State for War*. London 1870.

Page 164. The Ethiopian Emperor Johannes IV, the former Prince Kassai of Tigray and an ally of the British.
: Richard Pankhurst, Shiferaw Bekele, and Taddese Beyene, eds., *Kasa and Kasa: Papers on the Lives, Times, and Images of Tewodros II and Yohannes IV (1885-1889)*. Addis Ababa 1990.

Page 165. Prince Alemayehu, son and heir of Emperor Tewodros II of Ethiopia.
: Photograph by Julia Margaret Cameron.

Page 167. Letter from Laqiyaye to Victoria, Jan. 1870.
: Sven Rubenson, ed., *Internal Rivalries and Foreign Threats 1869-1879: Acta Aethiopia*. New Brunswick, NJ 2000.

Foreword to the English Edition

By Richard Pankhurst

The 1867-1868 Magdala expedition into Ethiopia was noteworthy in that it witnessed the use, by the British, of the first modern weapons extensively deployed on the African continent. The opening engagement, which was to prove decisive, was fought on 10 April 1868, when the invading force, which possessed quick-firing Snider-Enfield rifles, as well as rockets, attacked Emperor Téwodros's army on the nearby Arogé plain. An estimated seven hundred to eight hundred Ethiopian soldiers, including the cream of the Emperor's army, were killed, for a British loss of no more than twenty men.

This disparity in the number of casualties on both sides was to characterize European colonial wars for many decades. It found no less dramatic expression in the battle of Omdurman on 2 September 1898 when the British, thanks to their possession of Maxim guns which had by then been perfected, succeeded in slaughtering 10,800 Sudanese and wounding a further 16,000, for a total of only forty-eight British casualties.

Many European writers about the Magdala expedition were profoundly influenced by the imprisonment of Téwodros's European missionary craftsmen, and by their heartfelt appeals for freedom, as well as by the memoirs of the valiant British officers who traveled halfway across the world in difficult mountain terrain to liberate them. Such writers tended to ignore or underplay the above-mentioned disparity in casualties, and chose to present the expedition in highly emotive terms as no less than a crusade for freedom or almost a holy war. Professor Volker Matthies, by contrast, adopts a more dispassionate approach; he refers to the battle of Arogé bluntly for what it was—a "massacre."

Readers familiar only with the writings of Téwodros's captives may be surprised to read, in Matthies's carefully balanced narrative, that the captives, when freed, appeared well fed, and were accompanied by their families and numerous servants. Indeed, some ex-hostages wanted to remain in Ethiopia and resented the British commander's order that they should leave the country forthwith.

* * * * *

Volker Matthies, the first European writer about Magdala to make extensive use of Ethiopian sources, considers almost all aspects of the Magdala expedition, including its consequences for posterity. Looking at the conflict between Téwodros and the British government through twenty-first century eyes, he recognizes that the "massacre" of Téwodros's army in no way justified the looting, let alone the present-day retention, of the country's "treasures," and that there is therefore a strong prima facie case for the repatriation of the innumerable crowns, crosses, and manuscripts from Magdala currently held in British libraries and museums. The institutions holding Magdala loot include the British Library and Museum, the Victoria & Albert Museum, Cambridge University Library, the Bodleian Library in Oxford, the John Rylands Library in Manchester, and the Royal Library in Windsor Castle. If the British victory at Magdala was unusual in not resulting in a colonial occupation of Ethiopia, as many writers assert, it was no less remarkable for the extent to which the country was looted of its cultural heritage.

Ethiopia, like other countries of the Third World, has suffered considerably from such looting, both at Magdala in 1868 and half a century later during the Italian Fascist invasion and occupation of 1936-1941. Objects forcibly taken from the country in the latter period included the great early-fourth-century Obelisk from Aksum, which was transported to Rome in 1937 on the personal orders of the Fascist dictator, Benito Mussolini. The Obelisk was duly returned to Ethiopia in March 2005, as a result of international agitation. The engineers in Rome had first to cut it into three pieces. It then took three flights of an Antonov—one of the largest planes in the world—to bring back to Aksum the three parts, each weighing some 40 tons. There have likewise been numerous demands for the repatriation from Britain of the loot from Magdala, notably by international scholars arguing that Ethiopian children and others have the right to see the cultural achievements of their forebears. These appeals have prompted British institutions that had formerly displayed little interest in such loot to come forward with the novel claim that they were holding it not on behalf of Britain but as part of the world's cultural heritage. Other British curators have argued that their institutions have carefully preserved Ethiopian (or African) artifacts that might otherwise have been destroyed—to which advocates of repatriation reply, "Thank you very much for looking after our property; we are now capable of looking after it properly, so please return it."

We are indebted to Volker Matthies for a sensitive yet well-researched study that is both concise and comprehensive.

Addis Ababa, London
August 2011

Ethiopia today.

INTRODUCTION

A Curious Campaign

In 1867-1868, one of the strangest military campaigns in the history of the relationship between Europe and Africa took place. According to the English author Alan Moorehead (1910-1983), there has never anywhere been a campaign comparable to that of the British army in Ethiopia.[1] Further, the German expert on Ethiopia, Gerd Gräber, states that "In the scope of both its planning and its logistics, the British military expedition was one of the greatest enterprises of this kind in the nineteenth century."[2] With a "gigantic military machinery"[3] the British Indian Army pushed hundreds of miles from the coastal plains on the Red Sea into the Ethiopian highlands, advancing on the mountain fortress of Magdala. There the emperor of Ethiopia, Tewodros II, was holding a few British diplomats and European civilians hostage. The reason for the hostage-taking was Tewodros's anger at Queen Victoria's failure to respond to a letter he had sent her and the resulting diplomatic quarrels. Magdala was considered one of Ethiopia's most impregnable natural fortresses, which were frequently located on almost inaccessible mountain tops.[4] The liberation of the European prisoners was the declared goal of the Magdala campaign, which ended in a great success: the emperor's army was annihilated, the hostages were freed, the Magdala fortress was stormed, and the emperor committed suicide. The British Indian Army then marched back to the coast, got back on its ships, and sailed away from Ethiopia without having suffered major losses. The African country was thus not occupied long-term or subjected to colonial domination, but instead retained its independence.

This spectacular enterprise, which has been described as the "first great 'humanitarian' intervention in world history,"[5] has long interested historians and writers concerned with the history of African-European relations and

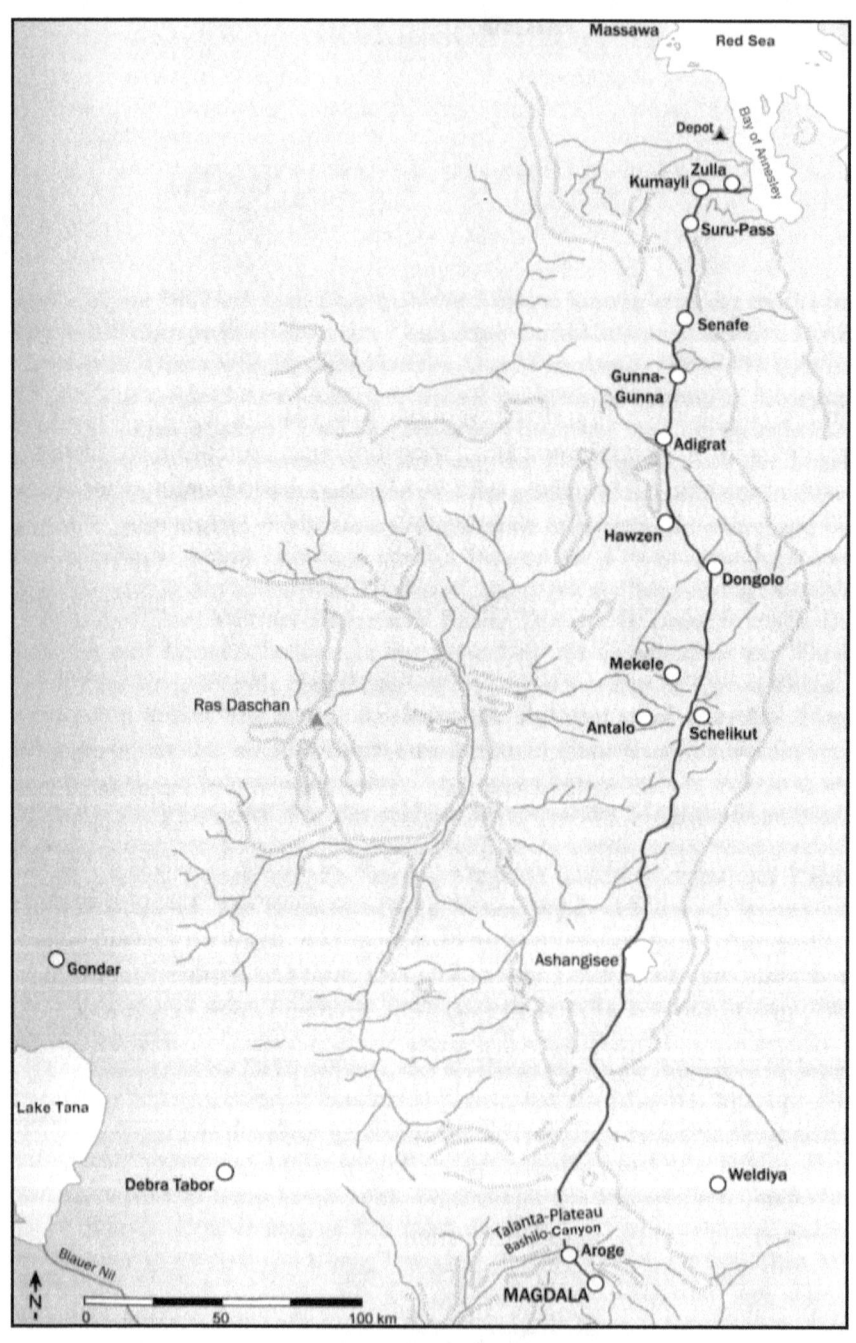

Map of Magdala expedition.

especially with British and/or Ethiopian history. Hardly any "incident in nineteenth-century Ethiopian history can surpass in drama the events that led to the British military expedition in Ethiopia at the end of the reign of King Tewodros II (1855-1868), the so-called 'Magdala campaign.'"[6] This campaign was one of "Queen Victoria's Small Wars,"[7] that is, one of a series of overseas "minor wars" that Victorian England waged all across the globe, in Africa, Asia, and New Zealand, and that were recorded in the relevant handbooks and lexicons of military history.[8] However, these military conflicts, which Europeans described at the time as harmless "small wars," were usually extremely brutal punitive campaigns or repressive measures taken against "rebellious natives."[9] These wars, especially in the course of the Magdala enterprise, involved a collision between the capacities and resources of non-Western, pre-industrial societies and the modern, technological, logistical, and armaments capacities of Great Britain, which was then the dominant world power and the leading industrial nation.[10] In them the incipient industrialization of war in the second half of the nineteenth century clearly manifested itself.

In European-Western societies, the special fascination of this campaign for the participants, contemporaries, and posterity proceeded from different factors: from the exotic nature of Ethiopia, which was at that time still a little-known, mysterious land called "Abyssinia," with its ancient Christian culture; from the dramatic nature of the human events (the uncertain fate of the hostages and the Ethiopian ruler's suicide); and finally from the figure of the illustrious commander-in-chief of the English forces, Sir Robert Napier, as well as from the victorious army's withdrawal from the country. Altogether, from a European-Western point of view, it was an adventurous, romantic scenario.[11]

The Magdala campaign was undertaken in response to a problem that is still with us: one country's citizens being taken hostage by rulers and violent actors in another country. At that time, questions that are still relevant were already asked: How can one cope with hostage-taking in a diplomatically and politically appropriate way? Should force be used to free the hostages?

In dealing with these questions, the prospects and risks of various approaches must be carefully weighed and compared with one another. With regard to the use of force to free citizens held in a foreign country, the Magdala campaign can be considered a "humanitarian intervention" in the strict sense. It points in an exemplary way to the explosive problem of military interventions based on humanitarian motives, with all their many dimensions: violent attacks on the sovereignty of foreign states, complex motivations and possible covert interests, the questionable nature of their "humanitarian" discourse of justification, the difficult decision processes, the role of the media and public opinion, the risks involved in carrying out the interventions, and the tense relationship between law and morality, between prospects and dangers, as well as between the costs and benefits of such enterprises.[12]

Since a certain number of journalists went along with the Magdala campaign, we can also speak here of an early episode of modern war reporting in the sense of "embedded journalism." Moreover, the Magdala campaign had enormous significance for the history of culture and science, and in this respect had "definite analogies to Napoleon's Egyptian campaign of 1798," which "prepared the way for modern Egyptology."[13] The campaign was accompanied by a scholarly staff that included some well-known experts on Africa and Ethiopia, so that in its wake Ethiopian studies—that is, the study of the history, culture, and language of Ethiopia—also bloomed as a result of newly acquired knowledge and confiscated cultural treasures. During the campaign, photographs of the land and its people were also made, and these are considered to be "among the earliest pictorial documents of this country and of East Africa in general."[14]

In both Ethiopia and England, the Magdala campaign is well known among scholars and large segments of the general public, and it is an important part of the historical memory and national mythology. From the Ethiopian point of view, Emperor Tewodros II is revered as a tragic hero, an anti-colonial freedom-fighter, and a martyr. In contrast, from the British point of view, Sir Robert Napier is admired as the glorious commander-in-chief of a victorious army that, to the fame and honor of the British empire, chastised an insubordinate African despot and succeeded in liberating its countrymen without great losses.

Outside Ethiopia and England, the historical significance of the Magdala campaign remained, however, more or less unrecognized. In Germany, this spectacular enterprise has thus far remained virtually unknown outside a small circle of specialists. Only a few Germanophone publications on the history of Ethiopia or Northeast Africa have given the Magdala campaign a certain amount of attention.[15] More specialized publications on the history of Ethiopia and/or Northeast Africa have been devoted to aspects of the campaign, for instance, the fate of the European hostages, the historical importance of the photographic documentation, or the expedition's staff.[16] Furthermore, the Magdala campaign itself had a significant "German" element. Among those participating in it were famous Africanists such as Johann Ludwig Krapf and Gerhard Rohlfs, as well as the Prussian military observers Count G. von Seckendorff and Baron Ferdinand von Stumm. From the Germanophone realm also came the Austrian military observer Theodor von Kodolitsch and the Swiss advernturer and scholar Werner Munzinger. Among Emperor Tewodros's prisoners, there were also "several German natural scientists and missionaries, including Wilhelm Schimper, Eduard Zander, and others whose names have now unfortunately been forgotten."[17]

The sources and literature on the Magdala campaign include a wide variety of accounts, points of view, and controversies. Not only participants in the campaign and the former hostages, but also contemporary and later historians and writers have discussed this exciting episode in African-European or Ethiopian-British relations. We find more or less subjectively colored accounts of personal experience (e.g., those of George A. Henry, Major Theodor von Kodolitsch, Clements R. Markham, Hormuzd Rassam, Gerhard Rohlfs, Count von Seckendorff, William Simpson, Henry M. Stanley, and Baron Ferdinand von Stumm),[18] splendid illustrated books,[19] and the fundamental two-volume official report on the campaign written by Thomas Holland and Henry M. Hozier,[20] as well as analyses and accounts by modern-day historians and writers (e.g., Percy Arnold, Frederick Myatt, Darrell Bates, and Alan Moorehead).[21] Most of these publications have been dominated by a Eurocentric perspective, that is, the "European way of seeing things" that has rightly been repeatedly criticized and now largely corrected by specialists in Ethiopian studies (e.g., Richard Caulk, Sven Rubenson, Richard Pankhurst, Bahru Zewde, and Gerd Gräber).[22] However, it is undeniable that the Magdala campaign plays "a central role in every historical study of modern Ethiopia."[23] By making use of fundamental sources and secondary works as well as studies of the campaign written by experts on Ethiopia, I have sought to take both points of view and their controversial assessments into account. In describing the course of the campaign, I have relied heavily on previously neglected and not easily accessible eye-witness accounts by "German" members of the campaign.

Almost all the drawings and illustrations reproduced in this book are taken from contemporary books, travelers' accounts, newspaper articles, and works by participants in the campaign, or from the official report on the Magdala campaign. By a rare stroke of luck, we have photographs of this campaign made by members of a specially established photographic unit of the Royal Engineers; they are taken from an album on the Magdala campaign that is now preserved in the Wallraf-Richartz Museum / Ludwig Museum in Köln.

The different spellings of the names of places, things, and persons found in the sources and literature pose a difficult problem for the author of a book on this subject. As far as possible, I have tried to regularize these spellings, but have not altered them in quotations and illustrations borrowed from other writers or on the maps reproduced here. In the interest of simplicity, I have also used the term "Ethiopia" throughout, without making a conceptual or linguistic distinction between the pre-modern empire—which in the nineteenth century was called "Abyssinia" by most Europeans—and the modern country of "Ethiopia." The geographical term "Ethiopia" is derived from the Greek "Aethiops," which means "man with a scorched face" ("black"). Geographically, the term originally referred to the whole of Africa south of Egypt, and later to the state or imperial union of the Christian inhabitants of the highlands in the Horn of Africa. The term "Abyssinia" supposedly goes back to the word "Habashat," which the Arabs used to refer to their trading partners on the African side of the Red Sea.

I would like to thank Regina Franck for her painstaking preparation of the camera-ready illustrations, Professor Bodo von Dewitz of the Wallraf-Richartz Museum/ Ludwig Museum for his kind permission to reproduce original photos of the Magdala campaign, as well as Fritz Zickermann and Walter Scholz for their preparation of camera-ready illustrations for the single-volume format. For the acquisition of literature, I cordially thank Antje Bütow and Patricia Milus. Special thanks are due to Dr. Stephan Lahrem and Dr. Angela Borgwardt for their dedicated supervision of the publication of this book. For critical comments, I thank Professor Bairu Tafla and Dr. Verena Böll. I warmly thank my wife Roswitha and my daughter Anja for giving the manuscript an initial critical reading.

CHAPTER 1

Mysterious Ethiopia

As seen by the West, the trackless mountain country of the Horn of Africa in which the Magdala campaign took place in the late 1860s was then still surrounded by an exotic aura. The march on Magdala required a climb from the coast into the high mountains. The Ethiopian highlands consist of a mountainous area with relatively high rainfall and peaks as high as 15,000 feet, which rise steeply from the surrounding arid lowlands. As a result of heavy, prolonged erosion the area has been cut into individual massifs and mesas that are called "amba" in Ethiopian. The seasons are marked by the alternation of rainy and dry periods. Precipitation is heaviest from June to September, and during this time, travel and transportation in the country are significantly more difficult. Therefore the British high command was determined to complete the Magdala campaign before the beginning of the great rainy season.

The geographical seclusion and broken-up nature of the region with its differing climatic and vegetation zones promoted the formation of a multitude of contrasting ethnic groups, cultures, forms of life, and economic activity. The agricultural societies of the Amhara and Tigray people, who adhered to Christianity, had traditionally occupied the northern highlands of Ethiopia, the ancient heart of Ethiopian-Christian culture. Its economic basis was agriculture, using ox-drawn plows to grow teff, the most important Ethiopian food grain.

The heirs of the ancient Aksumite Empire, the two ethnic groups together constituted, as so-called Abyssinians, the politically and culturally dominant "state people" and the politically and culturally dominant center of Ethiopia, to which peripheral and non-Christian people such as the Gallas were subordinate. The people formerly known as "Gallas" and now as

"Oromo" are the largest population groups in Ethiopia. Their original area of settlement was probably in the southeastern part of the country. Over time, some Oromo groups were Islamized, whereas others converted to Christianity and were assimilated into the Amhara culture.

The first state structure in the Horn of Africa was the ancient empire of Aksum, which was established in the first century C.E. in the northern highlands. In the fourth century, Christianity became the state religion of the Askumite Empire. The ecclesiastical leader was called the "Abuna." From that point on, the continuity of the historical tradition from the Askumite Empire to the medieval Christian Ethiopian Empire was communicated through the church. The rulers of Aksum bore the title "Negus Negasti" ("Ruler of Rulers" or "King of Kings," that is, Emperor), which the Emperors of Ethiopia also later adopted. From the end of the thirteenth century to the first half of the sixteenth, the Ethiopian Empire underwent an increasing expansion of political power and cultural blossoming. The famous work "Kebra Negast" ("Fame of Kings") was written at this time, codifying the ancient traditions of the origin and destiny of Ethiopia and becoming a basic legitimating document for the state, the ruling dynasty, and the church. However, increasingly powerful Muslim rivals to the Christian Ethiopian Empire in the highlands of the Horn of Africa arose on its coasts and lowlands, which led to belligerent conflicts. These conflicts reached their highpoint in the "Great War" (1529-1559) between Ethiopia and the Adal Sultanate, which under its ruler Ahmad Gran devastated, burned, and plundered large parts of the Christian highlands. In doing so, Gran was able to draw on the support of the expanding Ottoman Empire, which supplied him with firearms and mercenary troops via the harbor of Zeila on the Gulf of Aden (in modern-day Somalia). The intervention of a Portuguese expeditionary force that also had firearms played a less than insignificant role in saving Ethiopia from a crushing defeat.

Under Emperor Fasilades, the Ethiopian Empire underwent another flowering. The capital city of Gondar that Fasilides built served as the residence of the Ethiopian emperors for two centuries. However, after 1769, the central imperial power crumbled and gave way to a period of constant civil wars and wars for hegemony, the "Age of Princes" ("Zemene Mesafint"), in which various dynastic factions, princes ("rase") and regional warlords battled each other for power and influence. This protracted

The ox plow was one of the important tools for agriculture in Ethiopia.

phase of civil wars (from 1760 to 1769 and from 1784 to 1855) and peasant uprisings was also the great period of the "Shifta," the outlaws in northeast African societies. In terms of the criticism of domination and society, as rebels the Shifta fulfilled very important, widely recognized social and political functions, and in the Ethiopia of that time, their activity was considered a legitimate form of conflict management.[1] One of the Shifta leaders, Kassa Hailu of Gondar, demonstrated, even as a young man, extraordinary military and political talents and the qualities of a successful leader, emerging as a kind of "Ethiopian Robin Hood."[2] Starting in about 1845, he became an important participant in battles for hegemony being waged by the princes of northern Ethiopia, whom he subdued one after the other in various campaigns and battles. Shortly afterward, the victorious Kassa was crowned emperor of Ethiopia, taking the name of Tewodros (Theodore) II.

European travelers and scholars have always been fascinated by the ethnic-cultural diversity and peculiarity of the people of the Horn of Africa, and especially by the Christian Empire of Ethiopia, which was long little

The fortification of Gondar, which was for two years the capital city of the Ethiopian empire.

known. In the Middle Ages, the Portuguese set out to find Prester John, whose legendary, myth-enshrouded kingdom was thought to be in Ethiopia, among other places. The goal was to forge an alliance with this apparently powerful Christian ruler against the forces of Islam. Ethiopia, which was also increasingly threatened by Muslim powers, was interested in an alliance with European Christendom. Since the beginning of the fourteenth century, the Ethiopian emperors had repeatedly sought diplomatic contacts and alliances with the pope and with the Christian rulers of Portugal and Spain. In addition, they were also very interested in bringing in craftsmen, professionals, and above all, weapons technology (firearms) from Europe. Portugal's chief interest was in gaining control of the Red Sea, decreasing Muslim naval domination, and safeguarding their possessions in India. In 1541, when Ethiopia was overrun by the forces of the Muslim Adal Sultanate, Portuguese soldiers under the command of Christopher da Gama, the son of the famed seafarer, made a decisive contribution to the Ethiopian victory—and thus also to the survival of the Ethiopian state and its Christian culture.

Since the seventeenth century, more and more European travelers had been going to Ethiopia, including a number of Jesuit missionaries, but also adventurers and scholars: "They left behind factual material, part of which is of extraordinary value for historical research, and which was recorded in more or less extensive printed travel accounts. Particularly important are the books by James Bruce, Henry Salt, Eduard Rüppel, and William Cornwallis."[3]

In the nineteenth century there was a new wave of voyages of discovery, though now in the context of budding European colonialism and imperialism. Geographical and scientific expeditions pursued not only academic goals, but also diplomatic-political and economic ones. Increasing numbers of travelers, diplomats, missionaries, soldiers, scientists, and adventurers invaded the Horn of Africa and Ethiopia. The occupation of Egypt by Napoleonic France in 1798 moved England to establish contacts with Ethiopia, which lies south of Egypt. To this end and to promote diplomatic and commercial interests, Henry Salt accompanied the British aristocrat George Annesley (Lord Valentia) as his secretary and draughtsman when Annesley traveled to the Red Sea, Tigray, and Aksum in 1804. In 1809-1810, Salt again traveled through large parts of northern Ethiopia on a diplomatic mission for the British government. He reached Gondar and visited Aksum again, studied inscriptions, made drawings, and learned the local languages. In 1839, the English established themselves in Aden. This city at the southern tip of the Arabian peninsula, with its natural harbor near the point where the Red Sea opens into the Gulf of Aden across from the Horn of Africa, was then put under the administration of British India and developed into a major base on the route to India. From then on, the English also took an interest in political and commercial relations with the African coast on the other side of the Gulf. In 1841, England sent a diplomatic mission under Captain Cornwallis Harris to the Shewa kingdom in central Ethiopia and to its ruler, Sahle Selassie, whose chief interest was in obtaining modern firearms. Over the next two decades, until shortly before the Magdala campaign, Harris's notes were followed by other travel and research reports by adventurers, diplomats, missionaries, and scientists from various European countries (including Henry Dufton, Johann Ludwig Krapf, Théophile Lefebvre, Mansfield Parkyns, and Rochet d'Héricourt),[4] who disseminated knowledge about Ethiopia. In addition, in 1862, the German research traveler Theodore von Heuglin had sketched the first view of Magdala and its surroundings.[5]

Thus in the years preceding the Magdala campaign, a good deal of information about Ethiopia was already available and could be used in preparing this enterprise. Nonetheless, there were still many gaps in the knowledge of Ethiopia's geography, population, history, and culture. The campaign, which was accompanied by a scientific staff, thus had a very special significance for future scientific research on Ethiopia.

CHAPTER 2

Tewodros II Defies Queen Victoria

When in February 1855, the former Shifta Kassa Hailu of Gondar, after long years of waging successful wars against his opponents, had himself crowned emperor of Ethiopia, under the throne name Tewodros II, he could already look back on an illustrious career.

    He had been born into a noble family in 1818, near Lake Tana in Qwara province, in part of the Christian Amharan heartland. As a child, he was in the custody of his mother, who, having been divorced by her husband, supported herself by selling an herbal remedy ("Kosso"—from the flowers of the Kosso-Tree) for intestinal worms, and lived in relative poverty with her son. Later on, as the son of a "noble man," Kassa was raised as a warrior at the court of Qwara. He grew up at a time in which his homeland was threatened from several sides: the Muslim Turks and Egyptians repeatedly invaded Ethiopia from the coast of the Red Sea and from Sudan, and the Muslim Galla tribe that was expanding from Central Ethiopia also presented a constant danger. In the long period of wars for hegemony and the turmoil of war during the "Age of Princes," which was accompanied by famines, peasant uprisings, and scientific and cultural decline, Kassa quickly made a feared name for himself as a charismatic and successful Shifta leader. It was because of these experiences that after he had achieved imperial power, Tewodros's chief goal was to unify the Ethiopian Empire once again after long years of quarreling, to bring order to it, and to strengthen it against outside threats. In order to achieve this goal, he built a powerful, disciplined, and well-trained army, introduced fundamental reforms, and accelerated a modernization of Ethiopia along the lines of European technology. With a powerful army that at times consisted of more than 150,000 men, he succeeded in pacifying the country at least temporarily. Moreover, he sought to put an end to the slave trade, to curtail the extensive land holdings of the Orthodox Church, and to promote the use of Amharan as the "living" written language at the expense of Ge'ez as the "dead" ecclesiastical language. However, this policy of centralization and reform earned Tewodros II the bitter enmity of the provincial nobility and the church.

In order to modernize his empire, Tewodros also tried to revive the ancient Ethiopian effort to open itself to the West, in order to find there Christian allies in the battle against Islam and partners with whom he could cooperate in the realm of technology. Yet, ultimately none of his domestic and foreign efforts to this end had much success.

Thus in the last decade of his life, Tewodros found himself faced with increasing internal resistance in his capital city of Debra Tabor and demands made by foreign powers. Starting in 1855, the year of his coronation as emperor, the internal opposition on the part of the Church and the provincial nobility grew, and rebellions against his rule became increasingly frequent. At the same time, the European pow-

Tewodros setting an example to his men by building a road to transport cannons from Dabra Tabor to Magdala.

ers, whom he had asked for help and technological support, responded to his requests with rejection or indifference. In addition, more and more of his troops were abandoning him, so that by 1866 he could call upon an army of only about 10,000 men. Finally, his real sphere of domination consisted only of the Tabor-Magdala axis, and even this stretch of land was threatened by rebellions. Thus at the end of 1867, Tewodros saw himself forced to abandon his old capital city of Debra Tabor and retreat to Magdala. This retreat to an isolated mountain ridge symbolized the final end of his rule over Ethiopia and the end of his dream of modernization.[1]

Among both his contemporaries and modern historians, Tewodros's character and his violent acts have repeatedly been the subject of controversial debates and assessments.[2] Whereas one writer considers him "as a ruthless and unpredictable tyrant," others saw him "as a ruler who put an end to anarchy and restored the central power of the Negusa Nagast, the King of Kings."[3] No doubt Tewodros II was a complex and contradictory figure who invited both demonization and idealization. On the one hand he was a charismatic leader, a brave warrior, a brilliant general, a resolute unifier of the empire, a far-sighted reformer and innovator, as well as a proud, dignified, and sometimes also generous and humane monarch; on the other hand, however, he could also be an unpredictable, mistrustful, and extremely cruel dictator. The negative traits of his character seem to have grown stronger, particularly in his last years, a development to which the spreading intra-Ethiopian rebellions against his rule and the apparently insoluble conflict with England may have made a less than insignificant contribution.[4]

In the middle of the nineteenth century, the British empire had at first shown genuine interest in having friendly relations with all countries lying along the strategically important route to India. This held in particular for the region of the Red Sea and East Africa. From the vantage point of Aden, English diplomats' attention turned increasingly toward the African coast on the other side of the Gulf. Accordingly, in March 1855, the Foreign Office therefore sent William C. Plowden, the British consul residing in the harbor city of Massawa and engaging in trade with Ethiopia, to Gondar, where he was to conclude with Tewodros II a treaty of friendship and trade. Plowden, an experienced diplomat and expert on Ethiopia, and his secretary, John Bell, soon succeeded in winning the emperor's trust and estab-

Emperor Tewodros supervising the crossing of the Blue Nile.

lishing amicable relations with him. Bell, who was married to an Ethiopian and could speak the language, even became one of the Tewodros's closest counselors. Both Englishmen later lost their lives in battles against the emperor's enemies.

Plowden's successor as consul was Captain Charles Duncan Cameron, who traveled from Massawa and arrived in Tewodros's military camp on October 7, 1862. Cameron thanked the emperor for the honorable treatment of his predecessor and gave him a pair of silver pistols with an engraved dedication. Thereupon the emperor decided, on October 29, 1862, to write a letter to Queen Victoria, in which he emphasized his own importance as the ruler of Ethiopia and asked the "Christian queen" of England for support in his battle against Islam and the "Turks." Since this letter was to become the source of all the later misunderstandings, hostage-takings, and diplomatic quarrels with Great Britain, we may quote in full its most important passages here:

> King Theodore to Her Majesty the Queen.
> (Received February 12, 1863)
>
> In the Name of the Father, of the Son, and the Holy Ghost, one God in Trinity, chosen by God, King of Kings, Theodoros of Ethiopia, to Her Majesty Victoria, Queen of England. I hope your Majesty is in good health. By the power of God I am well. My father the Emperors having forgotten our Creator, He handed over their kingdom to the Gallas and Turks. But God created me, lifted me out of the dust, and restored this Empire to my rule. He endowed me with power, and enabled me to stand in the place of my fathers. By his power I drove away the Gallas. But for the Turks, I have told them to leave the land of my ancestors. They refuse. I am now going to wrestle with them. Mr. Plowden, and my late Grand Chamberlain, the Englishman Bell, used to tell me that there is a great Christian Queen, who loves all Christians. When they said to me this, "We are able to make you known to her, and to establish friendship between you," then in those times I was very glad. I gave them my love, thinking that I had found your Majesty's good-will. All men are subjected to death, and my enemies, thinking to injure me, killed my friends. But by the power of God I have exterminated those enemies, not leaving one alive, though they were of my own family, that I may get, by the power of God, your friendship.

> I was prevented by the Turks occupying the sea-coast from sending you an Embassy when I was in difficulty. Consul Cameron arrived with a letter and presents of friendship. By the power of God I was very glad hearing of your welfare, and being assured of your amity. I have received your presents, and thank you much.
>
> I fear that if I send Ambassadors with presents of amity by Consul Cameron, they may be arrested by the Turks.
>
> And now I wish that you may arrange for the safe passage of my Ambassadors everywhere on the road.
>
> I wish to have an answer to this letter by Consul Cameron, and that he may conduct my Embassy to England. See how the Islam oppress the Christian![5]

Cameron was supposed to deliver this letter personally to his queen. But he acted against the emperor's wishes, had the letter taken to England by a messenger, and continued his journey into the western territory along the border with Egyptian Sudan. There he conducted talks with the local authorities on behalf of his government, regarding measures to protect the Christian population of Bogosland (a region in present-day Eritrea) from the attacks of slave traders and also tried to determine the possibility of establishing commercial relationships in the Sudanese cotton trade.

The Ethiopian emperor's letter did reach England and the Foreign Office, but it was met with little favor. The British empire's interests in Northeast Africa and the region of the Red Sea were quite different from those of the Ethiopian emperor.[6] The English did not want to conduct a Christian "crusade" against Islam, but instead to cooperate politically, strategically, and commercially with the Ottoman Empire, Egypt, and Sudan. This was not only in order to protect the route to India. The Ottoman Empire was also supposed to be supported as a buffer against Russia's plans for expansion into Central Asia. As a result of the American Civil War, deliveries of cotton from the southern United States to the British textile industry were declining; thus the British were increasingly dependent on Egyptian-Sudanese cotton. In view of these interests, the English Foreign Office forwarded the Ethiopian emperor's letter to the India Office, where it was preserved but not answered.[7] Thus it was ultimately the incompatibility of the current interests of Ethiopia and Great Britain that provided the background for the escalating conflict between the two countries.[8]

When Emperor Tewodros received no answer to his letter and Cameron's travels in the Sudanese border region became known, he became increasingly disappointed, hurt, and mistrustful of the English government's behavior. Originally, the emperor had been very pro-British, not least as a result of his deep affection for Consul Plowden and his secretary Bell, both of whom had given their lives for him.[9] Tewodros admired Great Britain as a leading industrial nation and saw in the Christian kingdom of England a natural ally in the battle against the Muslim Turks and Egyptians. The queen of England's silence deeply wounded his pride and his dignity. In addition, he resented Cameron for not delivering his letter to the queen personally and instead traveling in the western region bordering on Sudan, which amounted to fraternizing with Ethiopia's arch-enemy. Therefore when Cameron returned from his trip in August 1863, Tewodros received him coolly. Yet, at first the emperor vented his frustration and humiliation on the Anglican missionary Henry Aaron Stern, who had been active among the Ethiopian Jews ("Falashas") since 1859. Stern had made himself a suspect not only by the photographic equipment he had brought with him, but especially by his good relations with the Abuna Salama, the patriarch of the Ethiopian Orthodox Church and one of the emperor's main opponents.[10] Moreover, Stern had published studies on Ethiopia containing passages that, in Tewodros's view, disparaged his ancestry and life and were therefore tantamount to a kind of lèse-majesté, which damaged the emperor's standing in England and in Europe in general. Therefore on November 20, 1863, he had Stern and his missionary assistant Rosenthal whipped and put in chains. When, toward the end of the year, a message from the Foreign Office reached the imperial court that contained no reply to Tewodros's letter but merely ordered Consul Cameron to leave Ethiopia and return to Massawa, the emperor had had enough. On January 4, 1864, Cameron and all his assistants were seized, put in chains, and later taken to Magdala, along with the imprisoned missionaries Stern and Rosenthal and other Europeans.[11]

Theodore's Charges against the Missionary Henry A. Stern

Stern had little respect for the emperor, and his imperious behavior offended many Ethiopians. Theodore questioned him about what he had written in his book *Wanderings among the Falashas in Abyssinia* about the emperor's origins and his behavior. Stern was charged by the king with having stated that his mother was a vendor of kosso and with having reflected on the king's ferocity. All enemies of Theodore professed the most supreme scorn for "the kosso vendor's son." In the above-mentioned book, Stern had written:

> King Theodore, the present ruler of Abyssinia, was born in QUARA, a small province on the western borders of AMHARA. His father, HAILU WELEDA GEORGIS, though a reputed scion of Queen Saba's royal line, acquired no distinction in life, and awakened no sympathy or regret at his death. The small fortune of the deceased nobleman was soon seized and wasted by greedy relations, and the poor mother of KASA (the surname of the future King), like numbers more in that demoralized country, . . . was, ere long, driven by want to eke out a miserable subsistence by the sale of KOSSO (the kosso tree grows at an altitude of about 8,000 feet. Its beautiful flowers, which hang in profusion on every branch, are a specific against the tapeworm, from which all Abyssinians suffer), whilst the tender object of her affection found a refuge in a convent at TSCHANGAR, twelve hours south-west of GONDAR. . . .
>
> The King . . . restored the blessings of peace and security to a long torn and bleeding empire, . . . when news of a rebellion in GODJAM forced him again to the field. Goaded to desperation by these perpetual revolutions, his fiery temper burst through every bond of humanity, and most atrocious and revolting deeds were, regardless of sex and station, perpetrated on the hapless victims of his vengeance. The rebellion was crushed in blood . . .

(Source: Henry A. Stern, *Wanderings among the Falashas in Abyssinia*; together with a "Description of the Country and its various Inhabitants," London, 1862, pp. 62-63 and p. 80.)

In his later book, *The Captive Missionary*, Stern wrote about the charges against him:

> Ten articles, I believe, were preferred against me. They were nearly all garbled, perverted, and disconnected extracts from notes and diaries, which the base minions of the tyrant, in the hope of favour and reward, had dexterously disposed to suit their own and their employer's murderous design. The most formidable crimes alleged against me were, that I had stated his Majesty had no good counsellors; that he had plundered various districts; . . . that I had said that at Dubark, on the Woggera plateau, the king had murdered in cold blood between 700 and 800 people; and, finally, that I was in correspondence with the Metroplitan, and had a few harmless letters from him in my possession.

(Source: Henry A. Stern, *The Captive Missionary: Being an Account of the Country and People of Abyssinia Embracing a Narrative of King Theodore's Life and His Testament of Political and Religious Missions*, London, 1868, pp. 96-97.)

In April 1864, Great Britain's political resident in Aden, William Merewether, communicated the news of Cameron's imprisonment to the government in London. The Foreign Office promptly drew up a letter bearing the royal seal. A small diplomatic mission consisting of a head, Hormuzd Rassam, and his two assistants, Dr. Henry Blanc and Lieutenant W. F. Prideaux, was then assigned to take the letter to Ethiopia and deliver it to Tewodros II, in order to secure an amicable release of the hostages. However, since Tewodros did not allow the English diplomats to enter his coun-

The house where Consul Cameron and the Rev. Mr. Stern were first imprisoned.

try until August, 1865, the arrival of Rassam's mission at the imperial court was delayed until January 26, 1866. After a quite friendly reception, the prisoners held in Magdala were at first released and brought to the emperor's military camp. However, when Rassam and his Ethiopian escort tried to leave Ethiopia, they were also held, evidently as a kind of pledge for further negotiations with England. Rassam wrote to Queen Victoria on behalf of the emperor. He told her about the release of the prisoners and also asked her to send craftsmen and all kinds of technological equipment in order to help modernize Ethiopia.[12] On April 21, 1866, two letters to this effect were sent to the English government, while the briefly released hostages were taken as prisoners again and taken to Magdala, along with the members of the Rassam mission.

On July 8, 1866, the letters reached the government in London, which at that point still clearly wanted to avoid an expensive and risky attempt to free the hostages by force.[13] Therefore craftsmen were recruited, and machines and tools were made ready and shipped to Magdala in November 1866. At the same time, in a letter of reply to Tewodros Victoria sharply condemned the hostage-taking, and indicated that she would allow the craftsmen to enter Ethiopia only on the condition that all European hostages were immediately freed. When in April 1867, the Foreign Office sent Tewodros a last letter to this effect, and in May 1867, the condition had still not been met, the craftsmen returned to England without having done anything. This marked the end of diplomatic efforts to arrive at a mutual, peaceful solution to the hostage problem.[14]

In the expanding hostage affair between Ethiopia and England—in April, Tewodros had more Europeans detained—an intellectual conflict in European-African relationships emerged that went beyond the previously mentioned incompatibility of interests. From the British point of view, the detention of diplomats and European hostages was a clear breach of established international law—a violation of the principles of immunity—as well as an offense against the code of behavior in civilized dealings between nations. From the Ethiopian point of view, the taking of hostages was absolutely in accord with the country's customs, which allowed groups involved in political conflicts to take members and relatives of the opposing party hostage.[15] Thus the hostages held by Emperor Tewodros in Magdala included not only his European prisoners but also dozens of high-ranking Ethiopians.

CHAPTER 3

The European Hostages

Even today, the total number and exact identity of the Europeans taken hostage by Tewodros remain unclear, especially if one takes into account their wives—some of whom were Ethiopians—and their children. The journalist Henry Morton Stanley, who accompanied the Magdala campaign, gave the number of the hostages released as 61, along with 187 servants.[1] Theophil Waldmeier and Georg Wilhelm Schimper, who were among the hostages, mentioned 59 and 64 hostages, respectively; Clements Markham, a scientist participating in the campaign, mentioned 67.[2]

In various publications focusing on the Magdala campaign, there are lists that give differing data regarding the total number, names, countries of origin, professions, marital status, and family relationships of the hostages. Finally, through photo-historical investigation and a comparison of the lists with other written sources, Gerd Gräber, an expert on Ethiopia, was able to arrive at a fairly precise identification of the former hostages in photographs and to discover previously unknown details of their biographies.[3]

In addition to the previously named Englishmen, a group of German and Swiss missionaries connected with the Protestant St. Chrishona pilgrim mission, based near Basel, was also drawn into the intensifying conflict. They had come to Ethiopia in 1856 to "work as simple craftsmen among the Ethiopian Christians," as they put it, "and thereby stimulate a 'revival' of the Ethiopian Orthodox Church."[4] Among these missionaries were Theophil Waldmeier, Christian Friedrich Bender, Johannes Meyer, and Johann Gottlieb Kienzlen. The Ethiopian emperor, who esteemed above all their technical abilities, willingly accepted these missionary craftsmen and assigned them a place to live and work in Gafar, not far from his residence in Debra Tabor. Tewodros wanted to establish a technology center there in order to modernize, with European help, his country and especially his army. Over time, an almost "European" settlement with a strong "German" component developed in Gafar, a kind of "oasis of European culture" in which not only the missionaries but also various other Europeans from England, France, Poland, and Switzerland lived with their families.[5] This European community gradually adapted to the local customs, some of it members learning the Amharan language, wearing the local clothing, and also marrying local (Ethiopian) women. However, conflicts repeatedly arose within this community, for example because of mixed marriages, behavior with respect to Emperor Tewodros, lack of money, and the failure of most Ethiopian Christians to respond to the efforts of the European missionaries. In addition, in 1859, rivalry between different groups emerged as a result of the appearance of the English Jewish missionary Henry Aaron and the subsequent defection of the Chrishona brother Martin Flad to the London Jewish Mission Society. However, Stern and Flad devoted themselves primarily to the Falashas, the Ethiopian Jews.

The village of Gafat, near Dabra Tabor, where Tewodros's craftsmen resided and where his cannons and mortars were cast.

From 1862 onward, the Chrishona brothers were occupied chiefly with the construction of cannons for the Ethiopian emperor, and they also accompanied him on his campaigns in order to maintain the artillery they had manufactured.[6] Moreover, Waldmeier also frequently served as Emperor Tewodros's interpreter. The German adventurer and naturalist Georg Wilhelm Schimper, a fellow prisoner, later described the fate of these craftsmen-missionaries and how they were forced to construct cannons:

> They were expected to fabricate cannons in accord with the emperor's command, a task they knew nothing about, and when they explained that they could not do it, they were locked up and their assistants were beaten. During their detention, when they were given their daily bread they were told: "Do it or you're dead!" A book with technological content happened to fall into their hands and became a kind of teacher that was their immediate salvation. . . . Soon thereafter they produced a four-pounder cannon, and now the emperor himself came to supervise the work and to accelerate it, that is, he beat these respectable men. . . . In order to make them more obedient, they were repeatedly locked up and their possessions, clothes, and food reserves confiscated until they completed another project. . . . There is no doubt that it was these respectable men who were the most grievously mistreated. They were Bender from Staufenberg in Baden, Kienzlen and Meier from Württemberg, Saalmüller from Saxony, and Waldmeier from Switzerland.[7]

Schimper himself belonged to a group of German adventurers and naturalists who had also been taken as prisoners, "whose life-histories have now fallen almost completely into oblivion, and some of whom had a significant influence on the development of Ethiopia in the nineteenth century. . . ."[8] For this reason two of these figures must be described in somewhat greater detail here: the previously mentioned Georg Wilhelm Schimper and Eduard Zander.

Schimper, a botanist born in Mannheim on August 19, 1804, first learned the turner's trade, then became a soldier, and later studied natural science.[9] After extensive travels around the Mediterranean, he arrived in Egypt in 1834, then spent a few months in Arabia, where he studied, among other things, the flora around the holy city of Mecca. In late 1836, he went to Massawa to study the Ethiopian plant world. He lived for some years in the city of Adwa in northern Ethiopia as a "physician" and "architect" (though without professional training in these professions), enjoyed the favor of Prince Ubie, and built a palace for the latter, receiving a few estates as his reward. In 1843, he decided to remain permanently in Ethiopia and to marry an Ethiopian woman. They had three children, a son and two daughters, who later married the German missionaries Bender and Kienzlen, who were living in Gafat. Schimper was able to follow the hostage drama at close range, especially since he himself was taken prisoner:

> When I tried to take my leave of Tewodros, I was ordered to stay. From 1863 to 1865 I had the opportunity to carry out my scientific work, but when Tewodros came to Gafat, this freedom ended, and I partly shared the fate of the other Europeans; I was forbidden to go out, but I was not forced to work. Finally Tewodros had the large province of Begemeder plundered, and was therefore forced to fortify to a certain extent his camp in Debra-Tabor, where we Europeans were being detained. In close company with foul and disgusting vermin, we had to spend the insalubrious rainy season from April to October shut up in temporary huts and tents, my unfortunate countrymen were forced to work day and night, but I was allowed to remain in my wretched hut, working on my trigonometric survey maps of Begemeder and Tigray. The preceding year, when Tewodros had finished completely looting the great province of Begemeder and burned all the villages, he headed for Magdala with his army, which was diminishing daily as a result of desertion; we had to go along and witness the destruction by fire of all the inhabited places and the murder of the captured inhabitants. Because roads were built during the march, we arrived in Magdala only on

March 26, 1868. Although I had been deprived of my freedom, up to that point Tewodros had treated me with a certain respect, but as the English troops approached I was imprisoned in an imperial arrest tent and closely guarded by a large number of soldiers, though for some unknown reason I was released soon thereafter, that is, I was allowed to return to my tent, where I was no less closely guarded, but felt somewhat relieved and could finish the botanical and geological studies I had written on the trip.[10]

Eduard Zander was a friend and close collaborator of Schimpers', who had spent altogether more than two decades with him in Ethiopia. Zander was multi-talented, an "adventurer, naturalist, painter, architect, and craftsman," but above all a painter and draftsman whose work provided the basis for many contemporary and later descriptions of the Ethiopian landscape and scenery.[11] He is said to have been born in Radegast (Anhalt) on October 22, 1813. In 1847, while on a journey of adventure, he met Schimper in Adwa and became the latter's closest collaborator. Like Schimper, Zander married an Ethiopian woman who bore him children. Later Zander was involved in the violent conflicts between Kassa (the later Tewodros II) and Prince Dajazmach Webe, whose artillery he commanded during the battle of Deraskie (1855). After the defeat of his master, he went over to Kassa, who made him the commander of the fortified Gorgora peninsula on Lake Tana. In 1859, Zander wrote in the mountain fortress of Magdala a work on "The Agriculture of Abyssinia," which was subsequently published in a popular contemporary German book on Abyssinia.[12] Later on, Zander was also taken hostage and was forced to construct cannons for Emperor Tewodros.

Among the diplomats held hostage, the most prominent figure was probably Hormuzd Rassam, a Christian from the Ottoman Empire. He was born in Mosul in 1826 and converted to Protestantism in his youth. While still a young man, he had assisted the English researcher and archaeologist Austin Layard in his famous excavations in the ancient Assyrian city of Nineveh (in modern-day Iraq). Later he served as England's diplomat in Aden and Zanzibar. In 1864, he was chosen, because of his knowledge of languages and diplomatic skills, to deliver Queen Victoria's letter to Emperor

Tewodros, who responded by taking him hostage.[13]

Faced with threatening dangers, this very diverse group of European hostages did not stick together but instead was often internally divided and cultivated its mutual animosities.[14] A French adventurer named Bardel was even thought to be a spy for Tewodros who denounced other Europeans and betrayed secrets. Obviously, in Gafat, the Europeans' cohabitation was already largely marked by "intrigues, petty jealousies, and slanders," which continued after the hostages were released.[15]

During the time they were detained, it may also have been due to the different ways in which they were treated. There were differing degrees of abuse and discomfort or of freedoms and comfort. One group of hostages, which Tewodros for the most part treated benevolently, was that of the Chrishona brotherhood. The group he most hated was the English Jewish missionaries, especially Henry Aaron Stern, whose writings he thought insulted him and disparaged his honor and dignity. He was just as hostile to the English diplomat Cameron and his staff, whose conduct and detention had led to the conflict with England. In contrast, he sometimes treated England's later diplomatic mission, consisting of Rassam, Blanc, and Prideaux, comparatively better. Finally, there were also the two German naturalists, Schimper and Zander, to whom Tewodros granted a relatively large measure of freedom.

To judge by various reports, the treatment of the hostages, with the exception of the English diplomats and missionaries, was evidently not quite

The British diplomat Hormuzd Rassam, who negotiated between Emperor Tewodros and Queen Victoria.

as dramatic as English propaganda often claimed.[16] The hardest part was probably the constant fear of the unpredictable moods of the emperor, who threatened them with torture or death.[17] Otherwise, the hostages were treated very well: they lived in huts of the usual local kind, with a certain degree of comfort (chairs, beds, tables, and cooking facilities), and also had access to their Ethiopian servants, their luggage, and their food reserves, and were able to eat quite well (home-baked bread, soup, fish, meals with several courses, dessert, cream cheese, honey-wine, arrak and rum). In addition, they were allowed to receive seeds from the British consular agent Merewether and to grow their own vegetables (peas, potatoes, and tomatoes). They were not permitted to leave their assigned housing, but they were still able to send reports to the coast or to receive reports from there. High-ranking Ethiopian figures were also commonly offered the company of young women as companions. On the whole, however, monotony and oppressive boredom prevailed, and this repeatedly led to dissensions among the hostages. Rassam was able to arbitrate or calm most of these conflicts. Apparently the English diplomats and missionaries functioned as a kind of "governing committee" for all the European hostages.

CHAPTER 4

The British Empire Prepares for War

After it became known in London that Tewodros had taken the British consul Cameron hostage on January 4, 1864, British politics constantly had to cope with the hostage crisis. Taking a British diplomat hostage was seen as a flagrant violation of established international law and also as a humiliating insult to England's national honor. It was only after three and a half years of futile diplomatic efforts to find a peaceful solution to the conflict that violent measures against Tewodros were considered. For a long time, the British shrank from resorting to a military operation to free the English and other European hostages. On the one hand, English politics and public opinion were still under the impact of the Crimean War, which Great Britain had waged against Russia, along with France and Turkey, from 1854 to 1856, and in which the British army had made a shameful impression. In addition to the incompetence of the military leadership, the chaotic organization of the operation and the wretched supply and medical care for the soldiers had been the subject of massive criticism.[1] On the other hand, the British were witnessing Napoleon III's disastrous Mexican intervention in Mexico.[2] The Austrian archduke Maximilian, who had been made emperor of Mexico in 1864 at the instigation of Napoleon III and with the support of French troops, ruled haplessly and ultimately had to yield to the pressure exercised by Mexican independence fighters and by the United States. The French troops left Mexico, Archduke Maximilian was taken as prisoners, court-martialed, and shot on June 19, 1867. It was feared that English troops might suffer a similarly humiliating defeat in Ethiopia. Finally, the immense cost of such a military campaign had to be taken into account; it was estimated that it would amount to millions of pounds.[3]

In parliament and in public opinion, all these arguments and reservations were the object of controversial debate.[4] As a result, there was steadily growing pressure on both the political class and the government to adopt a harder attitude in the hostage affair.[5] Neither the Liberals under William Gladstone nor the Conservatives under Benjamin Disraeli could escape this pressure. Above all, both the hostages' family members living in England and the press demanded more energetic action against the Ethiopian emperor.[6] The newspapers reported on the related parliamentary debates, provided their readers with up-to-date information about the condition of the hostages, and published the latter's letters of petition and complaint addressed to their relatives in England, making public discussion of the hostage affair more emotional.[7] The English attitude clearly hardened after it was learned that the diplomatic mission under Rassam, which was supposed to arrive at a mutual and peaceful solution to the hostage problem, had itself been taken hostage.[8]

Although in the public debate the prevailing opinion was that the main reason for the hostage affair and the coming war against the Ethiopian emperor was the British government's failure to deal properly with Tewodros's letter to the queen,[9] in view of the prolonged, fruitless negotiations with Tewodros, people were increasingly prepared to make an example of him. As the Austrian military observer Kodolitsch wrote:

> The petitions and pleas addressed to the English government by the prisoners, who had been for years in daily, indeed hourly danger of death, became increasingly urgent; a few influential men spoke out in the same vein and referred to the necessity of upholding the authority and dignity of the British name and the British national honor by means of an exemplary chastisement of behavior that mocked every human and international law, and thereby indirectly protecting the lives and security of so many hundreds of consuls exposed to half and wholly savage peoples, so many thousands of British subjects, and finally, trade and British industry. Soon voices were also heard in the press taking the same view, until finally the all-pow-

erful public opinion gave the government the final and decisive impetus.[10]

William Merewether, Great Britain's diplomatic resident in Aden, played a particularly important role in instigating the war, being one of the first to advocate the use of force to free the hostages.[11] He had argued for a military operation in a letter to the Foreign Office written on September 25, 1866, and in the spring of 1867 he recommended the deployment of an expeditionary force consisting of some 6,000 men. In addition, he repeatedly pointed to Emperor Tewodros's dwindling power base within Ethiopia and to the increase in desertions from his army, which would make forceful action against him easier. By publishing various articles in influential London periodicals, Merewether sought to spread a belligerent mood in public opinion. He repeatedly warned that adopting an indulgent position in the hostage affair would lead to a serious loss of British prestige throughout Asia and possibly to further rebellions in India.[12] A decade earlier, in May 1847, the British empire in India had been threatened by one of the largest and bloodiest anti-colonial uprisings of the nineteenth century, the so-called "Great Rebellion" or Sepoy Mutiny. Memories of this dramatic event were at that time still very much alive among the British people and in British politics.

It appears that the Foreign Office began to seriously consider a military option as early as April 1867. But not until the end of June 1867 was an attempt made to authorize the War Office and the India Office to initiate planning for such an option. There were still many reservations and thus considerable caution about making final decisions.[13] According to Captain Henry Hozier's ironic report,

> to the majority of men in England the Abyssinian Expedition appeared foolish and chimerical. Arguments repeatedly appeared against it in the daily journals. Letters from correspondents were inserted in their columns, which drew ghastly pictures of the malaria of the coast and the insalubrity of the country. At times the expedition was to die of thirst, at times to be destroyed by hippopotami. Every beast antagonistic to the life of man was, according to

these writers, to be found in the jungles or the swamps of that treacherous country. Animals were to perish by flies, men by worms. The return of the expedition was regarded as chimerical, the massacre of the prisoners as certain. The climate was hastily laid down as similar to that of the West Coast of Africa. Insurance offices raised their rates mercilessly to the officers volunteering for the service, who were regarded as rushing blindfold into suicide.[14]

Hozier, one of the two authors of the official report on the Magdala campaign, described the tedious, complex process of shaping public opinion and decision-making that led to the dispatch of the punitive expedition: at first, the statesmen involved were

> loth to thrust an expedition into a distant land, shrouded in mystery, where danger alone was certain. The disasters of the Crimea still hung heavy on men's minds. An idea was widely spread abroad not only in this country, but throughout Europe, that through some adverse disposition of the British character it was impossible but that England should fail in any military enterprise which depended more on the spirit of order than on the stubborn courage of her troops. Men in India, confident in the power shown in the suppression of the great mutiny, thought otherwise. Accustomed to treat princes of the more civilized East with a high and restive, who so much as lifted a voice against the English name, they writhed beneath the insult which a British envoy had received at the hands of an African savage. They loudly spoke out their opinions. These were carried home and acted as a stimulus on the minority of public opinion, which did not yet despair of the prowess of the country. The tiny band, which had always advocated the rescue of the captives by force, gained in numbers and brought its weight to bear upon the Government. Colonel Merewether, the Political Resident at Aden, perpetually urged upon the notice of the Foreign Office that force

alone would ever cause Theodore to yield up his prisoners. ... Had it not been for Merewether, the captives might yet linger in chains at Magdala. He was the author of the Abyssinian Expedition. ... It appears that towards the middle of April 1867, the Government first began to contemplate the possibility of an expedition to Abyssinia. ... It was, however, only reluctantly and dubiously that the Government determined upon sending an expedition.[15]

The Abyssinian War from an Abyssinian Point of View

In his article on "Popular Opposition in Britain to British Intervention against Emperor Tewodros of Ethiopia" (*Ethiopia Observer* 16, 1973) Richard Pankhurst wrote (p. 179): "The ranks of the opponents of the war were joined ... by Augustus F. Lindley, who ... attempted to see the dispute through Ethiopian eyes. He wrote a long article entitled 'The Abyssinian War from an Abyssinian Point of View.' ... This notable work ... was presented as having been written by an Ethiopian nobleman, who, inquiring as to the causes of the war, supposedly opens the publication by declaring:

I am what the English would call an Abyssinian, although really a native Amhara. I am a Chief —ARISTOS in my own country, and have been for many years principal counsellor of our brave Negus, Theodore the Second. Strange as it may seem, I have the power of thinking sometimes, and also of expressing my thoughts. At intervals—when the calm spirit of reflection stealeth upon me—I ask myself, whence and wherefore comes the well-armed and multitudinous array which is threatening our beautiful and plenteous land?

Who can it be that comes to injure us? What sin have we committed, that strangers from afar should seek to ruin our country? ...

We find that the fierce invaders ... are directed by the Government of a far distant land—a rich, happy, and powerful country, named Great Britain. It is a great Christian people— a people who make large professions of Christianity. I should like to know their interpretation of Christian doctrines; it is different from ours. Their spreading of the Gospel seems to be the making of wars and the slaying of men in every part of the world, from New Zealand to China, from the East Indies to Ashantee and our country. We are dark, they are fair; they call themselves civilized, us uncivilized: Do these things make all the difference? Yet, I ask, what have we done to offend this great Christian nation? At least our civilized invaders might have considered it courteous to inform us why we are to be killed. They have not deigned to make any official and authoritative declaration of war. What is the term for such style of conducting hostilities in Europe? Is it not brigundage, piracy or filibustering?

. . .

We—anxious to settle our doubts and be assured of your friendship or enmity—sent, through your Consul, an autograph letter from our ruler, begging for your friendly alliance— Well, what did you do with the courteous communication of the Negus? You treated it with the gross insult of silent contempt. This proved to us your inimical intentions, and that the Consul was not sent to us for the purpose professed, for he did not even receive from his government any acknowledgment of the receipt of the Negus's own letter.

. . .

I know your custom with foreign nations not so powerful or civilised as yourselves, O ye strangers from afar! You first send missionaries, then Consuls to support the Missionaries and stray subjects, then armies to support the Consuls, and so you seize upon your neighbour's land, or, if not sufficiently rich and fertile to suit you, kill its men, destroy its government, and leave it a devastated wilderness. This latter system seems to have become your favourite. Is it that of late your proud England has become so surfeited with wronged and stolen lands that her former aggressive and conquering policy—rendered almost sublime by reason of its magnitude—has sunk to the idle and wanton wickedness of waging war simply to maintain the phantom thing your politicians call prestige?

. . .

I have given you ample proof that we imprisoned the captives for seditious writings and treasonable acts; how can you find fault with us? Were you not, at the very same time, daily arresting and imprisoning many of your own people upon a mere SUSPICION of Fenianism? By what law, then are we supposed to be bound to tolerate the treacherous and suspicious acts of men who deliberately thrust themselves in our country, and mix in its concerns, without our permission and against our wish? The fact is that you have one law for the strong, and another for the weak.

. . .

We know that you are an aggressive nation; that in all your wars you are the first to begin—at all events, during the present generation. This is of sinister import and proves your quarrelsome, arrogant, aggressive character. Of late, you always choose weak antagonists upon whom you try your superior and ingenious weapons.

. . .

If the balance of power, the rivalry with other nations, or the trial of the Snider rifle, be not one or all of the causes of your making war upon us, then we must accept your own plea that it is for the keeping up of your PRESTIGE. . . . If you come to fight us to release the prisoners, you wage illegal war; if you are coming to maintain your PRESTIGE you also wage illegal war. You are wrong, whichever plea you choose.

. . .

I do not fear. I trust not in my own power: I trust in God, who says, if you have faith as a mustard grain you can remove mountains. . . . Not only at the time of Cameron—when they (the English) gave no answer to my letter in which I asked for friendship—did I find out that they were not my sincere friends, but I saw it even at the time of Bell and Plowden—those were my friends and out of friendship I treated them well. I leave it to the Lord and He shall decide between us when we are fighting in the battle-field."

(Source: Augustus F. Lindley, "The Abyssinian War from an Abyssinian Point of View," London, 1868, cited in Richard Pankhurst, "Popular Opposition in Britain to British Intervention against Emperor Tewodros of Ethiopia," *Ethiopia Observer* 16, 1973, pp. 179-183.)

After years of debates, fruitless diplomatic efforts, and delays, and after overcoming a great deal of skepticism and doubt, the British government ultimately decided, on August 13, 1867, to liberate the hostages by force. A corresponding ultimatum was sent by Great Britain to Emperor Tewodros II of Ethiopia on September 9, 1867. In this final decision for a solution by force, the government's growing irritation at the detention of its diplomatic envoys Cameron and Rassam played just as important a role as did the growing evidence of Tewodros's diminishing power within Ethiopia.[16] Above all, however, in the interim the considerations regarding the preservation of Great Britain's national prestige had eclipsed the original humanitarian motives in the hostage affair.[17] The "Abyssinian difficulty," as Benjamin Disraeli, the leader of the Conservatives in the House of Commons, called the hostage affair, had become a national issue of the first order: "England could in the course of extending its colonial power allow itself no loss of prestige in the area of the Red Sea, and all the more since this area had gained enormous importance through the construction of the Suez Canal, which was then nearing completion."[18] Whether and to what extent other domestic and foreign policy grounds and motives played a role in the decision to go to war is debated in historical research.[19] It may be that the war against the emperor of Ethiopia came at an opportune time for the political class, because it allowed the population to be distracted from social problems in England (e.g., demonstrations in Hyde Park in 1867 in connection with electoral reforms). Perhaps after the debacle of the Crimean War, England also wanted to show European nations, particularly expansionist France and Prussia, which was growing in strength, that it was absolutely capable of conducting an effective military action.

The responsibility for planning and preparing the Magdala campaign was put in the hands of the government of British India in Bombay and its army, whose area of responsibility extended as far as the Red Sea and Aden, where British India's greatest naval base with numerous transport ships and well-stocked storehouses was located. The native troops stationed nearby were considered loyal and brave, while the British units stationed there were already used to the tropical climate and had been tested in battles against rebellious tribes.[20] Sir Robert Napier, the commander in chief of the Bombay Army who had been designated as leader of the Magdala campaign, was regarded as an extremely competent and loyal officer who had proven his mettle in many wars in the service of the Crown and the Empire.

Sir Robert Napier

The Ethiopian emperor Tewodros's main opponent was General Napier of the British Indian Army, commander in chief of the Magdala campaign and later Field Marshal Lord Napier of Magdala. He was born in Ceylon on December 6, 1810, the son of a major in the Royal Artillery, and died on January 14, 1890 in London. He spent most of his life in military service.[21]

In the opinion of Count von Seckendorff, who took part in the Magdala campaign as a military observer, in deciding on Napier, the British government was counting on "a general with a long and outstanding record of service whose personality was happily chosen in every respect."[22] And Captain Hozier, who was also a participant, wrote "Rightly England made her choice."[23] By his experience, his capabilities, and his character, Napier was virtually predestined to assume supreme command of the Magdala campaign.[24] Then fifty-six years old, he had accumulated in the course of many years in the service of the crown an enormous amount of military, operational, and administrative experience; yet, it was nevertheless unusual for a member of the engineering corps to be chosen for such a command.[25] He was especially interested in and dedicated to engineering and medical services, as well as logistics, which was to prove particularly important for the success of the Magdala campaign. The writer Alan Moorehead compared Napier with generals such as Charles George Gordon and Horatio Herbert Kitchener, who later led military campaigns against the Mad-

Sir Robert Napier, the commander-in-chief of the British coalition troops in Ethiopia. He was later knighted as the "Lord of Magdala."

hists in Sudan, and attributes to him the same degree of competence, but also a friendlier nature and more modesty.[26] He could be sure of the respect and loyalty of both his superiors and his subordinates.[27]

At the age of fourteen, he entered the East India Company's military college in Addiscombe (Surrey) and was then assigned to the Bengal Engineers where he received training in engineering. In 1828, at the age of eighteen, he arrived in India. There he worked for many years in the department of public works as an engineer and sapper, and he accumulated a broad and varied practical experience by building roads, bridges, military camps, and defensive fortifications. He distinguished himself by his many innovations. For example, in 1842 Napier showed his talent by building a new kind of better-illuminated, airier, more spacious barracks that significantly improved the hygiene and quality of life of the soldiers who lived in them. These structures were later called "Napier barracks" in his honor.

Napier learned and practiced his particular brand of military craftsmanship in the British empire's various colonial-imperialist wars of conquest and repression. For example, in the Sepoy Mutiny in India and the Taiping rebellion in China, he participated, as a loyal soldier of the Crown, in some of the bloodiest and most brutal warfare, thereby earning his superiors' respect as a military technocrat. He first engaged in military action in 1845 as a young officer (captain and later major) of the military engineers in the Sikh wars, in which he was seriously wounded. When in 1857 the "Great Rebellion," the anti-British mutiny of the Sepoys (Muslim mercenaries employed by the British military), broke out and was cruelly crushed within a few months by British soldiers and loyal Sikh troops, Napier, who had been promoted to chief of staff, was part of the army that marched on the Indian city of Lucknow, which had been besieged by the enemy. In the course of the fighting, Napier suffered a second serious injury. After his recovery, he directed, as general and leader of the sappers, the successful works for the reconquest of Lucknow. During the battle for Lucknow, Napier had a series of mines lain that "were unparalleled in the modern art of war."[28] In 1860, during the repression of the Taiping Rebellion in China, which was directed against foreign domination by Europeans and the foreign dynasty of

> the Manchus (1852-1864), Napier commanded an infantry division that stood out in particular in the course of the storming of the Taku forts. The battles fought during the Taiping Rebellion resulted in high casualties among the native population and broad domination of China. For his new military achievements, Napier was promoted to the rank of major-general. After his return from China, he became a member of the General Governor's advisory council and then, with the rank of lieutenant general, the commander-in-chief of the Bombay Army. In this top position, Napier had many opportunities to acquire administrative and political competencies as well.
> The high point of his career, however, was the successful conduct of the Magdala campaign, which won him great honor and fame and the title of "Lord Napier of Magdala."

The British Indian Army, writes the German historian Dierk Walter, was "Great Britain's colonial army itself, and fought in this capacity in East Africa, the Near East, and in South Asia and East Asia. . . . India was the heart of the Empire, and a large part of Great Britain's imperial activities in East Africa and South Asia served indirectly to ensure its domination in India. Therefore it was ultimately only consistent that the sea route to India was defended by the Indian Army in East Africa and Arabia as well."[29] The Magdala campaign was thus unmistakably located in the political-strategic context of British India: "The political-administrative integration of the army into the British India government in Bombay was not only clear from the army leadership, which was basically deployed from India, but also from the participation of British diplomatic representatives from the area of the Indian government: for example, the resident Merewether from Aden was subordinate to the Indian government. Here, Ethiopia is an undeclared but nevertheless clearly recognizable part of British India's sphere of influence: the intervention served to protect India."[30]

In the run-up to the decision to embark upon the campaign, General Napier, together with his chief of staff Robert Phayre, assessed all the available information about Ethiopia and in early August 1867 presented an initial recommendation that already contained the basic outlines of the later mode of procedure.[31] A large base of operations was to be established on

The Port of Massawa on the Red Sea in modern-day Eritrea.

Egyptian-controlled territory near the Red Sea port of Massawa, as well as a further base in Antalo, half-way to Magdala, which lay about 400 miles from the coast. In addition, Napier specified the number and nature of the troops required, as well as their weapons, equipment, and transport requirements. Finally, he estimated that the campaign would take several months to complete, and also referred to the high cost of the enterprise. The British government was at first not exactly pleased with the unexpectedly large material, financial, and temporal magnitude of the undertaking, and seemed to prefer the option of a quick, small commando operation (a "rapid dash") that was frequently postulated at that time. But Napier firmly rejected the latter option and argued instead for a strong army that could, if necessary, march through hostile territory on its own.[32] However, to this end, a sound agreement should be achieved with the oppositional forces through whose areas the army would have to pass. But for Egypt, the condition for such an agreement and for permission to land military forces was nonetheless a clear statement that no permanent occupation or colonization of Ethiopia was sought, but only the limited goal of liberating the European hostages, which was to be followed by an immediate exit from the country.

This plan was ultimately adopted by the British government on August

13, 1867, and was subsequently put into effect. On August 18, Napier was officially appointed leader of the Magdala expedition and authorized to deploy his troops for use in Ethiopia. These were to be an Anglo-Indian army consisting predominantly of native Indian units. The combat troops (infantry, artillery, and sappers) totaled 13,088 men, including 9,050 Indians and 4,038 Englishmen. If auxiliary and civilian personnel are included, the expeditionary force amounted to 62,200 men in total.[33] In this colonial-imperial army, shaped and led by Britons, "colored" soldiers from India were supposed to fight against other "colored" troops in Ethiopia for the interests of their "white" masters. This was only one example among many of the use of "colored" soldiers recruited from the colonies in fighting in other colonial areas or, later on, on European battlefields.[34]

Transportation for the campaign was to be provided by 44 elephants, 5,735 camels, 17,934 mules and ponies, as well as 8,075 oxen and 2,538 horses. The troops, animals, and materiel were to be shipped from India to

The Harbor of Bombay, where elephants were taken on board for the Magdala expedition.

East Africa on 75 steamships, 205 sailing ships, and 11 smaller ships.[35]

In carrying out his planning, Napier encountered a number of major problems.[36] He had to cope with the demands of a difficult terrain and special climatic conditions, and also forestall possible illnesses among his men. In addition, there was the problem of apprehending Emperor Tewodros. It was to be expected that he would not remain in Magdala, but instead would conduct a mobile guerilla war and constantly evade his pursuers. The fate of the European hostages also remained uncertain, since they would be in constant danger of being killed. Finally, diverse questions of political and administrative authority and quarrels over the implementation of Napier's demands had to be settled. Despite all these problems, however, the preparations for the expedition slowly advanced.[37]

The Foreign Office secured permission to establish a temporary base on Egyptian territory on the Red Sea, and to send agents to Spain and the Middle East to purchase donkeys, mules, and other baggage animals. In addition, negotiations were begun with the Austrian Mint for the coining of half a million 1780 Maria-Theresa thalers, the only currency then accepted everywhere in Ethiopia. The Admiralty provided for the security of shipping in the Red Sea and made available cargo space and hospital ships, while the War Ministry provided, as arms for the expeditionary force, modern mountain artillery, rocket guns, and 4,000 new Snider-Enfield breech-loading rifles for the European combat troops.

The diplomatic and political negotiations with the Ottoman Empire and with Egypt proved to be particularly sensitive.[38] On the one hand, an agreement regarding permission to land troops had to be sought, and this was tantamount to an implicit recognition of Ottoman or Egyptian sovereignty over the African coast of the Red Sea—ultimately, from the British point of view, the Ethiopian area was "in the broader sense the 'hinterland' of India (and thus a British sphere of influence), far more than it was an area of interest for the ally Egypt . . . although the coastal area on the Red Sea, that is, the expedition's first main theater of operations, was formally part of a southern province of Egypt."[39] On the other hand, England wanted to maintain a political distance from Egypt, and certainly to avoid anything that would smack of a British-Egyptian alliance, fear of which was latent in Ethiopia. In any case, the English wanted to prevent any participation of Turkish or Egyptian troops in the Magdala campaign, no matter what form it might take. They were convinced that any such participation would cause the princes rebelling against Emperor Tewodros to go over to his side.[40]

As Wolbert Smidt, a Hamburg ethnologist, historian, and expert on Ethiopia, wrote in his lexicon of the important persons in the Magdala campaign, the list of the participating British and foreign officers can also be read "in part as a brief guide to Great Britain's colonial history in Asia—and still more as a supplement to the history of international wars; the officers had fought on battlefields from Mexico (Kodolitsch) to China (Napier). They therefore contributed to a military globalization that had begun with the intervention of British and European armies in America in 1776."[41] After Napier, the most important officers of the campaign were doubtless Colonel Robert Phayre and Lieutenant Colonel William Lockyer Merewether.

Robert Phayre (1820-1897) was chief of the general quartermaster's staff of the expedition to Ethiopia and had an important part in the success of the enterprise from the outset, as the contemporary Austrian military observer Kodolitsch wrote: "Colonel Phayre is a very energetic, enterprising, intelligent, and scientifically educated officer. His part in the enterprise was from the very beginning an extremely important one. He was a member of the reconnaissance commission under Brigadier Merewether that landed in Massawa on October 2, and he took a major part in all that was done, the determination of the landing point, the finding of the Koomaylo Pass and the choice of the same to reach the high plateau, the laying out of the road, and finally the construction of the large depot in Senafe."[42] William Lockyer Merewether (1825-1880) directed the political and reconnaissance department and was commander of the advance party. As a long-serving diplomatic representative of England in Aden, he was made director of the preparations for carrying out the campaign.

However, the most romantic and enigmatic figure among the British officers was probably Tristram Charles Sawyer Speedy (1836-1911), who became known as "Captain Speedy." Because of his exceptional size, this eccentric officer with a large, red beard made an imposing impression. In addition, throughout the campaign he wore Abyssinian clothing and carried a spear. The journalist Henry Morton Stanley was obviously very struck by Speedy's huge size ("six feet six inches") and enormous physical

The eccentric Captain Speedy, in one of his typical outfits made of lion skin, with a spear.

strength, which he compared with that of the ancient warriors Ajax and Hercules. However, Speedy was short-sighted and thus always wore glasses.[43] Captain Speedy joined the campaign as a substitute for the missionary Johann Ludwig Krapf, who had fallen ill, and served as an interpreter. Like Krapf, he had been in Ethiopia earlier and had learned Amharan at that time. Whenever necessary, Speedy translated into Amharan General Napier's English letters to the Ethiopian princes and translated their replies into English.

Speedy had an adventurous life: after serving in the British army in India's northwestern border province (1854-1860), he went on an elephant hunt in Ethiopia where he arrived at the court of Emperor Tewodros II.[44] The latter admired his imposing physical size and strength and took him into his service. Speedy fought in Tewodros's army, and the emperor rewarded his fighting ability and bravery by making him the commander of a larger unit. Because of the envy and resentment among the courtiers, Speedy decided to leave the imperial court and Ethiopia. Tewodros tried to keep him there, but failing to do so, he paid him his wages, gave him a horse, a shield, and a spear, and then let him go. Afterward, Speedy acted as British vice-consul in Massawa, substituting for Consul Cameron when the latter was away. In early 1864, Speedy went to New Zealand, where he fought against the Maori as captain of the Waikoto militia. At the beginning of the Magdala expedition, General Napier tracked Speedy down there and won him "as a priceless acquisition for the enterprise because of his precise knowledge of the country, the people, and the language," as Kodolitsch wrote, adding "I believe that he really rendered outstanding services that allow us to excuse his somewhat ludicrous habit of always wearing an Abyssinian costume with a lion's skin, and even appearing barefoot on great occasions."[45]

In addition to the British officer corps that was actively responsible, a dozen foreign military observers from various European armies also took part in the campaign, including officers from Prussia, Austria, Italy, France, Spain, and Holland. Four officers from the German-speaking realm were accredited members of the expedition. From Prussia came Count G. von Seckendorff and Baron Ferdinand von Stumm; from Austria came Theodor von Kodolitsch, a lieutenant in the Hanoverian Hussar regiment no. 15 who had already gained diplomatic and military experience in Mexico, along with Corvette Captain Count von Kielmannsegg. It is not entirely clear why the British military leadership invited foreign military observers to join the expedition. The most probable reason is that they were reasonably sure of succeeding and wanted to impress European governments after the dishonorable performance of the British military in the Crimean War.

The expedition was also accompanied by a small civilian scientific staff, which was supposed to make new contributions to research on northeast Africa. The co-author of the official report on the expedition, Captain Henry Hozier, described the "scientific" character of the campaign somewhat euphemistically: "The troops of Sir Robert Napier were not only liberators of their countrymen, but were explorers and pioneers in an almost unknown land. A vague charm was presented to the men who comprised the Expeditionary Force. The theatre of their operations was little better understood than when it was supposed to be the seat of empire of the mythical Prester John."[46]

In history there have always been military campaigns in the course of which the commanding officers or the accompanying scientists systematically gathered information regarding foreign countries, societies, and cultures, carried booty home, wrote studies, or even carried out archeological excavations, and thus contributed to their own societies' knowledge of parts of the world that had up to that point been unknown. Famous examples of this are Alexander the Great's campaigns in antiquity, and in modern times, Napoleon's Egyptian campaign, which led to the rise of modern Egyptology. The British Magdala campaign had similar effects on research, especially concerning the history and culture, but also the geography, flora, and fauna of Ethiopia; thus the campaign had a significant effect on the development of modern Ethiopian studies. However, these achievements were ultimately responsible for the extensive plundering and violent, predatory appropriation of Ethiopian cultural artifacts.

The scientific staff of the Magdala expedition included more or less well-known figures such as its geographer, Clements Robert Markham (Royal Geographical Society), its archeologist, Richard Holmes (British Museum), its zoologist, W. Jesse (Zoological Society), its meteorologist, Dr. Cook (Bombay Indian Army), and its geologist and naturalist, William T. Blanford (Geological Survey of India).[47] The most remarkable personality among these scientists was undoubtedly Clements Robert Markham (1830-1916).[48] In his youth, Markham had traveled widely in South America and had taken a special interest in the Incan ruins in Peru. Later on, he entered the service of the East India Company. In 1860, he acquired a collection of cinchona trees and their seeds in the eastern Andes, with a view to acclimatizing these trees in India in order to improve the supply of quinine. Then he became geographer of the India Office and accompanied the Magdala campaign in this capacity.

The British government and the army also consulted other contemporary scholars, travelers, and missionaries who had already had experience in East Africa and especially in Ethiopia, and invited some of them to join the expedition as advisors and interpreters. Among these were such well-known people as the British East Africa scholars, travelers and explorers Samuel Baker, James Grant, and Dr. Charles T. Beke, the Swiss scholar and diplomat Werner Munzinger, the German African explorer Gerhard Rohlfs, and the German Protestant missionary Johann Ludwig Krapf, who played an important role in the expedition.

Krapf (1810-1881) grew up near Tübingen and became famous both for his geographical discoveries and for his linguistic and ethnological research. Krapf made numerous trips to northeastern and eastern Africa, and on December 3, 1849, he discovered the snow-cappedd Mt. Kenya. Like Livingstone, Krapf—according to the historian Hanno Beck—was "both a missionary and important Africa scholar. . . . He had a high regard for knowledge, studied the atlas while still a child, read contemporary travel accounts very carefully, and above all mastered foreign languages very quickly because of his natural talent for them."[49] Krapf lived in Ethiopia for three years (1839-1842), in Ankober, the capital of the Shoa kingdom, whose king, Sahle Selassie, he accompanied on several campaigns against the Gallas. However, he devoted himself primarily to missionary work and the study of this people. In 1841, he served as an interpreter for the British Ethiopia expedition under Major William Harris and also aided the latter in the composition of his travel report. In 1855, on behalf of London's Church Missionary Society and the Swiss St. Chrishona Pilgrim Mission, Krapf traveled to Ethiopia once again (along with Johann Martin Flad), where he was warmly received in Gondar, north of Lake Tana, by King Tewodros, who had, in concert with the Abuna Salama, expelled the Catholic missionaries. According to Beck, Krapf was moved "neither by ambition nor by scientific geographical concerns, but solely by his religious mission."[50] But to fulfill this mission, Krapf was also always prepared to put himself at the service of the political interests of the British empire, as he demonstrated through his activity as an interpreter during the Magdala campaign.[51]

Krapf was evidently very much liked by participants in the campaign, and especially by his fellow Germans. In addition, he provided priceless services to the English. For example, Gerhard Rohlfs wrote that "Krapf received us with exceptional courtesy and we found in him a true countryman who considered it an honor to be a German. I listened with admiration to this elderly man, whose mind seemed much younger, speak about his plans for further travels, and who knows whether he himself might have taken part in new voyages of discovery had not illness forced him to return to his homeland.... We received letters from General Merewether informing us that Dr. Krapf had left for Germany, an irreparable loss for the English, because he was the only European who could write Amharan well and had a fundamental knowledge of the country, its inhabitants, and its customs."[52]

Count von Seckendorff also lamented the departure of Krapf, who was replaced by Captain Speedy: "Since there was a great lack of interpreters and guides in this unknown country, the loss of Dr. Krapf, who was known for his many trips through Abyssinia, was a very serious one."[53]

The most famous person among all the Africa experts accompanying the expedition was doubtless the Scot Major James Augustus Grant (1827-1892). Under the sponsorship of the Royal Geographical Society and together with John Hanning Speke, whom he knew from their common service in India, he had sought the source of the Nile from 1861 to 1863 and finally discovered it in Lake Victoria; he had also studied the landscapes, peoples, and cultures of East Africa.[54] After this expedition, he became England's leading expert on Africa. Grant served as an interpreter and intelligence officer on the Magdala campaign.

The English author Alan Moorehead (1910-1983) particularly emphasizes the thoroughness and precision of the Magdala campaign's organization, which seem almost "modern." In his view, the Allies' landing in Normandy in 1944 could hardly have been more thoroughly planned and prepared.[55] A multitude of already available information—such as the old reports of W. James Bruce and Henry Salt, who had traveled through Ethiopia—was systematically analyzed in order to plan the expedition with an almost scientific seriousness: "All the books and records that the library of the Bombay Asiatic Society and the archives the Government could supply were placed in the hands of the Quartermaster-General. Colonel Phayre waded through a vast mass of travels and correspondence, and condensed the result of his investigations in a brief report."[56] Napier himself concluded from the quite incomplete meteorological tables drawn up by the 1841 Harris Mission to Ethiopia "that the troops would be obliged to encounter both rain and cold, and that it was absolutely necessary that the soldiers should have their tents, warm clothing, and a waterproof sheet for each man."[57]

In the realm of geography and cartography as well, great efforts to be of use to the expedition were made using the Royal Geographical Society's library and map collection, as the leading German cartographer of the time, the anglophile August Petermann, noted: "When it was learned that the English government had decided to take military action against Abyssinia, the available maps of this country were sought out. . . . In England, new maps were drawn up. . . . Using both lithographic and mimeographic processes, the topographical department of the English War Ministry provided with great rapidity a significant number of maps by taking the best available specialized maps and copying and reproducing them in precise facsimiles."[58]

For the specific, operative preparation of the expedition, however, the close collaboration of William Merewether with Werner Munzinger, a Swiss scholar and diplomat, proved to be of great importance; according to Rohlfs, they were, along with Robert Phayre, the "soul of the expedition."[59] Furthermore, Sven Rubenson, a modern Swedish historian of Ethiopia, still considers Munzinger a "key figure" in the Magdala campaign.[60]

Munzinger was born in 1832 in Olten, the son of the Swiss finance minister Joseph Munzinger. He studied at the universities of Bern, Munich, and Paris, and concentrated on the study of oriental languages. In 1852, he traveled to Egypt as the representative of a trading firm, and in August 1853, he went on to Massawa on the Red Sea. In 1854, he journeyed into the interior of the country, to the city of Keren in "Bogosland," a highland area that is now part of Eritrea, where he lived among the Bilen people who had settled there, took a wife from the region, and became familiar with the local customs and traditions. In July 1861, Munzinger took part in the search party to look for the lost researcher Eduard Vogel that was organized by the Duke of Sachsen-Coburg-Gotha and was led by the Africa scholar Theodor von Heuglin.[61]

During the many years he

The Swiss adventurer Werner Munzinger, who served as a consultant and translator for the British during the Magdala campaign.

lived in northeast Africa, Munzinger was also very active as a scientist, and the numerous works he published on the linguistics, ethnography, and geography of the regions he investigated are still considered valuable. His important *East African Studies* was published in 1864. He also acquired an extensive knowledge of the Arabic, Tigray, Tigrinya, and Amharan languages. Moreover, Munzinger had an outstanding knowledge of the land and people of Ethiopia, not least because of his local family relationships. In addition to his work as a scientist, Munzinger was active as a diplomat and politician, first in the service of European powers, and later in the service of Egypt. In the 1860s, he was appointed "double consul" for England (vice-consul from 1864 on) and France (vice-consul from 1865 on) in Massawa. Given his excellent knowledge of the country and its languages, it is hardly surprising that Munzinger took part in the Magdala campaign as an interpreter and political advisor.

According to the Austrian military observer Kodolitsch, Munzinger made

> very extraordinary contributions. One can hardly follow him in all his travels back and forth to find the best routes and the most convenient crossing points, to meet with chieftains, sometimes on political missions, sometimes in order to get them to provide food supplies and forage. He surely traveled the road from Zula to Magdala, with all its detours, at least three times. His peregrinations ranged as far as Adowa and Axum in the west and deep into the land of the Gallas in the east, often—even among the thieving and treacherous tribes in the east—with only a few companions and servants, which was not without great personal danger. He was a scientifically educated man equipped with an extensive knowledge of languages, was advantageously known as a writer, and contributed a great deal to knowledge of that part of Africa.[62]

While his diplomatic and political activities continue to be the object of conflicting assessments, Munzinger's merits as an orientalist, linguistic researcher, and ethnographer are still recognized today. On the one hand, he is seen as an unscrupulous "adventurer," an enemy of Ethiopia, and an "agent of imperialism" in the service of Europe and Egypt; on the other hand, he is seen as a liberal modernizer and administrator who had the welfare of the local population at heart, who opposed the slave trade, and who was concerned, above all, with the economic and infrastructural development of the areas under his administration.[63]

If we review the meticulous preparations, we can say that in its transport systems, logistics, and weapons technology the Magdala expedition was certainly a "Victorian triumph," as the Ethiopian expert Richard Caulk puts it.[64] Captain Hozier, one of the authors of the official British report, listed with visible national pride the utilization of the latest scientific knowledge and achievements in military technology for the Magdala campaign:

> The various departments of the Government assisted each to the best of its ability. As Abyssinia has no sea-board, the Foreign Office obtained permission for disembarkation on Egyptian soil. It also engaged its agencies in the Mediterranean ports to aid in the purchase of animals for the transport service of the expedition. The War Department laid open its stores and arsenals to supply the demands from Bombay. The Admirality took measures for lighting and buoying the approaches to Massowah (Massawa) through the intricate and dangerous coral reefs, which abound on the western margin of the Red Sea. Vessels were chartered by that department for the conveyance of animals from the ports of the Mediterranean and Levant to Alexandria. Other vessels teeming with warlike cargoes were engaged to sail from the Thames to Bombay. They carried clothing, ammunition, and breech-loading arms for the British troops who were to be thrown into the unknown region. Three large ships were dispatched to act as floating hospitals in the port of debarkation. The climate of the seaboard was supposed to be almost deadly to the European constitution. Every precaution was adopted to lessen and alleviate its baneful effects. These ships were fitted with every appliance which science could suggest or experience

dictate for the restoration of the sick and the comfort of the suffering. Tried and skilled surgeons were stationed on board of them. Nor were the researches of science adapted to minister to the comfort of the sick and wounded alone. Vast stores of coal were sent to the Cape of Good Hope, Bombay, and Aden to provide the motive power for the transit of troops and the means of condensing from the sea fresh waterfor the use of men and animals. The electric fluid was pressed into the use of the campaign, and a telegraph was constructed suitable for service in the field, to connect the office of the commander with the vessels of the fleet. The discoveries of chemists were combined with the skill of the mechanician to enable the outposts by means of lamps to flash instantaneously their observations to head-quarters. By another arrangement, for Theodore was reported to be daring in attacks conducted under the cover of darkness, the whole of the country adjacent to a camp could be illumined by a light as useful as the sun. The power of steam was not to be limited to the sea alone. Preparations were made for sending out a railway to connect the landing place with the interior, but these were rendered unnecessary by its being obtained from Bombay. Condensers such as the latest experiments of science, which had proved to be the most efficacious, were supplied for use on shore. Piping of iron many miles in length was sent forth to collect the slender rills of the African mountains, and carry their waters to the stations of the British troops. Carts for the conveyance of supplies, and ambulances for the carriage of the wounded, with the harness for their draught animals, were sent forth from the storehouses of Woolwich, while the factories of Enfield hurried to supply the Europeans of the expedition with breech-loading firearms. Special artillery, fitted for mountain warfare, was prepared at the Royal gun factories, and equipped for transport on the backs of mules. Wells were obtained for finding water in inland positions, and power-

THE BRITISH EMPIRE PREPARES FOR WAR

ful pumps for forcing it to the surface within the easy reach of thirsty claimants.

It was necessary that the army should be provided with treasure. Without the means of paying its way, it could have obtained no supplies in the country. The natives would have withered away before its presence. No coinage was current in Abyssinia except the Maria Theresa dollar of Austria. To obtain these, British agents were employed to buy all that they could obtain in Southern Germany, and British influence set the machinery of the mint at Vienna in motion. These dollars were shipped from Trieste to Alexandria, thence conveyed to Suez, and dispatched to the scene of operations.[65]

These were truly trail-blazing achievements of industrial logistics.

The British expanded the village of Zula into a major port city as part of their massive logistical campaign during the Magdala expedition.

CHAPTER 5

A Harbor City Built Overnight

In early October 1867, the expedition's advance party, which had sailed on ships named "Coromandel" and "Euphrates," reached Massawa, a harbor on the Red Sea under Egyptian control. This party was composed of a committee, attended by an escort of marine infantry and some cavalry. The president of the committee was Lieut.-Colonel Merewether, C.B. "The members were Lieut.-Colonel Phayre, Quartermaster-General of the Bombay Army; Lieut.-Colonel Wilkins, Royal Engineers, the senior naval officer, and the senior medical officer.... Officers were dispatched with the reconnoitering party to draw up special reports, each regarding his own department. The reconnoitering party was authorized to take into employment such portions of the native tribes under Egyptian rule as might be found necessary and expedient for guards for forage parties and escorts."[1]

The following day, a search was made for an appropriate landing place in Annesley Bay, about seventy miles southeast of Massawa. The bay was named after the English traveler George Annesley, who arrived there on May 19, 1804. A few miles further inland, the officers found on a broad, open plain near the village of Zula (whose indigenous name was Mulkutoo) an ideal place for the establishment of the camp.

After the cavalry escort had disembarked, the participants in the advance unit began a more precise examination of the surrounding area. In doing so, they made contact with the local population, the Sahos, a Muslim nomadic group living between the coastal plain and the mountains. The Sahos were hesitant at first, but, when offered the prospect of rich rewards, they proved cooperative and showed the English soldiers the nearby water sources and the appropriate mountain passes for climbing to the Ethiopian highlands. Thus the greater part of October was spent in reconnaissance work and the search for the most suitable pass and the best route. The Kumayli Pass, which led to Senafe, was finally chosen. In the following weeks it was finally possible to unload the first materiel and military engineers, and to begin constructing the harbor installations, loading facilities, and storehouses.

Commander-in-Chief Napier and his staff landed only on January 2, 1868, in Zula, which had in the meantime become a genuine harbor city. British agents were already establishing contacts with Ethiopian princes who opposed Emperor Tewodros. In addition, the advance party had already reached Senafe, which lay in the mountains, about forty miles from the coast, and begun the construction of a camp there. Napier remained in Zula for a few weeks to deal with administrative matters and to plan the future advance of his troops into the interior.

The landing in Annesley Bay and the sight of Zula with its busy life and activity must have made a deep impression on all the participants in the expedition. For example, the Prussian military observer Count von Seckendorff wrote on arriving in the bay: "Before us lay Zula, the landing place of the English expeditionary force. There were swarms of people and animals on the coast, in the Annesley Bay harbor almost seventy ships were anchored, and there was life and activity everywhere. We had reached our long yearned-for goal!"[2] The physician Dr. Josef Bechtinger, an Austrian who served in the English army, described his impressions similarly:

> In the roads, two hundred ships were majestically anchored—true paragons of the English navy. . . . But what was most surprising was the busy life on the ships that had just arrived; the enormous number of camels, pack and draft oxen, horses, mules, etc., that were continually being lowered onto landing craft and lighters and then unloaded on the dike; the number of small boats that hurried back and forth and in the confusion, often could not find their ships, the shouting and noise of the sailors, the huffing of the steamers, five of which worked continuously day and night to convert the salty sea water into drinking water, all that was highly impressive.[3]

Zula was not only a debarkation and landing point for the expedition's troops, but it was also their main depot, the central food and materiel magazine for the Magdala campaign. The later re-embarkation and transportation of troops and materiel out of Ethiopia also took place from Zula. Thus a stable settlement had to be established for the whole duration of the campaign, and therefore an artificial harbor city had to be built almost overnight. At first, this involved major problems because firm leadership and oversight were lacking. The landing facilities proved to be inadequate so the arriving ships could not be unloaded swiftly enough. The bodies of dead animals were not disposed of in an orderly way, which resulted in hygienic and health problems. All of these deficiencies were only solved in early December, with the arrival of Major General Charles Stavely, on whom Napier had bestowed unrestricted powers until his own arrival. Under Stavely's command, the necessary works rapidly proceeded in an orderly way, even if they were very arduous as a result of the tropical heat and the noticeable lack of water: "The work on the landing place," Count von Seckendorff wrote,

> basically extended as far as the construction of a stone jetty 350 yards in length, for which stone had to be brought from the island of Disse, 28 English miles away. Later a second jetty built on pilings was constructed; both of them were provided with filtration machines. Two railway tracks led directly to the magazines. The arduous construction of these jetties was useful in every way and made it easier to disembark men, animals, and materiel. . . . Natives were employed in the earthworks and in transporting stones, whereas the construction of the magazines, the railway, and the drinking water facilities were carried out by sappers. . . . The lack of water in the bleak coastal area was particularly palpable. It was only possible to meet the great needs to some extent because all the ships delivered desalinated water, and two large filtration machines were operating at the same time on the coast.[4]

A bridge for the railroad track built especially for the Magdala campaign by the British.

Captain Hozier also found the "physical labour . . . excessively severe," but he left no doubt as to the necessity of the works: "the railway and roads had to be made, and made they were."[5]

The most conspicuous sign of the industrialization of war that took on shape in the Magdala campaign was probably the railway, which was built exclusively to meet the need for military transportation from the base camp at Zula through the arid coastal areas to the edge of the Ethiopian high country. According to Seckendorff's report, the "Chinese, who are known as outstanding workers,"[6] were brought in to build the railway. This "first railway in Africa" was, however, a kind of flash in the pan, because at the end of the campaign it was completely dismantled and carried away.[7] No doubt constructing and putting into operation this stretch of railway, seventeen kilometers long (not counting spurs) was a significant engineering achievement. Since the Suez Canal was opened only in 1869, all the construction material, the locomotives, and the cars, as well as the technical equipment and the corresponding civilian skilled employees, had to be brought from India to East Africa. Lieutenant Ferdinand von Stumm was impressed:

> If one walked down to the sea, one soon came across rails, which ran out some three hundred paces into the shallow bay on the carefully constructed jetty, and connected the unloading sites with the storehouses. By April 11, the railway was completed over a distance of nine miles, on May 2, as far as the camp at Komayloo, and was twelve English miles long in all. Although the railway could be used only for a short time, it nonetheless significantly aided the advance of the expedition, and after a few weeks, the cost (the earthworks ran to only £ 5,000) was more than covered. The baggage animals were thus spared the march between Komayloo and Zula, so that the costly consumption of water in the latter place could be limited to a great extent.[8]

The railway was also used on the march back to the coast in order to get the victorious troops and the liberated hostages to Zula as quickly as possible. All in all, during the six months the campaign lasted, the railway transported 63,756 men (14,700 combat troops and 49,057 non-combatants and auxiliaries).[9]

Count von Seckendorff was deeply impressed by the outstanding organization and almost luxurious care given to the sick in Zula:

> For receiving the sick there were field hospital tents on land and hospital ships in the Annesley Bay harbor, three for the European troops, and one for the native regimentals, camp followers, et al. The three ships "Golden Fleece," "Queen of the South," and "Mauritius" were rented from a company and fitted out for the expedition in London. . . . On the ships there was no lack of baths, rooms for bandaging and operations, or storerooms. In addition, each ship had an ice room and several ice machines. Several arrange-

ments were available to move the ill from the lower rooms in the ship to the top deck, as well as tents on the foredeck to protect them from the sun.[10]

For Hozier, Zula was "the heart from which the life-stream flowed that must pulsate through the long artery of the line of communications and carry food to the farthest outposts."[11] The Austrian military observer Koloditsch was overcome upon seeing in Zula the "mountains of sacks, bales, and boxes, the endless rows of barrels, metal crates, cans, carts, wheels, tools of all kinds, and the ant-like activity of the individuals of all countries and colors who were doing the loading and unloading."[12]

In Zula, a colorful society was composed of British Indian troops, the labor and auxiliary personnel, the natives, and also the adventurers and wheeler-dealers from all over the world, a society that settled in as best it could and arranged its common life under the adverse conditions of extreme heat, humidity, and the omnipresence of sand. Thus, as the military physician Josef Bechtinger wrote, "instead of the deserted beach where shortly before lions and hyenas had roamed the muddy coast, there arose a small, respectable city" whose pulsing center was the so-called bazaar.[13]

According to Kodolitsch's report, this bazaar was the

> place assigned for the traders' huts, where the businessmen were allowed, in exchange for a fee, to set up their shops and sell their wares. . . . The bazaar was subject to inspection by its own inspector, who had the corresponding camp police force under him, and enforced very strict rules. . . . In the bazaar there was a relatively great orderliness, and in particular excesses or theft did not occur, so far as I know, and one can imagine what a rabble from all master countries was gathered there, naturally keeping its distance from the representatives of a few very respectable trading houses. The prices were on the whole not excessive, and the French house of Bazin & Co.—which, may it be said in passing, did an exceptional business—provided very outstanding wines, preserves, dried vegetables, etc. . . . All the facilities that were by nature more inclined to produce

Hindu troops, who were included in the multicultural British invasion army during the Magdala expedition.

evil miasmas or effluvia, such as the bazaar, . . . the latrines, the cemetery, and the slaughterhouse, were downwind and at a distance from the camp proportionate to the harmfulness of their exhalations. . . . The cleanliness of the camp left nothing to be desired.[14]

Lieutenant Stumm described the scene in the bazaar somewhat sarcastically. It consisted, he wrote, of two wide, dusty streets of straw and mat buildings "in which Indians and Europeans sold off their treasures at the most fabulous prices, partly to their own countrymen, partly to the astonished Saho people who streamed down from the mountains. Two German traders sold Liebfrauenmilch wine, genuine Johannisberger wine, matches that would not burn, cigars that didn't draw, shirts that fell apart the first time they were put on, stale mixed pickles and all the nameless junk that can be found only in an Abyssinian grocer's shop."[15] And Bechtinger also regarded the bazaar with skepticism: "Day after day, people came over, mostly from Suez, Aden, and Bombay, to speculate on English rupees. . . . Portuguese, French, Arabs, Turks, and Abyssinians competed to sell their little goods and to outdo each other in prices and fraud."

In the hustle and bustle of the harbor city, prostitutes from Egypt also turned up, but they were not tolerated in Zula and had to return to their homeland. In Bechtinger's opinion, the most unusual establishment in the bazaar was a tavern named after the Ethiopian emperor Tewodros: "In the 'Tewodros II' tavern there were no members of the Abyssinian elite, but rather a peculiar society of captains, sailors, officers, and workers. The owner, a cunning English trader in liquors, knew from the outset how to go about his business and had given his tavern a striking moniker. . . . He was also the only man in Zula who had all kinds of iced drinks, which he produced artificially by means of an ice machine."[16]

The multicultural composition of the troops posed a significant problem for the logistics department:

> There meat, flour, bread, peas, dried vegetables, butter, sugar, rum, tea, coffee, potatoes, pepper, salt, and rice were distributed, and the funniest thing was that each of the various nationalities and religious sects had to have its own

special rations. The Europeans were given different foods than the Arabs, the Muslims different foods than the Hindus, while the latter were given different foods than the Brahmins, and so on. Naturally, all these differences made the work of the commissary officers infinitely more difficult and confusions could not fail to occur.[17]

According to Bechtinger, the officers made better arrangements for themselves when they could:

> The officers in the camp built their own clubs, corresponding to the staff to which they were assigned. They had their mess there in groups of eight to twelve, which remedied some small problems and was supposed to result in better food, since the kitchen, which usually consisted of a walled-off adjoining area, could be entrusted to a Hindu familiar with the art of cooking. In its immediate proximity was another small area that will better remain unnamed. Thus the tent of the officers who remained permanently in Zula was fortunately surrounded by agreeable-smelling areas such as the stables, the kitchen, . . . etc., which disseminated their peculiar fragrance, depending on the capacity of the owners, at temperatures that often reached 116° F.

In order to escape these not very comfortable living conditions, the officers went on hunting and reconnaissance excursions in the surrounding area, and they also visited the nearby ruins of the ancient harbor city of Adulis. Such distractions were denied ordinary soldiers. Thus, they were all glad to finally be able to march into the cooler uplands, while their comrades permanently stationed in Zula looked longingly after them.

CHAPTER 6

Embedded Journalists

The Magdala campaign is a highly interesting but up to now little-noticed chapter in the history of war reporting.[1] The expedition was accompanied by half a dozen "specials" (special war correspondents) who were assigned by their respective newspapers to write eye-witness reports of the events and to provide critical observations on the behavior of the British army for their readers. Through their articles, the readers of the various newspapers were able to virtually participate in the "adventure" of the Magdala campaign. These war correspondents who traveled with the troops to the most advanced front, as "embedded journalists," as it were, were considered the elite of the journalistic profession. Among them was Dr. Charles Austin (for the *Times*, the most sophisticated newspaper for the educated elite and upper class of England), George A. Henry (for the *Standard*, a paper close to the Tories and a conservative competitor of the *Times*), W. Owen Whiteside (for the *Morning Post*, which had a conservative-imperialist slant), Alex Shepherd (for the *Daily News*, a liberal paper whose first publisher was Charles Dickens), and Lord Adare (for the *Daily Telegraph*, a thrifty "penny newspaper" for a less educated readership). The only non-British correspondent was the (naturalized) American Henry Morton Stanley, who later became famous as an Africanist (for the *New York Herald*, a well-financed, inexpensive daily paper that had the largest readership in America, and already used headlines, photographs, interviews and even comic strips and cartoons). The *Illustrated London News* sent the painter William Simpson, the "Pioneer of War artists,"[2] who had already made a name for himself with his illustrations of the Crimean War and the Sepoy Rebellion of 1857-1858. In comparison with painting, photography was then still under-developed as a visual medium for war reporting, and was used primarily for

63

The *Illustrated London News* with several illustrated reports about the Magdala expedition.

military purposes.[3] However, Simpson joined the campaign only after the storming of Magdala.

All of these journalists traveled at the expense of their newspapers and had no status as combatants. All the same, among them were adventure-loving persons who did not shrink from any personal risk during the campaign and accepted, without complaint, the usual hardships, privations, and inconveniencies of the march, the accommodation, and the food. Their reports, which often had literary pretensions, were definitely critical of the military, but also often humorous and colored by their own personalities. However, as a result of their lack of knowledge of the language and the country, their descriptions of the customs and traditions of the Ethiopian people are not infrequently marked by serious distortions and moral arrogance.

To communicate their reports and news, the correspondents were dependent on written dispatches that had to be sent by military or diplomatic post through Suez and Alexandria to Europe. Because of its high cost, the

The New Pier at Annesley Bay in Abyssinia was primarily used by the British Navy to unload army supplies.

telegraph was at first infrequently used to transmit news. However, news could also be sent by telegraph cable to Europe from Suez, by way of Alexandria and Malta. If the telegraph was not out of order at the time, it took about four weeks for news to reach London.

The standards for modern war reporting had been set during the Crimean War (1853-1856) by the English journalist William Howard Russell, who was at that time reporting for the *Times*.[4] Russell lived with the troops and wrote eyewitness accounts of the fighting, the incompetence of the British generals, the soldiers' miserable living conditions, and the scandalous treatment of the wounded. These critical reports impressed readers, the public, and members of Parliament, but they also led the military to accuse Russell and the *Times* of giving aid and comfort to the enemy by their unsparing revelation of Britain's weaknesses.[5] Later on, Russell also reported on the repression of the Sepoy Mutiny in India and on various wars in Europe. Had Russell not stood for a seat in Parliament precisely in 1867, the *Times* would have sent him, as a prominent and experienced war reporter, on the Magdala expedition as its special correspondent.

War reporting can have fundamentally ambivalent functions. On the one hand, as a critical agency, it can reveal the backgrounds of wars and discover the misconduct of the parties waging the war. On the other hand, as a result of hindrance, manipulation, or censorship by the parties to the conflict, war reporters run the risk of becoming more or less involuntary supernumeraries or even propagandists for wars.[6] In addition, some reporters are inclined to have too high an opinion of themselves and present themselves as heroes. The reporters' triumphs and tribulations against the background of the war thus become more important than the war itself. There is an unmistakable conflict of interest and a latent tension between journalists and the military that can be observed throughout the history of modern war reporting. Whereas journalists are bound primarily to tell the "truth" of the war and to report it as objectively as possible (the "watchdog" function), the military are primarily concerned with successfully fighting the enemy, the victory of their own forces, and a positive image of themselves. Journalists are repeatedly accused by the military leadership of revealing important information about their own side's intentions and weaknesses to the enemy through their critical reports, undermining their own soldiers' morale, weakening support for the army among the public and in the politics of their homelands, and thereby ultimately harming their own side. The logical result of this conflict of interests was perpetual attempts to control war reporting.

The British army had certainly gained, at least since its experiences with the media during the Crimean War, a great respect for the power of the press and its influence on public opinion. The dispatching of the previously mentioned representatives of the press to Ethiopia was the result of the British public's marked interest in the Magdala expedition. The African explorer Gerhard Rohlfs remarked ironically that the English officers on the march to Magdala probably were more afraid of their own press than of Emperor Tewodros.[7] The officers accordingly treated the war reporters courteously during the Magdala campaign. In the reports of a few participants in the expedition, we can discern occasional glimmers of resentment against some of the representatives of the press, who behaved with considerable self-confidence and sometimes even with a certain arrogance. Thus the Austrian military physician Bechtinger, who was in the service of the English, points to an understandable distance between the British officers and the press: "They avoid all publicity and try to pay no special attention to newspaper reporters, book-scribblers, and writers of reports. They may have been right to do so; they wanted to be spared and cope with their difficult task without supervisors."[8]

Gerhard Rohlfs also was annoyed by the preferential treatment accorded a war correspondent and was generally critical of the work and appearance of journalists: "Most of these correspondents usually see things only through the eyes of the superior officers. I knew one who had the [officers'] reports given to him, simply embellished or perhaps worsened them, and then sent them on to his newspaper as his own work. Many were also extremely presumptuous and when their wishes, for example to be with the vanguard or to be attached to some particular unit, were not immediately granted, wrote the most mendacious reports regarding rough treatment by superior officers, etc."[9]

The German Lieutenant Stumm saw things quite similarly:

> A very remarkable kind of men arrived along with the headquarters, a legion of newspaper correspondents who accompany the English army as the monitoring represen-

tatives of a sovereign people, so to speak. I always found it incomprehensible that these men, who did not hesitate to disseminate the crudest lies and to deliver positive or negative judgments regarding military affairs about which they knew nothing at all, could be treated with so much respect and attention. Some of these same men did not hesitate to spread in their newspapers revolting, often dishonoring rumors about even outstanding figures in the expeditionary corps who had by some accident incurred the scorn of these literary heroes.... Once, we foreigners also had to enjoy the kind attention of these gentlemen. Despite its ludicrousness, the report that the Prussian officers had left the English camp because of their poor treatment there and had gone over to Tewodros's camp made the rounds of Indian, English, and German journals, indeed in England people had nothing better to do than to immediately demand very officially that Sir Robert Napier explain this mysterious affair. Naturally, this judgment regarding the English correspondents does not apply to all of them, and I recall a few who were very agreeable persons.[10]

Commander-in-Chief Napier was held in great respect by all sides for his skillful handing of the correspondents during the Magdala campaign.[11] He had already had a great deal of experience with the press during the Sepoy Rebellion in India, when he was the officer responsible for the journalists present there. Napier had learned how to use the publicity gained through a cooperative relationship with the press for his own purposes. The war correspondents, who all respected Napier, unanimously praised his competence, patience, courtesy, and generosity. Napier regularly invited representatives of the press to dine with him and his officers.[12] During these meals together, he repeatedly impressed the correspondents by the soundness of his education and the number of the subjects in literature, botany, geology, and landscape painting, which he could discuss knowledgeably. However, General Napier's generosity was sometimes limited with respect to giving out information, as Stumm noted: "The reason for this was first that Napier did not usually declare his intentions and plans even to his own staff, and also that he had to be extremely cautious with newspaper correspondents because of their indiscretion."[13]

In general, war correspondents accompanying the Magdala expedition enjoyed a high degree of freedom in their journalistic work, which took place in the "golden age" of early war reporting, when there was still no formal political or military censorship and hardly any supervision by the editorial staff at home.[14] They wrote critical reports on the initial organizational defects of the expedition, about what they sometimes saw as all too hesitant advances, and sometimes as excessively long marches that overstrained the soldiers. With their vivid eye-witness reports, they shaped their readers' notions of the land and people of Ethiopia and the "glorious" British army in "deployment abroad" in defense of "national interests," and also often propagated and conveyed—particularly through the reports of George Henry and Henry M. Stanley—typically "Victorian" paternalistic ideas concerning the superiority of Western civilization and of the British empire in comparison to non-Western societies and cultures.

Stanley—who was then still a young, hardly known journalist working for the *New York Post* as the only non-British correspondent participating in the Magdala Campaign, and who afterward wrote a book about it—emerged a few years later as one of the great explorers of Central Africa. The later Sir Henry Morton Stanley was born in Wales in 1841, under the name John Rowlands. After a deprived childhood and a difficult youth in the workhouse, in January 1859, he sailed as a cabin boy to New Orleans, where a childless businessman named Henry Hope Stanley gave him a job and adopted him. Stanley fought in the American Civil War, at first on the side of the South, and then as a sailor on the side of the North. Later he became a journalist and through his travels, he became acquainted with large parts of the Americas, Spain, and the Near East.

The frequently arrogant and elitist British correspondents and officers of the Magdala campaign obviously did not much care for Stanley, with his American accent, rudimentary education, and humble social ancestry; the feeling was mutual.[15] Anti-American sentiments collided here with anti-British feelings. This probably had more than a little to do with the recent American Civil War, in which the British upper class had favored the South. In addition, Irishmen who had immigrated to the United States were supporting anti-British uprisings in the old country.

On career grounds, Stanley apparently was not always entirely scrupulous with regard to the journalistic process of determining the truth, as Lieutenant Stumm warned. Stumm was displeased that the "correspondent of an American paper" telegraphed to his readers the "most appalling boasts," the "most ludicrous reports on great battles," and the "most impossible incidents in the course of the expedition." Stumm says that when Stanley was asked about this, he replied: "In America people want excitement, and if I reported the truth, they would consider it all very boring and pointless, and wonder how a New York paper could have sent such an untalented correspondent here."[16]

Sir Henry Morton Stanley

Sir Henry Morton Stanley was a journalist, explorer, and author who trekked across the African continent, helped claim the Congo for the Belgian king, and left a trail of death and destruction in his wake, yet he is best known for uttering a phrase he probably never voiced.

Born in Wales on January 28, 1841, Stanley moved to New Orleans at age 18. He fought with the Confederate army in the Civil War, then deserted and joined the Union navy, and then deserted again. At the conclusion of the war, he decided to pursue a career in journalism.

Sir Henry Morton Stanley

From the start, it was clear that press conference and city hall coverage was not what Stanley had in mind. He led a journalistic expedition to the Ottoman Empire that, in a preview of things to come, ended dramatically with his imprisonment. He was later employed by the *New York Herald* as a foreign correspondent, and he was soon assigned to find the Scottish missionary David Livingstone, who had disappeared somewhere in Africa.

Stanley traveled to Zanzibar in grand fashion, with 200 porters, many of whom quickly died or deserted. He treated his African porters brutally, flogging and, according to some accounts, even shooting them "like monkeys." In 1871, he found Livingstone in modern-day Tanzania and may or may not have asked him famously, "Dr. Livingstone, I presume?" After another African expedition, starting in 1874 and lasting 999 days, he was approached by Belgian King Leopold II, who encouraged him, under somewhat false pretenses, to do his work in the Congo. There, he inadvertently spread disease and indirectly helped claim the territory for Belgium. In 1886, he led a similarly problematic expedition to southern Sudan to rescue the governor of Equatoria, before returning to Europe in 1890.

He served as a member of Parliament in the Liberal Unionist Party from 1895 to 1900 and was knighted in 1899 for his exploits in Africa. He died in 1904.

CHAPTER 7

The Long March to Magdala

On January 25, 1868, Commander-in-Chief Napier and his staff left Zula and set out for Senafe, where he arrived on January 29. The advance of the expeditionary corps met no resistance, but the troops had to cross extremely difficult terrain and sometimes suffered from a lack of water and food. By February 14, the vanguard had already reached Antalo, about 200 miles from the coast. The climb from the coastal plains into the mountains was made over steep, rough passes, but also provided marvelous views. After the first, quite desolate stretch of the way, the marching columns encountered more agreeable landscapes with rich vegetation and thickly populated settlements.

The second largest camp after Zula was Kumayli (*Koomaylo*), which also served as a staging area for the baggage animals: "Because of its situation on the edge of the desolate coastal area and the entrance to the pass, through which the English army was to reach Abyssinia's high plateau, because of the abundance of drinking water found there, and finally because of the circumstance that Koomaylo was railway's terminus, this place acquired a very special importance."[1] The camp in Senafe was the expedition's third largest camp; it became the base of operations on the high plateau and served as the main depot in case the campaign had to be continued beyond the rainy season. Further, large camps were established in Adigrat and Antalo. The "availability of drinking water and the avoidance of floodwaters were the main principles guiding the choice and determination of the camp locations, along with the simple availability of adequate room for the camps, which was not always easy to find in rocky ravines that were often miles long."[2]

The officers' faulty information regarding the troops' ability to march the often excessive distances between camps and regarding the frequently exceptionally bad condition of the roads and the lack of drinking water were repeatedly the occasion not only for discontent among the soldiers, but also for critical reporting by the newspaper correspondents accompanying the expedition.[3]

The organization and everyday life during the day's march was vividly described by the Austrian military observer Kodolitsch: "First came, of course, the vanguard composed of infantry and cavalry, ... with the cavalry usually at the head of the column, followed by the artillery, and finally the infantry. So far, it was going very well, and the forward units, with the band in the lead, strode along merrily. But then came the baggage train, the field hospital, the regimental infirmaries, the camp followers—in short, the whole dreadful ballast of every operating army, incredibly magnified by the circumstance that all this had to be carried on baggage animals, and the ill on men's backs."[4] Naturally, when obstacles blocked or narrowed the way, moving forward became still more problematic: the animals became restive, "loads were taken off, and confusion seemed to have reached its highpoint. I saw departures in which it took four to five hours to get the whole column in movement. But finally, it happened. However, disorder then infected the column itself, separations occurred, and everything marched pell-mell, the slow water oxen holding up the faster mules, the camels preventing the pack horses from maintaining their pace, and when a few huffing and puffing stretcher-bearers crowded in, any advance was out of the question."[5] The temporary marching camps

> were usually set up as far as possible from the permanent camps for the guard posts and garrisons, first because the air around the latter was not so pure, but mainly on account of the natives who, because a permanent market for food, forage and wood was held there, often sat and lay around in large numbers and had dreadfully many vermin on them. These natives were truly a local plague, and they could not be completely excluded even from the marching camps, first because it was certainly not desired or permissible to do them any harm, and secondly because it was nonetheless agreeable when these natives sometimes

brought milk, eggs, or honey, or even animal skins and other objects for sale.[6]

The expedition's special logistical demands were emphasized by Captain Hozier, who thereby in no way denied the initial shortcomings and transportation problems, which were also criticized and censured by the war correspondents and by the foreign military observers: "Never were operations carried on in a country so unfavourable to war."[7] Major Kodolitsch arrived at the same assessment:

> Here I come to the most important part of the expedition in Abyssinia. The baggage train system is in general one of the most difficult branches of an army's organization and also one of the most decisive in carrying out its operations, and this was the case in Abyssinia as well, and because of the peculiar conditions in the country, even more than usual.... The success or lack of success, indeed the very possibility of carrying out the whole enterprise, depended on the good or bad organization of the overland transport system, on its continued functioning or its breakdown.[8]

According to Hozier, this organization "was lost through the want of proper superintendence; ... at the close of January its deficiencies were being corrected and its organization assimilated to that which would, had Sir Robert Napier's advice been accepted, have been in complete working order in the beginning of October."[9]

One of the main logistical problems was the provision of the necessary means of transportation on a large scale. General Napier had urged that

> this factor not be underestimated. Unfortunately, his suggestions were not adopted.... If the number of mules, asses, horses, oxen, camels, and elephants is reckoned to be about 36,000, perhaps 12,000 to 15,000 of these died, so they were truly not too many. Not anticipating such dimensions, the necessary number of officers and drivers

Thirty thousand transport animals were used by the British army to carry supplies.

had not been foreseen; the latter were a rabble that came from all countries and spoke a hundred different tongues. Therefore it also happened that the difficulties at the beginning of the expedition, particularly with regard to the baggage train, seemed overwhelming, and it owed only to the great energy of the commander that after his arrival everything had to move forward.[10]

In addition to its own personnel, the expeditionary corps drew on native resources for transportation and food supplies: "We must also take into account the numerous caravans of cattle, mules, asses, and burden-bearing women with which the natives contracted to transport food supplies and forage,"[11] because "contracts were made with the chiefs of the larger districts, and these then conveyed the goods consigned to them across their area, handing them over to the neighboring chief for the same conveyance. Thus the endless train of asses, mules, cattle, or burden-bearing Tigray people moved through the country and punctually delivered grain and flour in large amounts to the designated large storage sites."[12]

Foreign observers were deeply impressed by the excellent care for the sick. Thus Kodolitsch emphasized that great attention was given to providing for the ill, and that "in general this care was very good. In all the hospitals, ambulances, and troop units there were large provisions of all kinds of preserves, meat-extract, arrowroot, lemonade concentrate, chocolate, port wine, porter beer, cognac, and rum, which were distributed to the sick in generous amounts. Particularly valuable were Liebig's meat extract, which produced a very strong broth when boiled in water, along with the dried vegetables, a kind of julienne from the Collet factory in Paris. These provisions were called "medical comfort" and every distribution of them to the healthy after long privation of these luxury articles was a joyful event on the return march."[13] Count von Seckendorff also praised the good medical care: "There were depots for field hospital supplies in Senafe and Antalo. So-called medical comforts consisting of wine, rum, meat extract, lemons, chocolate, arrowroot and other things were taken along by the healthcare department and packed in eighty-pound crates in order to make them easier to load onto mules."[14]

Both the participating correspondents and the foreign military observers suffered from the tedious, time-consuming communication systems, and they criticized the corresponding problems and the military postal service. It could take as long as five weeks to get reports to London. Thus, for example, Count von Seckendorff complained about the straggling and time-consuming connections with the outside world: "It is about 2,320 English miles from Bombay to Annesley Bay, and fourteen days' travel time. Unfortunately the telegraphic connection is not convenient. Messages going to England had to be sent to Suez, and during the expedition it repeatedly happened that the Alexandria-Malta line was interrupted, so that a delay of several days occurred."[15]

Lieutenant Stumm made similar complaints, though with more humor, regarding the expedition's postal service:

From then on there was, at least nominally, a regular postal connection between Zula, Atigerath, and Antalo, and letters from the latter place were supposed to reach the coast in four days. But the sad fact was that letters frequently were lost after the first stations, or very quickly became undeliverable. They were stuck into a sack that the horseman charged with transporting it did not hesitate to use as comfortable padding for his saddle. The sack, kneaded like steak-tartare, naturally contained nothing but torn envelopes and loose papers that the unfortunate postman in Zula was not in a position to send on to their distant destinations. Moreover, sometimes the mail went to Aden and Bombay rather than to Suez, and our letters made the most enviable voyages.[16]

While the English army advanced from the coast toward Magdala, Emperor Tewodros's troops were also approaching Magdala from the interior of the country. A few days before the British landing in Zula in October 1867, Theodor had set out after the rainy season from Debra Tabor. Before the end of the year, he received information about the advance of the English. Thus there emerged a kind of "race" between Napier and Tewodros.[17] Napier marched warily and cautiously, because he did not know the terrain well enough. Tewodros knew the terrain, but he did not advance quickly. Ultimately, the Ethiopian emperor had a harder time of it in his own country than did the British general, who had disciplined and loyal troops, along with access to plentiful supplies.[18] Tewodros, on the other hand, could no longer trust his own soldiers, large numbers whom deserted when the opportunity arose; he had to march through long stretches of enemy territory and ward off hostile peasants. He had no elephants to transport his heavy artillery and constantly had to use force to acquire food. Every day he had to supply food and forage for ten thousand people—men, women, and children—as well as huge herds of cattle. The army rolled across the land like a huge reptile, but in good order. Every morning at seven o'clock the march began, and covered as much as thirty miles a day. Tewodros himself often helped elderly women and children at difficult crossings of ravines and rivers. At night, 20,000 tents and huts were put up. Day by day, groups of

Dragging Tewodros's great mortar "Sebastopol," named after the battle in the Crimean War, from Dabra Tabor to Magdala.

warriors swarmed into the surrounding areas to get the necessary food and supplies by stealing it. The military road that Tewodros and a few European hostages, who were experts in the subject, planned for the last section of the route was very admired and appreciated by the participants in the Magdala campaign—thus Kodolitsch wrote enthusiastically that "This military road of Tewodros's, called the King's Road, was certainly one of the most unusual and, in its brutal-barbarian but savagely clever design, most marvelous structures in the world."[19] In March 1868, Tewodros reached Magdala with his troops and ten thousand civilian followers, only a few weeks before the arrival of the English expeditionary force.

The staff of the British troops reached the Antalo camp on March 2. There they stopped for several days and reduced their marching packs and rations in order to advance more quickly. In addition, the combat troops were regrouped. On March 12, they resumed their march and after eight days reached Lake Ashange, where further reductions of the baggage and rations were made. The pace of the march was also increased, especially since Napier learned that Tewodros had won the "race" to Magdala and had already occupied the mountain fortress. The terrain was steadily becoming more difficult and with long marches and short water rations, there were even grumbling and disciplinary problems among the soldiers in a few units.[20]

Nonetheless, during this protracted and difficult march to Magdala, some participants in the expedition repeatedly found occasion and time to leave the wayside or camp to make "touristic" excursions into the nearby or more distant surroundings in order to see, admire, and describe Ethiopia's landscapes, natural beauties, and cultural sights.[21] These began with excursions from the base camp in Zula to the ruins of the ancient harbor of Adulis, and continued during the stages of the march to Magdala with further visits to churches, markets, and settlements, as well as descriptions of the landscape, flora, and fauna of the regions of Ethiopia through which the expedition was passing. Through the vivid and partly illustrated reports that they published during or after the campaign (for instance in the *Illustrated London News*), they helped shape the contemporary picture of Ethiopia in European societies. Among these temporary "tourists" on the Magdala Expedition were not only its civilian advisors, interpreters, scientists, journalists, draftsmen, and painters (notably William Simpson), but also its officers and foreign military observers. During "touristic" excursions, some of these apparently hardened warhorses proved to be well-educated, sensitive people who were eager to learn, and some of them also sought to establish contact with the local population.

After the initial climb through a barren, arid landscape into the Ethiopian highlands, the participants took increasing pleasure in the charming flora and fauna of the areas through which they passed, as Captain Hozier's description of the landscape makes clear:

> Above Undul Wells there was a small plain in the pass, which from the number of birds of that kind found there, received the name of Guinea-Fowl Plain. Here, the previous desert character of the pass was lost, and beautiful vegetation commenced. The tulip tree of enormous size, the acacia, and the oleander clustered along the side of the way. The cactus rose stiff and hard among schistose rocks.

Going up to attack Magdala.

> Animals were abundant. The antelope occasionally bounded across the road; the boar and elephant had their haunts in the hills beside. Baboons and monkeys barked from the cliffs, and crowds of bright humming birds flashed their gorgeous plumage in the dazzling sunlight.[22]

Lieutenant Stumm was also "delighted by the splendidly unexpected environment," when, in early March 1868, he gazed at the landscape near Antalo.

> Across from the camp the round straw roofs of the little village of Garadigdig peek out from the undergrowth; farther on, a green side valley closed off by huge trees and impenetrable thickets, over which tower the mountains with their lush green slopes. Everywhere splendid water springs up and is carefully guided by the natives through long ditches to their fields and gardens. That was really tropical vegetation, an Abyssinian landscape as one dreams of it, that we enjoyed twice as much after the barren plains and mountain ranges that we had crossed during the preceding weeks. Who would have expected to find such a paradise in the blue mountains that looked so rough and unreal and that stretch away like an uninterrupted wall south of Antalo?[23]

The participants in the expedition were particularly impressed by Ethiopia's sublime mountain landscapes. Thus Gerhard Rohlfs raved about the landscape around Gunna-Gunna: "Until our baggage came, we had time to visit the lovely waterfall of Gunnagunna, which spills over an eighty-foot high cliff through blooming roses, jasmine, and aloes and then meanders away through a valley full of olive trees and castor bushes. . . . The route was, as always, extremely romantic, and especially as we moved west, the view of the mountains of Adua, whose tops towered jaggedly and steeply and provided an enchanting image of the unbending defiance of Tigray's inhabitants."[24] On the way to Lake Ashenge, he was again impressed by the beauty of the landscape: "Up as far as Messino the vegetation was even lusher than in the lower parts of the valley and a place full of splendid wild olive trees, sumac, mimosa, and laurels, closely woven together by creeper vines, completely hid the view of the valley walls, and one might have thought one was in a primeval forest on the banks of the Benue or the Niger rivers."[25] But Rohlfs also already made critical observations regarding the harmful ecological consequences of the slash-and-burn clearing practiced in the country: "If this kind of burning and scorching continues in Abyssinia, after a few centuries the whole country will be a desert, because most of the mountains are too steep to retain the humus layers during tropical rainstorms.... In a country that consists of such absolutely steep mountain soils, plant growth must be very carefully preserved to provide a permanent source of irrigation for the valleys, and to retain thick topsoil in the mountains."[26]

Gerhard Rohlfs

Gerhard Rohlfs was born on April 14, 1831, in Vegesack (near Bremen, Germany), the son of a physician. With Heinrich Barth and Gustav Nachtigal, he is one of the most important German Africanists, who succeeded in exploring large parts of the Sahara and Sudan. Rohlfs led the life of an adventurer at first, breaking off his studies of medicine to join the French Foreign Legion and go with them to Algeria: "He was at first the prototype of the adventurous European daredevil in the age of "Africa fever," but no one else so tirelessly made so many and such long voyages between the Atlantic and the Red Sea."[27] However, later on, the adventurer shifted to voyages of discovery. His great crossing of North Africa from the Mediterranean to the Gulf of Guinea in 1865-1867 made him known throughout the world and put him in the first rank of African travelers: "In addition to Livingstone, Speke, and Grant, and setting aside Clapperton, no educated European had so completely explored that part of the world."[28] In later years, Rohlfs devoted himself primarily to research on the eastern Sahara and the Libyan desert. Although he could never entirely overcome the shortcomings of his scientific education, his fascinating books nonetheless made him one of the popular German travelers in Africa. Rohlfs took part in the Magdala expedition as an interpreter "on behalf of His Majesty the king of Prussia," as he himself wrote: "Through Krapf's mediation, I was recommended to

> accompany the observer Phayre as an interpreter, and I was able, through an Arab who knew the Abyssinian language (Tigray) and an Abyssinian who spoke adequate French, to communicate with the natives."[29]
>
> In April-May 1868, during the return march, Rohlfs took the opportunity to make a trip to the west of the march route by way of Lalibela and Sokota, passing through a still little-known region to reach Antalo,[30] where he rejoined the English expeditionary force. He said that he had been greatly impressed by Lalibela's rock-cut church and also visited Aksum, the former capital of the ancient empire of the same name in northern Ethiopia.[31]

The participants in the expedition—especially Richard Holmes of the British Museum and William Simpson—sought out churches in the area they traversed. Lieutenant Stumm described such an excursion:

> Very nearby lay a few churches on a . . . thickly overgrown hill, surrounded by the dwellings of the monks, and I climbed up there almost every morning . . . , in order to talk or to barter for curiosities. Among the latter was a little cross of iron or copper worked in a pretty form, such as every priest or monk carries with him in a small leather pouch. In addition, little books written on parchment with wooden covers, and long, narrow scrolls with psalms and remarkable pictures that are kept in leather boxes and tied with knots, so that they can be carried around the neck by their owners. The churches themselves had the usual form, only here the cross-shaped outer wall was made of latticework, and at the top of the conical straw roof particularly dainty eight-armed crosses were attached and amply provided with bouquets of flowers.[32]

The participants in the expedition were also strongly attracted to the local markets, whose hustle and bustle was described extremely vividly and colorfully. Thus Rohlfs, for instance, reported on the market in Antalo:

"Every Wednesday a market is held in Antalo that draws people from the whole surrounding region; one finds there all sorts of local products, kinds of grain, onions, garlic, brown cabbage . . . , cotton fabrics, small baskets woven of colored straw, incense, antinomy, sulfur, butter, milk, hydromel or honey-water, which, when it has fermented a long time, is intoxicating, and finally, outstanding coffee from Gondjam and the lands of the Gallas."[33] Stumm compared the activity in the market of Antalo with that of the Leipzig fair:

> The news of a weekly market in Antalo led me to return to this place a few days later. From a distance we could already see long lines of natives with their wares, or hurrying with big burdens of salted goods to the market, which was to be held on a large square in the middle of the city. There might have been two to three thousand men gathered there, and, from a distance, the noise of the sellers and buyers resembled the humming of an immense swarm of bees. Traders of both the female and male sexes squatted in long lines and had placed their wares in front of them in baskets or animal skins. The bargaining and haggling and arguing and gesticulating was no less lively than that at the Leipzig fair, and one could see that when it comes to fleecing one's neighbors, people proceed in the same way throughout the world. . . . The main items being traded were grain, peas, bread, honey, butter, onion, white and dark brown cotton goods, tanned hides, crude iron objects such as swords, spears, and large hairpins, tobacco, and a few things in worked silver.[34]

In a few cases, direct contact was even made with the local population. In a place called Shelikut, the curious Ferdinand Stumm and one of his friends enjoyed a feast to which Ethiopians had invited them. He described the encounter with humor but also with certain condescension:

> Meanwhile, a glistening beauty began to stir water, flour and pepper in a pan, and put the devilish brew on the

quickly kindled fire. In a few minutes the dish, whose elaboration we observed with a shudder, was ready; damp, somewhat greenish-looking flatbreads appeared in a shallow basket; small pieces of the bread were torn off, rolled up, and filled with the hot pepper mixture and hand-delivered to our mouths by the housewife. . . . The large quantities of honey-wine consumed gradually put the guests in the best of moods; a musician appeared who drew three constantly repeated notes from his one-stringed instrument. Several members of this strange society were soon enchanted enough to sing a few national songs, and when my companion and I, so as not to be outdone in politeness by our hosts, did our best to sing a few English and German melodies, the merriment reached its peak. It was high time to avoid the increasing intimacies . . . and in the evening [we reached] the camp, where we recounted our strange experiences to an astonished assembly.[35]

The fact that participants in the expedition were able to move so freely through the country was due, not least, to the effects of British propaganda. In October 1867, the British leadership had made a diplomatic and political agreement with the native population, local potentates, and important provincial princes to protect the march from the coast to Magdala and to provide a reliable supply of food and forage. At Napier's behest, Colonel Merewether had distributed two documents throughout the country: a proclamation addressed to Tewodros as well as an appeal to the Ethiopian people announcing that the English army was going to war against Tewodros alone, and that no friendly citizen of Ethiopia would be harmed.[36]

> *To THEODORUS, KING OF ABYSSINIA*
>
> I am commanded by Her Majesty the Queen of England to demand that the prisoners whom your Majesty has wrongfully detained in captivity shall be immediately released and sent in safety to the British camp.
>
> Should your Majesty fail to comply with this command, I am further commanded to enter your Majesty's country

at the head of an army to enforce it, and nothing will arrest my progress until this object shall have been accomplished.

My Sovereign has no desire to deprive you of any part of your dominions, nor to subvert your authority, although it is obvious that such would in all probability be the result of hostilities.

Your Majesty might avert this danger by the immediate surrender of the prisoners.

But should they not be delivered safely into my hands, should they suffer a continuance of ill-treatment, or should any injury befall them, your Majesty will be held personally responsible, and no hope of future condonation need be entertained.

R. NAPIER, *Lieut.-General, Commander-in-Chief, Bombay Army*

To THE GOVERNORS, THE CHIEFS, THE RELIGIOUS ORDERS, AND THE PEOPLE OF ABYSSINIA

It is known to you that Theodorus, King of Abyssinia, detains in captivity the British Consul Cameron, the British Envoy Rassam, and many others, in violation of the laws of all civilized nations.

All friendly persuasion having failed to obtain their release, my Sovereign has commanded me to lead an army to liberate them.

All who befriend the prisoners or assist in their liberation shall be well rewarded, but those who may injure them shall be severely punished.

When the time shall arrive for the march of a British army through your country, bear in mind, People of Abyssinia, that the Queen of England has no unfriendly feelings towards you, and no design against your country or your liberty.

Your Religious establishments, your persons, and your property shall be carefully protected.

> All supplies required for my soldiers shall be paid for. No peaceable inhabitant shall be molested.
>
> The sole object for which the British Force has been sent to Abyssinia is the liberation of Her Majesty's subjects.
>
> There is no intention to occupy permanently any portion of the Abyssinian Territory, or to interfere with the government of the country.
>
> R. NAPIER, *Lieut.-General, Commander-in-Chief, Bombay Army*

In dealing with the Ethiopian princes, the British military leadership thus followed a policy based on the principle of "divide and conquer."[37] Many of these princes were in open revolt against Emperor Tewodros, and the English made skilful use of this fact. The most powerful of these princes was Wagshum Gobaze, the ruler of Lasta, which lay about fifty miles from Magdala, and Dajazmach (Prince) Kassai of Tigray.[38] The British made it clear that they were not going to war against the country of Ethiopia and its people, but only against Emperor Tewodros, who was thereby politically isolated. Moreover, they emphasized that the goal of the Magdala campaign was not a permanent occupation and subjection of a foreign people, but only a temporary, limited action to free the hostages and punish an insubordinate ruler. Therefore the British sought the princes' neutrality and offered them these alliances. They tried to cooperate with almost all the more important rulers and warlords along the route of their march and to conclude agreements to safeguard their communications and supply lines as well as to provide for food and forage for the expedition. This also holds for the two female rulers of the Muslim Gallas, Werkait and Masteeat, who were particularly willing to grant the English free passage through their territories and to provide them with food supplies. Moreover, they were prepared to cooperate militarily with the English army.

The most important actors in this diplomacy were Werner Munzinger, who had been sent to Lasta to make contact with Wagshum Gobaze and Major James A. Grant, who was supposed to negotiate with the Galla queen Masteeat regarding the participation of her warriors in the siege of Magdala—successfully, as it turned out, since the queen's troops were later to block the escape route from the mountain fortress to the south.[39] Whereas Gobaze himself kept his distance from the English, he contacted them through his representative Mashesha and agreed to a meeting between the latter and Napier in Santara, on March 29, 1868. The most important goal was to arrive at a satisfactory agreement with Kassai of Tigray, since the latter at that time ruled over what was probably the most powerful Christian province of Ethiopia, and about half the route of the march passed through his territory. Nevertheless, by way of his envoy Mircha Werque, who as a liaison and interpreter remained constantly with the expedition, Kassai set conditions for his cooperation with the English. The latter were to leave the country as soon as possible after Tewodros had been overthrown; in addition, the Egyptians were not to be aided in their expansion plans against Ethiopia, and after their withdrawal, the English were to leave no consul behind them. Hence, before the final decision to cooperate was made, there was to be a personal encounter between Kassai and Napier, which was prepared by a British delegation under Grant and Munzinger, and took place near Hawzen on February 25-26, 1868. Kassai also took the occasion to request Britain's support against his rival Wagshum Gobaze, which Napier refused, however, because he did not want to get involved in intra-Ethiopian power conflicts, in order to avoid endangering the success of his campaign. But Kassai was promised an ample reward for his cooperation, which he was to receive after the end of the campaign against Tewodros. Thus the meeting ultimately proved successful, and Kassai became a reliable ally for the British troops, for whom he delivered 15,000 kilos of grain per week to the storehouses in Adigrat and Antalo and protected their supply and telegraph lines.

Through the far-sighted diplomacy of the British, who counted on the support of the Ethiopian princes willing to cooperate with them, the expedition was transformed from an apparent invasion of a whole country into the conquest of a single mountain fortress that was defended by only a few thousand warriors.[40]

The non-violent and liberal treatment of the people also paid, if not in hard cash, at least in a great increase in reliable security and steady delivery of resources. On the other hand, the Ethiopian people along the march route benefited from hard cash, since the English paid for all their food and forage as well as for services, and paid for them in Maria-Theresa thalers, a significant number of which the British army had brought along with it, and which were the usual currency used in the country. In addition, stealing from or mistreating natives was subject to severe punishment. Overall, in this way, the participants in the expedition were able to establish and maintain a good long-term agreement with the local population that contributed greatly to the success of the Magdala campaign.

Maria-Theresa Thalers in Exchange for Food

An unusual and noteworthy characteristic of the British Magdala campaign was the deliberate choice not to appropriate by force the resources necessary to sustain life. In the history of wars in Ethiopia, this was something new. Times of war had always resulted in heavy burdens on the traditional economy and the people of the country. Warriors or soldiers "lived off the land," plundering the peasants, whether their own or those of the enemy country. Taking booty and pillaging, stealing food and livestock, and destroying settlements were seen as "normal" everyday events in wartime. The consequences of this way of waging war were the impoverishment of the rural population, famines, epidemics, refugee movements, and the devastation of whole areas of land.[41]

There were two chief reasons for the British army's decision not to use force to provide for itself and to pay for all deliveries in cash with the Maria-Theresa thalers in current use in the country. First, given the long supply lines and limited resources of their own, the British were extremely dependent on a constant and reliable local supply of food for the men and forage for the animals, which would have been imperiled by the use of force. Second, the British wanted to ensure a good and cooperative relationship between the foreign soldiers and the native population. In this vein, Captain Hozier praises the conduct of the British army: "Honesty was, however, the English General's best policy; for a single day of plunder would have driven the people, with their cattle, into the hills, the supply of meat would have been cut off, and the few provisions which were obtained from the natives could no longer have been procured."[42] According to Lieutenant Stumm, the English observed the wise principle of not making any requisitions, paying for everything in cash and generously, and the property of the localities was protected by English guards against the theft that could so easily have occurred with an army composed of so many different elements. Thus the agreement between the foreigners and the natives was the best solution, and during the later advance, only the army's reputation for handing out money, which spread throughout the land, was able to overcome the suspicions of the inhabitants and get them to provide supplies.[43]

Maria-Theresia silver dollars were the most commonly used currency in 19th-century Ethiopia.

However, such peaceable behavior on the part of the troops with regard to the people, which was in fact widely maintained, could be guaranteed only through a high degree of discipline, morale, and supervision, as Captain Hozier emphasized: "the discipline of the army was strict; no plundering took place.... It said much for the discipline of the army that when forage was desperately scarce, no horse wandered from the road to feast upon the tempting provender which lay so close within reach. But nowhere was the least damage done to the property of the inhabitants...."[44] Furthermore, sexual aggressions against the female population seem to have occurred hardly at all. According to Hozier, "no swarthy damsel was subjected to any rude gallantry on the part of the red coats."[45] However, now and then, Ethiopians offered to prostitute themselves, as Lieutenant Stumm reports: "The husband offers his wife, the brother his sister, as a worthless commodity, and I still recall a repulsive, vicious-looking fellow who moved through our camp with his barely adolescent daughters, offering in a loud voice to sell them at the price of one thaler apiece."[46]

Regarding the use of Maria-Theresa thalers during the expedition, Count von Seckendorf remarked:

> The Abyssinians were always extremely careful when they were paid with the aforementioned coin. They began by turning the thaler over in their hands for a long time, counted the pearls in the empress's crown, and only if the p. F. and the year 1780 were correctly imprinted did they accept the coin at full value. . . . Money, money, and yet again money, that was the solution here, because the Abyssinians sold their goods at high prices and seemed to think we were all as rich as Croesus. Every little article cost a thaler, and they refused to take any other coins.[47]

However, the British army's rejection of the appropriation of resources by force and its generous outlay of money also damaged its image and encouraged false impressions among the local population, as Lieutenant Stumm complained:

> As they knew, we had come to liberate our countrymen and to make war on the Negus, and instead of waging war in accord with the principles with which they were familiar, that is, by murdering, pillaging, and destroying, we moved peaceably through the country, handing out money. Thus it happened that Tewodros's spies reported to their exulting master that the English were no soldiers at all, but only a troop of unskilled traders who allowed themselves to be quite bravely deceived by the Abyssinians. . . . The great patience with which the English treated the inhabitants also had disagreeable consequences that inevitably accompanied this wise but often unbearable system. Thefts were committed in broad daylight with the greatest impudence in the camp, where the natives were allowed to sit around and loiter as much as they wished. Some individuals who wan-

> dered off to greater distances unarmed were even murdered, and the body was always found completely naked and abominably mutilated.[48] Captain Hozier also complained that the local inhabitants "extorted enormous prices from the soldiers, and, in return, despised an army which paid and did not take."[49]

The agreement at which Napier and Kassai of Tigray arrived on February 25-26, 1868, near Hawzen was extremely significant and strategically important for the success of the expedition, and it must be reproduced here in detail according to Captain Hozier's report, since his description is one of the most detailed and colorful accounts of the campaign:

> It was arranged that the meeting should take place on the banks of the Diab, a small stream, which runs from south to north, about midway between Adabagi and Hauzzein. Soon after daybreak on the 25th, the British troops were under arms, and . . . moved towards the Diab. The ground was rough and stony, but in the cool morning the troops . . . quickly traversed the distance, and while the sun was still low, their camp was pitched in some gently undulating ground laden with tall grass, about half a mile from the eastern bank of the Diab. On the further side of the rivulet . . . the Abyssinian camp was to be placed, for it was agreed that the rivulet should separate the troops of the two armies. . . . A little before eleven o'clock, a message came in to tell that the Abyssinians' vanguard was in sight . . . and shortly afterwards a dark group crowned the slope opposite the British camp, where a red tent was quickly pitched. A red tent is the sign of a king's residence in an Abyssinian army. In about half an hour the news was received that Kassai's main body, with drums beating and standards flying, was moving towards the Diab. In a short time, the group of men round the tent was largely swollen, and soon about 4,000 soldiers could be made out on the

summit of the hill. A few minutes before mid-day the army of Tigre began to advance down the slope towards the river. It numbered about 4,000 men, who moved steadily in a long deep line, to the music of rude kettledrums. Two yellow and red pennants, borne aloft in the center, marked the position of the chief. As soon as the Abyssinians began to move, the British troops got under arms, and in a few minutes, from the opposite direction, were moving down towards the water. They halted about 100 yards from the stream, where a large tent had been erected for the meeting. The British Commander-in-Chief mounted on an elephant, and, followed by his staff, rode down to the banks of the rivulet. The elephant was used on this occasion to impress Kassai, as the Abyssinians fear these animals much, and have never attempted to tame any of them. Close to the stream, he dismounted from the larger animal, and mounted his horse, lest the approach of the huge earth-shaking beast should create a panic and cause disaster among the cavalry of Tigre. By this time, the Abyssinian line was within 100 yards of the stream; it suddenly opened out in the centre, and Kassai, surrounded by his immediate counselors and guard, rode forward on a white mule, with a crimson umbrella borne above his head. He forded the stream, and was

Prince Kassai of Tigray, one of the most important allies of the British against the Emperor Tewodros.

received by Sir Robert Napier. Mutual salutations were exchanged, which, no doubt, were quite as sincere as those in daily vogue in the civilized world, although the words of each were quite unintelligible to the other. Kassai was then conducted to his tent, where he was received by a salute from a guard of honour. The unexpected rattle of the musketry blanched his cheek; doubtless a fear of treachery flashed through his mind. Then all dismounted, the British Commander led Kassai into the tent, and seating himself in a chair, placed Kassai in a chair on his right hand. Their respective officers ranged themselves on opposite sides of the tent – those of Kassai squatting on the floor, while those of Sir Robert Napier adhered to their more usual, although, perhaps, less natural, erect position.

Kassai was a young man of thirty-five years of age. His face, of a dark olive colour, was intellectual, but bore a careworn and wearied expression which justified the statement that he did not desire power, but that it was thrust upon him by the people of Tigre. He wore the Abyssinian costume, a white robe or toga embroidered with crimson, round his body, and the flowered silk shirt which marks those in high office round the king. His dark black hair was arranged in careful plaits by a piece of riband round the back of the neck.

The conversation was conducted through an interpreter. At first it consisted of almost meaningless enquiries about health. But the Abyssinians soon threw out hints for presents of firearms. These hints were adroitly fenced, and the conversation turned to the subject of our mutual Christianity. In this subject neither the chief nor his followers appeared to take nearly so much interest as in that of firearms, but they were held to it until it was suggested that a private interview would be desirable. The presents to be given to the Abyssinian chief were then brought in. They consisted of a double-barrelled rifle and some jugs and globets of Bohemian glass. They were laid on the floor at Kassai's feet, and, after inspection, were removed by one of his servants. The most valuable present of all could not be brought into the tent, but was surveyed through the doorway, as Sir Robert Napier gave to him a fine Arab horse, which had been his own charger. The goblets were brought back for use, and port wine, which seemed much enjoyed by the Tigrean courtiers, was served out to them. According to Abyssinian custom, the Commander-in-Chief had to drink some to prove that it was not a poison. ... The tent was then cleared of all but the Prince, the Commander-in-Chief, and two officers on either side, when serious matters were discussed.

Kassai was very anxious that the British army should undertake to guarantee his dominions against any invasion of his rival the Wagshum Gobaze. This Sir Robert Napier unhesitatingly refused, but promised that as far as advice and persuasion could go, he would endeavour to secure peace between them; he also assured Kassai that he was sensible of the friendship of the people of Tigre during the passage of the army through that territory, and drew to his notice the fact that all supplies were honestly paid for, and that no native had cause of complaint for a blade of grass or an ounce of food taken wrongfully by either troops or followers. Kassai was also informed that plenty of supplies could be brought from the ships, but that the army would have to be longer in Tigre if no supplies could be found in the province, and he was requested to send grain to the posts at Adigerat and Antalo, being assured that if he did so it would be remembered in his favour when the British left the country, and that the Queen would reward him in some way which would please him.

Kassai was then left alone to rest, and about an hour later was summoned to witness a review of the British troops. The 3rd Bombay Light Cavalry, clad in light blue and silver, the 4th King's Own, in scarlet, the gunners of Murray's battery, in dark blue and red facings, and a small detachment of the 10th Native Infantry, with scarlet coats and white turbans, formed a picturesque and compact, though small force. The cavalry charged, the infantry skirmished and formed square, much to the admiration of the Abyssinians; but these were chiefly delighted and impressed by the Armstrong guns. Kassai dismounted and closely inspected the pieces, handled the shells, and looked through the rifled barrel, while some of his followers remarked that the English must be good Christians or Heaven would not grant them intelligence to mold such wondrous weapons. It appeared that to their view, the greatest blessings, which could be vouchsafed to Christian morality, are firearms and gunpowder.

When the review was concluded, Sir Robert Napier and the officers of his staff accompanied Kassai to the rivulet, and there, they intended to bid him farewell. At the point of parting, however, an urgent invitation was given that the English officers should visit the Abyssinian camp. The rivulet was crossed, and in a moment they found themselves in the middle of the army of Tigre. All were astonished at their appearance and armament. They clustered round the few Englishmen in dense but ordered masses. Their heads were bare, except for their plaited hair; their costumes were picturesque, long white togas embroidered with scarlet; they were nearly all possessed of firearms of every description, from the matchlock to the double-barrelled rifle, but by far the greater number had double-barrelled percussion guns of English or Belgian manufacture. Many had pistols, and all had the long crooked swords worn from the right side, a cut from which it is said to be impossible to guard. The few – but there were very few – not armed with firearms had the sword, spear, and shield. Of the four thousand now present, about four hundred were cavalry, mounted on mules or ragged wiry ponies. The horsemen were armed similarly to the foot soldiers. These men were truly an enemy not to be despised. Hardy mountaineers, quick in scaling the most difficult paths of their rugged country, they would give an infinity of trouble to any European force. Had Theodore's army been as well equipped, and more attached to their leader, much British blood might have been spilled before Magdäla fell. Nor numerically were the soldiers of Tigre contemptible. At Adowa, his capital, Kassai had some six thousand more equally well armed. Their discipline was good, and in their short visit they showed a power of manoeuvring which would not have disgraced the forces of a civilized nation. Their serious error was that at night no sentries or pickets were posted outside their camp. Hence the wonderful effect of Theodore's night attacks, for which he became famous, may be accounted for. He himself always adopted these necessary precautions.

Up the hill went the English staff with the drums beating in front of them, surrounded by dense clusters of wild warriors until they approached close to Kassai's tent. Here they dismounted and were bidden to enter. At the further side of the circular tent was a small couch covered with silk cloth on which the Prince took his seat and placed Sir Robert Napier at his side. The Abyssinian officers of high grade sat round the tent on the floor at the left-hand side of their chief, while the English also seated themselves on the ground to the left of their commander. The scene was mixed and striking. The afternoon sun shone through the red tent, and lighted up with a crimson hue the robes and silken shirts of the Abyssinians and the uniforms of the Englismen. Girls bearing large baskets of Abyssinian bread and curry came in and placed them on the ground in front of the visitors, who were requested to eat. The Bread was brown, formed in flat circular cakes about a foot in diameter, and had a slightly sour taste. Very little sufficed to gratify curiosity, although it was permitted that each guest should help himself. In general, in Abyssinia, the servant, who brings in the loaves and curry, rolls some of the latter in a piece of the former, and after kneading it into a ball, thrusts it into the mouth of each diner. After enough had been eaten, other girls entered bearing huge bullock horns filled with "tedj", a drink made from fermented honey. This "tedj" or hydromel was poured into Florence flasks, one of which was given to each guest. It was expected that the recipient should bow towards the Prince and then empty his flask. No sooner, however, was the vessel emptied than it was seized by a watchful servant and again replenished. Each had to drink several flasks of the liquor, which tasted not unlike small beer, but rather sour. After a while, when many flasks had been emptied, musicians were introduced. The band consisted of six men who played on long pipes which uttered wild but not unpleasant music. A war song was then sung by a minstrel, and all the Abyssinians joined in chorus. The entertainment was now drawing to a close, and the presents were brought, in which were to be bestowed upon the British Commander-in-Chief. He was first invested with a silver-gilt armlet, the sign of a great warrior. Then a lion's skin and mane, the mark of a fierce fighter in battle, were placed upon his shoulders, a sword was girt upon his side, and a spear and shield for him were handed to one of his staff who acted on the occasion as his armour-bearer. The meeting then broke up. Kassai, after frequent hand-shaking, accompanied the General to the door of the tent, where a grey mule caparisoned with Abyssinian saddlery and housings was waiting. On this, Sir Robert Napier had to mount, and again accompanied by the Abyssinian army, rode down to the Diab, where the Abyssinians halted. The English General and his staff rode into their own camp, but the shades of approaching night prevented the soldiery from witnessing the return of their leader in such an unwarlike guise.

Early the next morning, Kassai paid a farewell visit to the British camp and had a second private interview with Sir Robert Napier, at which he promised to afford security to convoys and to threaten with severe punishment any who should endeavour to molest the telegraph through his dominions. He also promised to deliver three thousand madrigals of wheat and barley weekly, equivalent to about sixty thousand pounds, half at Adigerat and half to Antalo, for which he was to be paid. Such results of the interview were of no slight importance, for in a country where every man is a soldier, and a well-trained soldier, convoys would have to be most carefully guarded, posts well watched, strong and frequent garrisons maintained, and the line of telegraph continually patrolled if the population were hostile or even inclined to be unfriendly. Yet even the most sacred promises of the Prince of Tigre could not permit Sir Robert Napier to dispense with troops in position along the line of communication.

The friendship of Kassai was of the utmost value; he was a chief over whose country the road of the army lay for above 150 miles, and whose refusal to allow the soldiers to have free access to wood and water would have involved a campaign in Tigre as a preliminary to the advance on Magdäla. Yet, his friendship might prove fickle; he was young and newly seated on the throne, and he had several advisers who would have had him resent the entry of a foreign army into his dominions. His jealousy of Gobaze might rouse his anger against the English if they entered into friendship with the Wagshum, as they expected to be obliged to do, to secure similar advantages for the march through Lasta as the loyalty of Kassai would insure in Tigre. Even if Kassai meant and attempted to carry out his professions sincerely, whether he had the power to prevent attacks being made upon the convoys was open to doubt. The petty chieftain of any small district, eager for plunder and careless of his prince's orders, might lead his clansmen to assault the convoys of stores in their passage from Senafe to the front. Thus, though it was probable that Sir Robert Napier would gain something from his interview with Kassai, and the consequent friendship of the latter, and it was certain that at least a temporary quiet in the line of communications would be assured, his only real security was in being armed at all points, and in rendering himself, by his own judicious precautions, independent of all extraneous assistance.[50]

The meeting between Prince Kassai and Sir Robert Napier in February 1868 near Hawzen.

After this memorable encounter between Kassai and Napier, the English expeditionary force now advanced steadily toward Magdala. On April 5, Napier sent a messenger to Emperor Tewodros with the formal demand that the prisoners be immediately and unconditionally released: "By command of the Queen of England I am approaching Magdäla with my army, in order to recover from your hands Envoy Rassam, Consul Cameron, Dr. Blanc, Lieutenant Prideaux, and the other Europeans now in your Majesty's power. I request your Majesty to send them to my camp as soon as it is sufficiently near to admit of their coming in safety."[51]

Tewodros received Napier's message early in the morning of April 10, 1868. He brusquely rejected it and sent it back intact to the British commander-in-chief. At this time the Ethiopian emperor's behavior was characterized by changing moods and dispositions.

A photo of Prince Kassai and his officials posing with the British officers of the Magdala expedition.

An Unpublished Letter from Emperor Tewodros to Sir Robert Napier

An important, but hitherto unknown, letter from the Emperor has recently come to light. . . . The text, like that of most of Tewodros's letters, is in Amharic, and is undated. It was, however, probably written on or immediately after the dispatch of Napier's letter of the 5th of April, in other words little over a week prior to the battle of Mäqdäla and his suicide on the 13th of April. . . . The letter's fate is obscure. It seems evident from British accounts--and from its absence from British archives--that the letter (which was sealed and folded for dispatch) never reached its destination. The reason for this can, however, only be a matter of speculation. Was it dispatched and somehow intercepted; did Tewodros change his mind, and not send it; was its raison d'etre overtaken by events, and in particular by the approaching armed confrontation? We cannot say. . . .

The letter . . . is important in that it reveals its author's thinking prior to the battle of Mäqdäla. He seems to have been imbued with a deep and on-going desire-- unrealistic as it may now seem--to become friends with the British. This hope sprang largely, it would appear, from the fact that he had only a few years earlier befriended the former British Consul Walter Plowden (whose surname is rendered as Buladin). . . .

Tewodros clearly, if mistakenly, seems to have assumed that the friendship he had thus forged with the British envoy was an enduring one. He presumably felt that it would survive--and override--British displeasure at the detention of Rassam, Cameron, Blanc, Prideaux, and the other Europeans referred to in Napier's letter of 5 April--and whom he so pointedly ignored in his letter.

Tewodros, in his letter, thus reiterates that he had befriended Plowden "and others"--a reference perhaps to his other English friend John Bell (though the latter is not expressly mentioned by name). He goes on to express his confidence that the British commander would reciprocate by affording him (Tewodros) comparable friendship.

This friendship with Plowden (and Bell) was clearly an important factor in Tewodros's thinking. He had referred to it in his famous letter of 1862 to Queen Victoria--to which the British Government had not replied, and which thus led to his quarrel with London. . . .

The Emperor and/or his scribe were doubtless unfamiliar with the name Napier, and found it difficult to transcribe. The letter is thus addressed to Käbilafer. . . .

The letter, in English translation, reads as follows (translator: Alula Pankhurst):

> In the name of the Father, the Son, and the Holy Spirit, One God, King of Kings Tewodros. May it reach the servant of the Queen of England, the head of the appointees Käbilafer. How are you? I, thanks to God, am well. I have received the letter you sent me for our friendship. I am happy, by the Power of God, to have found your friendship. Previously I befriended Ato Buladin (Mr. Plowden) and others, in wanting your friendship. Now, by the Power of God, we are friends. And now, by the Power of God, you will be my friend, and I will be your friend. Make me friends with the Queen too.

> (Source: Richard Pankhurst, "Two Unpublished 19th Century Ethiopian Letters: From Emperor Tewodros to Sir Robert Napier, and from Däggazmac Naguse to Naib Hasän Bey," *Aethiopica* 11, 2008, pp. 61-64.)

On April 8, in a flight of generosity and clemency, Tewodros had freed a few hundred of his Ethiopian prisoners (including 186 women and children). On the next day, April 9, he ordered the release of the remaining Ethiopian prisoners—with the exception of those whom he continued to hold as political prisoners. When some of those released complained loudly about their chains, poor food, and lack of water, Tewodros became so furious that he broke in upon them with armed force. His soldiers followed the example of their leader and in the end, 200 to 300 dead and dying people were thrown over a steep mountain cliff.[52] Almost all of those killed were Gallas, who, as "unbelievers" (Muslims) and archenemies of the Christian Amharans, were the first to suffer Tewodros's wrath. Understandably, on learning of these events, the European hostages were deeply shocked by the emperor's unpredictable behavior and, in view of the approach of the English troops, now feared for their own lives. At this point, Napier received reliable reports that the Galla warriors had blocked the escape route from Magdala to the south, which was an important precondition for a successful attack on the fortress.

CHAPTER 8

The Aroge Massacre

The British army marching on Magdala was confronted by various problems.[1] Between the Bashilo River and Magdala there were no sources of water. The supply of food and munitions was not yet satisfactorily guaranteed. Furthermore, what would happen to the hostages could not be predicted. Was it possible that they might be massacred, following which Tewodros would attack the British, or would he perhaps attempt to escape with them? At that point, Napier still had no reply to his last message to Tewodros. Swift action therefore seemed indispensable, but the opposing forces must not be underestimated. In open battle, the British were sure of victory, but the uneven terrain in front of the mountain fortress of Magdala was still a cause for concern. Scouts' reports estimated the strength of Tewodros's army at more than 10,000 warriors.

The Magdala mountain fastness was the easternmost part of a mountain range that was difficult to access and had three towering peaks (the so-called Ambas): Fahla, above the Aroge plateau, which provided the only practicable access to Magdala, the neighboring Selassie in the middle, and the high plateau of Salamge. On Fahla, Tewodros had his cannons and mortars, which had been made by the German hostage Eduard Zander and his son-in-law Moritz Hall, placed in firing position. In addition, he had tested the fortifications and defensive works and increased the fighting morale of his soldiers by offering them the prospect of future victory and booty.[2] He concentrated his troops on Fahla and Selassi, whereas Salamge and Magdala, where the group of civilians was located, had only a minimal covering force.[3] Therefore General Napier rightly saw the high crests of Fahla and Selassie as the key strategic sites for his attack on Magdala, which had to be made from the west, especially since the allied Galla warriors had blocked the access routes to both the east and south of the fortress.[4]

On April 9, Napier, who was still twelve miles from Magdala, gave his commands to the 4,000 combat troops designated for the attack on the fortress. The infantry and artillerymen consisted primarily of British troops, while the cavalry and the sappers consisted largely of Indian units.[5] Colonel Phayre, commanding a small mounted vanguard, was to reconnoiter the Aroge plateau and the Fahla crest. The next day, April 10, 1868, Phayre set out shortly after dawn, and the infantry slowly followed him. Upon receiving Phayre's positive report that the Aroge plateau seemed to be free of enemy forces and secure, Napier ordered the mule train with the troops' baggage and the cannons to set out, but was completely surprised when he found no English soldiers posted to secure the deployment zone.[6] In addition, Napier obviously had no intention of fighting a battle there on that day.[7] But his opponent's behavior finally forced him to do so.

It seemed to Emperor Tewodros, who was observing the approach of the British troops by telescope from Fahla, that there was a favorable opportunity for an attack by his own troops. He believed that by seizing the apparently unprotected mule train he could easily gain a rich booty. Therefore he ordered—probably not least as a result of the pressure of his impatient warriors—his favorite general, Fitawrawi Gabriye, to storm down the mountain with 500 subordinate officers and 6,000 warriors and attack the mule train. The emperor himself remained on Fahla, in order to direct the fire of his artillery from there. The first salvo landed near General Napier's staff and disconcerted the English because they thought they were out of the range of the emperor's guns. However, General Napier had already swiftly given the necessary commands to defend against the impending Ethiopian attack.

This is how Gerhard Rohlfs described the beginning of the battle and the first salvos of the Ethiopian artillery:

> It was 4 p.m., and Sir Robert . . . had also arrived, while Phayre was still busy in the triangle between Selassie and Fahla. But Tewodros had seen us coming; we could clearly perceive people moving about on the Fahla plateau, and since Phayre could not, because he was too close to the foot of the mountain, Tewodros showed him by a cannon

shot, the ball hurtling far over the few cavalrymen, that he would not tolerate such temerity. –The first shot had thus been fired, it was 4:15 p.m. . . . But the retreating Phayre now had Tewodros's soldiers on his heels; they poured down from Fahla like a swarm of ants and were so eager for battle . . . that hardly ten minutes later they arrived in the triangle that Phayre had just left with his small number of cavalry.[8]

The Ethiopian artillery, to whose construction Emperor Tewodros had so intensively devoted his efforts, proved not to be very effective.[9] The cannons produced under the guidance of the hostages Saalmüller and Waldmeier were aimed too high and were loaded with too much powder, so that the balls flew too far and did no damage. His notorious "secret weapon," a seventy-ton giant mortar, cracked the first time it was loaded. On the Aroge plateau, the Ethiopian warrior groups now faced the well-disciplined, well-trained, and well-armed British-Indian combat troops. The marine rocket batteries and the other artillery pieces shot salvo after salvo into the attacking ranks of the Ethiopians and then onto the mountain peak of Fahla, nearly striking Emperor Tewodros himself. In addition, the English infantry unit "The King's Own" fired on the Ethiopian troops with their Snider-Enfield rifles, so that the opposing attack gradually stalled, but it was by no means over. Instead, the concentrated fighting now dissolved into multiple battles on the uneven terrain. A few of the Indian units (the Sikhs and Punjabi sappers) were forced to engage in hand-to-hand bayonet combat with the enemy, as Captain Hozier remarked:

> A large body of Abyssinians bore down upon the position occupied by Milward's guns and Chamberlain's Pioneers. Notwithstanding the effects of the mountain artillery, they continued to advance with much determination and order. Chamberlain, with his Pioneers, advanced promptly to meet them; both sides rushed in fearlessly, and a close contest ensued between spears and bayonets; for the men of the Punjab did not possess breechloading arms, and could not load so rapidly as the European soldiers. Not without

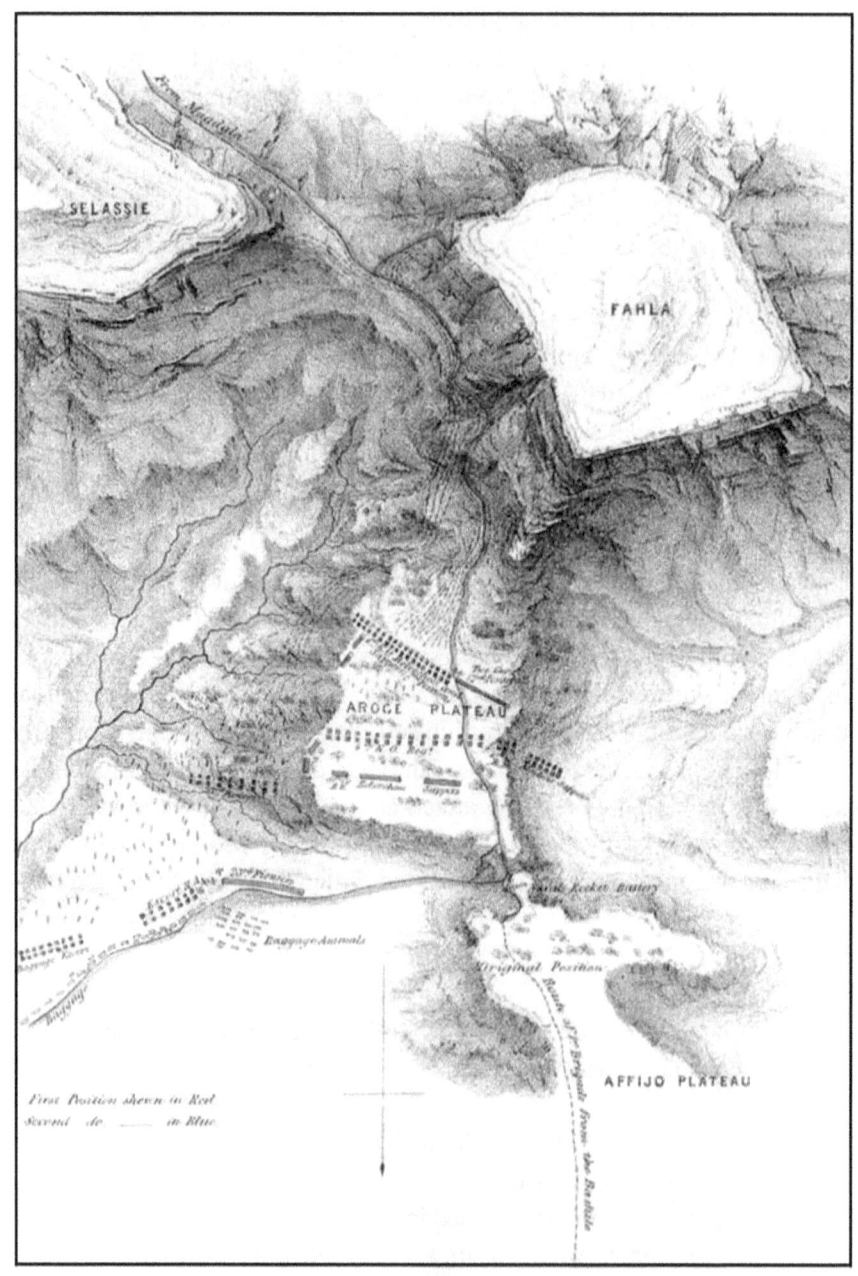

Attack plan of the British troops on the way to Magdala.
In the center is the plateau of Aroge.

a gallant resistance, in which many spear-wounds were received, were the Abyssinians forced off, and urged with great slaughter into the ravines on Chamberlain's left front.[10]

In close combat with the physically larger, robust Sikhs, the rather gaunt, slender Ethiopian warriors hardly had a chance.[11]

Lieutenant Stumm gave a vivid eye-witness description of the battle:

> It was an indescribable sight, when the terrain allowed us to see it, with this barbarian army advancing toward us with frenzied rapidity and bellowing like cannibals, overflowing the path and covering the steep slopes with its masses. As if they could not reach the enemy fast enough, individual cavalrymen and foot soldiers rushed ahead, swinging their lances and encouraging the others to hurry. ... While ... a lively rifle-fire was beginning and the first artillery shells were landing among the enemy, the first rockets whizzed in high arcs overhead and threw the enemy, which had been sure of victory, into a panic. The warriors in the van immediately paid for their temerity with their lives, and the others hastened, as quickly as they had come, back toward the foot and the slopes of Fahla, and only from there did they return the fire of the Snider-Enfield rifles with their own poor matchlock rifles; another part of them rushed into the ... ravine, where they shared their comrades' bloody fate. ... They suddenly found themselves attacked from three sides in the narrow ravine. A terrible bloodbath was inflicted on these unfortunates by our rapid-firing infantry, which had only to aim into the masses crowded together there. ... The din of the rattling rifles and the booming of the cannons was soon accompanied by the thunder of a violent storm that broke out over the two parties to the battle and momentarily darkened the battlefield with an intense hail and rain shower.[12]

As it grew dark, the fighting slowly ebbed, and the end of the battle approached: "It was four o'clock in the afternoon when the first gun, which announced the opening of the engagement, was fired from Fahla; it was seven o'clock, and nearly dark, before the Abyssinian soldiery were completely driven off. A thunderstorm and heavy rain had continued during the greater part of the action. When finally repelled, the troops of Theodore spread in no hasty or disorganized flight; they returned again and again to the attack, wherever the ground favored them."[13]

For reasons of security, the English soldiers spent the night on the battlefield, ready to fight.[14] It was a miserable night's rest. Most of them had still had nothing to eat or drink all day long. They were not allowed to light any fire, and tents were not available because of transportation delays. Thus the soldiers bivouacked in the open and had to sleep in the damp and cold on the naked ground. Moreover, in the darkness they heard the cries of the hyenas and jackals as well as the groaning cries of the wounded Ethiopians, and in the distance they saw the torchlight of the Ethiopian search parties trying to recuperate their wounded and bury their dead. Emperor Tewodros spent the night with the remains of his defeated army on the high ridge of Selassie. He lamented the losses suffered that day, but, above all, he mourned his favorite general, Fitawrawri Gabriye, who had fallen in the battle. This old warhorse had fought in the van and with great bravery, but he was finally hit in the temple by a bullet from a Snider-Enfield rifle and killed.[15] His body was found in a splendid robe of silk and gold alongside his dead horse.

The outcome of the battle was clear. Despite the courage of his troops, Emperor Tewodros had suffered a devastating defeat, lost about half his army, and forfeited the strategic advantage of his defensive position in the Magdala mountain fortress. The artillery he had held in such high regard had proven largely ineffective because of inadequate training and experience on the part of its Ethiopian crews (as well as possible sabotage by the hostages Saalmüller and Waldmeier).[16]

Altogether, about 700 to 800 Ethiopian warriors were killed and 1,200 to 1,500 wounded, most of them seriously, while on the British side there were only twenty casualties, two fatally wounded men, nine seriously wounded, and nine lightly wounded.[17] Nonetheless, the wounded "were promptly attended to after the action, and many wounded Abyssinians were also carried off the field by the British troops and were carefully tended to in the British hospitals."[18] The English soldiers expressed their admiration and respect for the fact that not a single Ethiopian fighter had thrown away his weapon to run away.[19] The weapons of both the dead and the wounded were still in their hands or lay next to them. The great endurance and bravery of the Ethiopian opponents were generally recognized.

The next morning, the horror on the battlefield was evident:

> Tracks of blood marked the courses of the wounded, who had spent their last efforts in feeble attempts to crawl back to the fortress and live, or to gain the shelter of some neighbouring bush to die. . . . On the left, where the Pioneers and baggage-guard had been engaged, the dead lay thickest. Along the ravine where the bayonet-charge was made, men and horses were heaped in tens and twenties. . . . On the right, where the firing had been at longer ranges, the tale of the dead was not so great, and more wounded men lay around, awaiting without a murmur or repine the approaching termination of their sufferings. The claims of these to sympathy were not disregarded. Many a dying man was turned to ease his pain, and many a flask was emptied of its precious contents, at the dumb request of some fevered lip or parched tongue. In addition to those that lay there, hundreds had been carried into the fortress during the night.[20]

Before a week elapsed, "the sleek wolves and greedy vultures deprived the field of much of its horror, giving it the appearance, which it long will retain, of a place of skulls".[21] The British sent out special teams to retrieve the last wounded and bury the dead (probably for hygienic reasons). According to Stanley, after three hours' work seventy-five wounded Ethiopian warriors had been brought to the field hospital and 540 dead buried.[22]

The enormous discrepancy in the losses alone makes the glaring asymmetry in military tactics and weapons technology between the opponents obvious.[23] Captain Hozier observed that "the great disparity of loss was due to the determined and persistent attack of the Abyssinians against the better-disciplined and better-armed force of the British, and to the invincible courage with which the Punjab Pioneers, whose smooth-bore musket was hardly equal to the double-barrelled percussion-gun of the Abyssinians, repaired the deficiencies of that weapon by a stern use of the bayonet."[24] Against this background, Aroge acquired the unmistakable character of a testing ground for new, modern European weapons. A special unit of the Magdala expedition consisted of the Royal Marine Rocket Brigade, which had been formed from the available officers and sailors of the British navy and the warships lying in Annesley Bay, as the Austrian military observer Kodolitsch reported.[25] Thanks to its excellent training, desire to go into battle, and strict discipline, this unit was considered an elite one among the expedition troops.[26] It was used to handle the Hale rocket batteries.[27] According to Kodolitsch, the rocket batteries fired 300 rockets during the Battle of Aroge on April 10, 1868, and 200 during the taking of Magdala on April 13, 1868.[28]

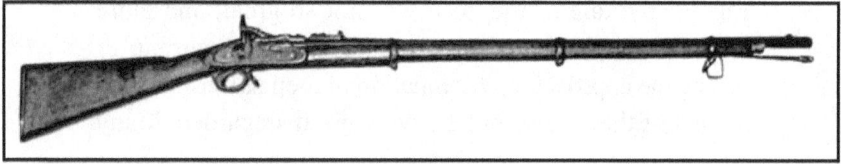

A quick-firing Snider-Enfield rifle, which was used for the first time in the battle of Arogé during the Magdala expedition. The breech-loading feature (the gun was loaded in the rear of the weapon instead of in the muzzle) allowed for faster reloading.

However, the newest weapon system used in the Magdala campaign, and the most important for the Battle of Aroge, was the Snider-Enfield rifle, a modern breech-loading, rapid-fire weapon that was used almost exclusively by the white British infantry units, and not by the colored British Indian troops, who were equipped only with older types of weapons (muzzle-loaders). Four thousand of the modern weapons were issued to the British troops on the Magdala campaign.[29] The Snider-Enfield was a redesigned, modernized version of the older Enfield rifle commonly used by the British army. In 1866, the Snider-Enfield had been produced by the Royal Small Arms Factory (RSAF). As a modern breech-loader, this rifle was effective up to a distance of about 500 meters and could fire more shots in quick succession, so that the rapidity of fire and the firepower of the troops equipped with this weapon were several times greater.[30] "On average," Kodolitsch estimated, "we can assume seven shots a minute, which is probably more than enough,"[31] and after inspecting the wounds this weapon inflicted on the bodies of the enemy, he noted: "The Snider-Enfield's wounds were small on entering, but terrible, because the bullets caused devastating damage inside the body."[32] According to the Prussian military observer Count von Seckendorff, the British infantry equipped with the Snider-Enfield fired a total of about 18,000 bullets during the battles at Aroge.

Various reports on the battlefield of Aroge indicate that the rocket batteries also had devastating, primarily psychological effects. Thus Captain Hozier wrote: "The rockets and shells left abundant testimony that the consternation and dismay which they had caused among the Abyssinians were far from groundless. Many a charred mass and mangled heap showed how terrible was the havoc, how awful the death they carried wherever they sped."[33] The military physician Bechtinger arrived at a similar estimate:

The Battle of Aroge, April 10, 1868. In the foreground, slain Ethiopian warriors.

"The Snider-Enfield, which like the rockets was used here for the first time, wrought terrible devastation among the attackers, they decimated dreadfully the brave ranks of these brown fighters. . . . The rocket batteries, spewing fire and flame, also quickly spread such terror and horror among the Abyssinian troops that they shortly afterward fled in haste; few escaped, because they were caught, along with another Abyssinian unit, in such a heavy canister fire that almost none were spared."[34]

Nonetheless, Count von Seckendorff was not particularly impressed by the use of the new British weapons system: "One cannot say that the Abyssinian expedition has taught us much about tactics or weapons technology. No judgment can be made regarding the Snider-Enfield rifle or the effects of the new seven-pounder mountain artillery. For that, the two engagements, the Battle of Aroge and the assault on Magdala, were too unimportant."[35]

However, Tewodros's Ethiopian warriors had nothing, as opposed to these modern European weapons systems, other than their eagerness to attack, their courage, and their boldness. On the whole, the Battle of Aroge, the only real and at the same time decisive encounter between Tewodros's forces and the English expeditionary army, was more the stronger's massacre of the weaker than a battle between two equally strong opponents.

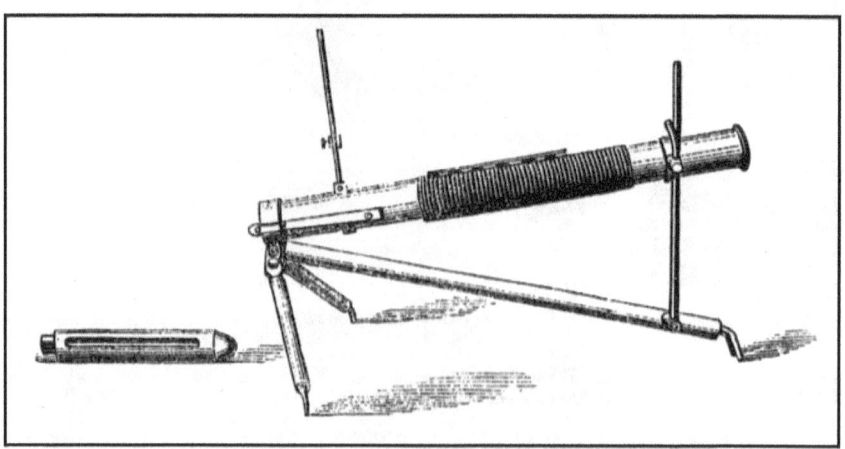

A rocket of the naval brigade, one of the new weapons developed during the Magdala expedition, had disastrous effects on the enemy.

CHAPTER 9

The Assault on the Fortress

On April 11, 1868, when Tewodros became fully aware of his defeat, he tried to gauge the possibilities of arriving at a peaceful settlement of the conflict. He asked the advice of the English diplomat Rassam, whom he was holding hostage, and on the morning of April 11, he sent two British hostages, Martin Flad and Lieutenant Prideaux, along with his son-in-law Dajazmach Alame, to Napier, with the oral message that he wished to arrive at a settlement with the English.[1] However, Napier insisted on the immediate release of the hostages and an unconditional surrender, though he promised to treat the emperor and his family honorably.[2] At the envoy Alame's request, he also agreed to grant Tewodros forty-eight hours' time to think over his offer. In addition, Napier had Tewodros's son-in-law shown the cannons, to demonstrate British superiority in weapons and to make it clear that there was no chance of resistance being successful.

Thereupon, the British supreme command sent the messenger back to the Ethiopian camp with a letter to Tewodros: "Your Majesty has fought like a brave man, and has been overcome by the superior power of the British army. It is my desire that no more blood may be shed. If, therefore, your Majesty will submit to the Queen of England, bring all the Europeans now in your Majesty's hands, and deliver them safely this day in the British camp, I guarantee honourable treatment for yourself and for all the members of your Majesty's family."[3]

Emperor Tewodros rightly interpreted this message as an ultimatum, which he, as a proud ruler, rejected as an unacceptable humiliation. He had Napier's letter returned in the same envelope, which amounted to a deliberate insult to the British commander-in-chief and which understandably enraged the latter.[4] Furthermore, along with the envelope, Tewodros sent

Tewodros with two of his lions. The lion was a symbol of royalty (Massaia VII, 59).

his own message, in which he addressed himself, in the form of a testament to the Ethiopian people and also to the English,[5] expressly declaring that he refused to hand himself over to the enemy as a prisoner:

> *In the name of the Father, and the Son, and the Holy Ghost, one God in His Trinity and His Unity:*
>
> Kasa, whose trust is in Christ, thus speaks:
> O people of Abyssinia! Will it always be thus that you flee before the enemy, when I myself, by the power of God, go not forth with you to encourage you?
> Believing that all power had been given to me, I had established my Christian people in this heathen spot. In my city are multitudes whom I had fed – maids protected and

maidens unprotected; women whom yesterday made widows, and aged parents who have no children. God has given you the power. See that you forsake not these people. It is a heathen land.

My countrymen have turned their backs on me and have hated me, because I imposed tribute on them, and sought to bring them under military discipline.

My followers, who loved me, were frightened by one bullet, and fled in spite of my command. When you defeated them I was not with the fugitives.

Believing myself to be a great lord, I gave you battle; but, by reason of the worthlessness of my artillery, all my pains were as nought.

The people of my country, by taunting me with having embraced the religion of the Franks, and by saying that I had become a Mussulman, and in ten different ways, had provoked me to anger against them. Out of what I have done of evil towards them may God bring good! His will be done! I had intended, if God had so decreed, to conquer the whole world, and it was my desire to die if my purpose could not be fulfilled. Since the day of my birth till now no man has dared to lay hands on me. Whenever my soldiers began to waver in battle, it was mine to arise and rally them. Last night the darkness hindered me from doing so.

You people, who have passed the night in joy, may God do unto you as He has done to me! I had hoped, after subduing all my enemies in Abyssinia, to lead my army against Jerusalem, and expel from it the Turks. A warrior who has dandled strong men in his arms like infants will never suffer himself to be dandled in the arms of others.[6]

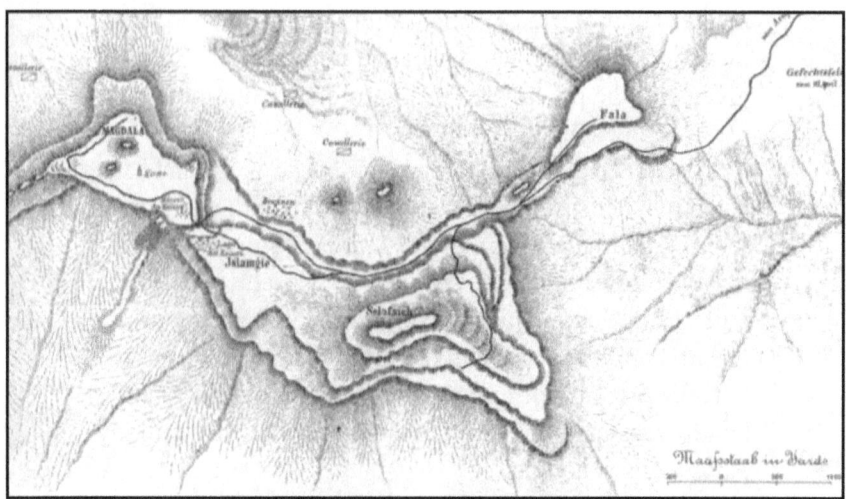
Map of Magdala and its surroundings.

Tewodros's Letter of Easter Saturday
(Amharic Original)

The letter . . . was written on Easter Saturday after the disastrous battle of Aroge and just before Tewodros's unsuccessful attempt to commit suicide. . . .

Since the letter was sent in reply to Napier's demand that he surrender, the last sentence, as well as some passages earlier on, carried the message that he would commit suicide rather than hand himself over to the British. Whether this was understood by the British commander or not is another matter.

Now that the Amharic original has been found and published, the impression that this letter was written (in fact dictated) by someone who was literally at his wits' end is confirmed. The translation is substantially correct though far from literal. The scolding of his countrymen is there—for resistance against his policies, for lack of courage in the final battle (which was certainly unfair) and for accusing him of apostasy.

So are the references to his great ambitions and plans, including the delivery of Jerusalem from the hands of the Turks. But the language is more terse and the tone is much more subdued than in the English text. The impression remains that Tewodros accepted the outcome basically as his own personal failure; therefore, "Kasa, whose trust is in Christ" instead of "King of Kings Tewodros"—and the expressed wish that God would grant his people "something good out of the evil I have done." A significant mistranslation at the time concealed the fact that Tewodros expressed the same kindly sentiments towards his enemies, the British. He wrote, "(You) people, who have spent the night in joy, may God not make you like me," in other words not permit the British to suffer defeat as Tewodros himself had done. The translation has the unforgiving ". . . may God do unto you as He has done to me" (C. R. Markha, *A History of the Abyssinian Expedition*, London, 1869, p. 331).

In his final hours of despair, Tewodros was looking back across the years of hard work: the introduction of new technology, the roads and the cannon; the attempts to create a disciplined army and a modern administration, even a more enlightened and tolerant attitude in religious matters; the many battles he had fought, in person, in order to unify the country in the face of external threats which he perceived clearer than his countrymen. It was all there in that letter which he believed to be his last. When he decided to use "Kasa" and not "Tewodros," it must also mean that he had returned in his thoughts to the days of his youth when everything had seemed possible.

(Source: Sven Rubenson, "Meqdela Revisited," in Taddese Beyene, Richard Pankhurst, and Shiferaw Bekele, eds., *Kasa and Kasa: Papers on the Lives, Times, and Images of Tewodros II and Yohannes IV (1885-1889)*, Institute of Ethiopian Studies, Addis Ababa, 1990, pp. 17-18.)

A short time after dictating this letter, Tewodros attempted to kill himself, but failed because he was thwarted by his secretary, Prince Ingeda, and his soldiers.[7] The Ethiopian ruler had sat in the open air for a long time, said a prayer, thrice bowed down, drunk a little water, and then suddenly drawn his pistol and put it in his mouth. But his men knocked the weapon out of his hand in time. This failed suicide attempt apparently made a deep impression on Tewodros and strengthened both his self-confidence and his hope for a peaceful settlement of the conflict with the English.[8] The suicide attempt proved to be an extremely critical moment for the European hostages. Most of Tewodros's advisors had recommended that the hostages be immediately killed and the English resisted to the bitter end.[9] But the emperor decided not to follow this advice and ordered the release of the Europeans, who dribbled into their camp unharmed on Easter Sunday, April 12, 1868, to the cries of joy of the English troops. Tewodros obviously hoped that releasing the hostages would favorably impress the English and lead to a peaceful solution. To this end, he wrote the same day a conciliatory letter to Napier, in which he also announced that he was sending him a gift: he intended to send him cattle for the Easter holiday.

In Napier's tent, this memorable letter was first translated from Amharan into Arabic, and then into English, and read as follows:

> *In the name of the Father, the Son, and the Holy Ghost, one God:*
>
> The King of Kings Theoderos:
>
> May it reach the beloved servant of the Great Queen of England.
>
> I am writing to you, without being able to address you by name, because our intercourse has arisen so unexpectedly.
>
> I am grieving at having sent you my writing of yesterday, and at having quarreled with you, my friend. When I saw your manner of fighting, and the discipline of your army, and when my people failed to execute my orders, then I was consumed with sorrow to think that, although I killed and punished my soldiers, yet they would not return to the battle. Whilst the fire of jealousy burned within me,

Satan came to me in the night, and tempted me to kill myself with my own pistol. But, reflecting that God would be angry with me if I were to go in this manner, and leave my army without a protector, I sent to you in a hurry lest I might die, and all things be in confusion before my message should reach you. After my messenger had gone, I cocked my pistol, and, putting it in my mouth, pulled the trigger. Though I pulled and pulled, it would not go off. But when my people rushed upon me, and laid hold of the pistol, it was discharged, just as they had drawn it from my mouth. God having thus signified to me that I should not die but live, I sent to you Mr. Rassam that same evening, that your heart might be made easy.

Today is Easter; be pleased to let me send a few cows to you. The reason of my returning to your letter yesterday, was that I believed at that time that we should meet one another in heaven, but never on earth.

I let the night pass without sending for the body of my friend Fitaurari Gabri, because I thought that after my death we should both be buried together; but since I have lived, be pleased to allow him to be buried.

You require from me all the Europeans, even to my best friend Waldmeier. Well, be it so; they shall go. But, now that we are friends, you must not leave me without artisans, as I am a lover of the mechanical arts."[10]

Napier replied to Tewodros only by an oral message in which he repeated and confirmed his earlier demands. But on listening to the messenger, the emperor got the impression that the British Commander-in-Chief was willing to accept the gift he had proposed. In this belief, he let the last European hostages go free. As a friendly gesture of gratitude, Napier ordered the mortal remains of leader of the Ethiopian army, Fitwrawri Gabriye who had fallen in the battle, to be handed over to the emperor, but otherwise maintained his hard, uncompromising attitude and thus ultimately sent back the gift in the form of a herd of livestock (about 1,000 cattle and 500 sheep). This behavior of Napier's aroused in his own time, as well as in ours, controversial assessments and critical commentaries.[11] In the eyes of some historians, Tewodros's noble act of releasing the hostages contrasts unfavorably with Napier's scandalous betrayal.[12] But it seems possible that Napier initially considered accepting Tewodros's gift, especially since it appears that at first he was not aware of the scope and political significance of doing so. Only when his advisors and Ethiopian experts had explained to him that in terms of Ethiopian customs the magnitude and kind of the gift could be seen as an offer of peace and reconciliation, did he inform the camp's pickets to send back the herd of livestock. In the rediscovered original Amharan text of Tewodros's message, only "cattle" are mentioned, without any indication of the quantity.[13] According to other historians, it is undeniable that Tewodros was tricked by the English, but it still remains unclear whether this happened deliberately or unintentionally, and who bore the main responsibility for it.[14]

Tewodros's Peace Offering of Easter Sunday

One issue over which there was much controversy at the time is whether Napier, in order to get all the Europeans safely to his camp, deliberately deceived Tewodros into believing that the latter's peace offering of 1,000 cows and 500 sheep for Easter would be accepted as such, and that Tewodros would therefore be spared an attack on his fortress. Napier defended himself against the accusation by saying that Tewodros's letter mentioned only "a few cows," and that he had been led to believe that the gift in that case was of no "significance."[15]

The problem is that Napier originally reported that Rassam and some others had simply "acquired the impression" that he had accepted the "offering of a few cows," and that Waldmeier, who was also present, recalled that Napier had said that he would refuse to accept them *until* all the foreigners had reached his camp in safety. According to Markham, finally, there were two translations of the sentence about the gift in Tewodros's letter of Easter Sunday, the one with "a few cows" and another with "1,000 cows and 500 sheep, as a breakfast for the troops."[16] The fact that the Amharic originals of the two letters that Tewodros wrote to Napier on 11 and 12 April never reached the official archives and have eluded discovery until now made many . . . suspicious about their exact content.

It is therefore a cause of great satisfaction that the originals of these very important letters have finally surfaced and been published.[17] We now know that Markham was wrong: Tewodros's written message has no numbers and no reference to the British troops. Nor does it, however, have any word corresponding to "a few." It reads, "Today is Easter, so permit me to send you heifers."[18] This does not prove that Tewodros was not deceived, only that Napier may not have known the size of the gift when he stated that he believed the matter to be of no consequence.

(Source: Sven Rubenson, "Meqdela Revisited," in Taddese Beyene, Richard Pankhurst, and Shiferaw Bekele, eds., *Kasa and Kasa: Papers on the Lives, Times, and Images of Tewodros II and Yohannes IV (1885-1889)*, Institute of Ethiopian Studies, Addis Ababa, 1990, p. 16.)

After Napier's unequivocal rejection of his "peace gift," it was clear to Emperor Tewodros that the English army's final attack was imminent. Therefore on Easter Monday morning (April 13, 1868) he attempted to escape to the southeast of the fortress, but this attempt stalled at the outset because most of his demoralized soldiers refused to obey him, apparently out of fear of the Galla warriors lying in wait for them out there.[19] Thereupon, he dissolved the rest of his army and urged his followers to see to their own safety. Many of his leaders and warriors subsequently surrendered to the English troops, while only a handful of loyalists and his personal entourage remained with Tewodros, in order to make a last stand against the enemy with him. When Napier heard about Tewodros's attempt to escape, he promised the Gallas a princely reward (50,000 thalers) if they managed to capture the emperor, and he accelerated his preparations for storming the fortress.

On the morning of April 13, Napier had already decided to storm Magdala without further delay, especially since there was a danger that Tewodros might yet succeed in escaping.[20] The attack began on Easter Monday, at about 9 a.m., and the plains of Islamgee were soon filled with the expeditionary army's forces. There, the English soldiers found the battered and decomposing bodies of the hostages whom Tewodros had massacred on April 9. Around noon, the advancing troops were met by parts of Tewodros's dissolving army, thousands of Ethiopian warriors and their families who had to be disarmed: "The numerous Abyssinians coming down the road, many of whom wore red woolen shirts and thus identified themselves as the emperor's soldiers, had to lay down their weapons at the foot of the mountain and had soon deposited large heaps of shields, spears, and curved sabers."[21] Lieutenant Stumm had joined the advancing British troops.

> After an hour and a quarter of arduous climbing, the attacking column reached the ... saddle linking Fahla with Selassie, and without having encountered the slightest resistance, we suddenly found ourselves in the teeming camp, surrounded by howling men, women and children who had lived here for months in the small, round straw huts or brown tents, and who covered the plateaus and slopes in countless numbers. Eleven prisoners with more than 1,500 armed men immediately presented themselves and handed over their weapons. It was hardly possible to make one's way through the dense masses of animals and humans who were hurrying back and forth, or trying to save their meager possessions from the expected plundering.... I very quickly caught up with the advance cavalry unit, and for the first time I now glimpsed Magdala, which lay in front of us like an inaccessible eagle's nest.... The foot of the fortress is reached by passing over a flat area one and a quarter miles in length; here lay the emperor's real camp, and, as we approached the people in it, fled in

all directions. Only at the foot of the mountain did there remain a group of about a hundred cavalrymen, from which a few shots were fired at us when we halted about 1,500 paces away from them. . . . Then four riders suddenly emerged from the mass; the shimmering silver plate on his shield and saddle and a fluttering white mantle distinguished one of the men, and as the skilled riders approached us, the natives hurried behind the shelter of the rocks, shouting: Negus! Negus! (king! king!). It was the emperor himself, who was making his last bravura performance and challenging his hesitating enemies. The little group halted two hundred paces away from us, fired its rifles at us, and as quickly as it had come, returned to the others, who received them with shouts of joy.[22]

The British army bombarded the fortress of Magdala for several hours before beginning the actual assault on it. Lieutenant Stumm used this time to inspect the camp the Ethiopians had abandoned. "One could have made a fine ethnological collection of all the implements and weapons that the frightened Abyssinians had left behind. . . . The place where some of the Europeans had lived was particularly interesting, and it was strange to suddenly find, among Abyssinian household effects and the like some German travel account or a volume of Becker's world history."[23]

The subsequent assault on the fortress of Magdala, which began around 4 p.m. and lasted exactly a quarter of an hour, was described by Captain Hozier this way:

> On arriving at the gateway, the progress of the assailants was arrested, for it was closed, and, for the moment, the engineers had not at hand the powder-bags with which to blow it in. The crowbars were, however, set to work, and the gate was broken down, when it was found that the path of the gateway, fifteen feet deep, was filled up with large stones to a height of twelve feet, which formed an almost insurmountable obstacle. While the Sappers were engaged upon the gate, the garrison maintained a constant fire upon

them through their loopholes, and during that time nine officers and men received wounds or contusions. Meanwhile, some of the men of the 33rd, turning to the right, found a point where the wall and fence were sufficiently low to be surmounted by means of a scaling-ladder. Here they entered, and, taking the defendants of the gate in flank, drove them up a narrow path, which, twisting through rocks and soldier's huts, led to another narrow gateway, seventy yards higher up. Through this the leading men of the 33rd rushed, close behind the rearmost fugitives; and being followed by the whole regiment, the summit of the fortress was quickly occupied, the standard of England was planted upon the African rock which had so long been the prison-home of British envoys, and Magdala was captured. The followers of Theodore immediately threw down their arms and prayed for quarter, which was of course granted, and no further loss of life occurred.[24]

Theodor himself continued to fight for only a short time, and then, in view of the hopeless situation, he released his last loyal comrades-in-arms from their duty to support him and forced them to flee.[25] He made it clear that he did not want to be taken alive by the enemy, took his pistol, put the barrel in his mouth, pulled the trigger, and fell to the ground. With this act of self-destruction, he deprived the British of their last and final triumph, taking him alive; at the same time, he laid the foundation for the legend of his unconquerability and became the symbol of the Ethiopians' unswerving independence.[26]

Lieutenant Stumm, an eyewitness, described the discovery of Tewodros's body:

> Climbing a narrow rock stairway, we advanced quickly toward a second gate, through which we passed without meeting resistance. About a hundred paces beyond it lay the half-naked body of the emperor himself, who had taken his own life with a pistol shot. A strange smile was on the remarkably young and attractive-looking face, and I was

THE ASSAULT ON THE FORTRESS 127

A drawing of the suicide of Emperor Tewodros on April 13, 1868.

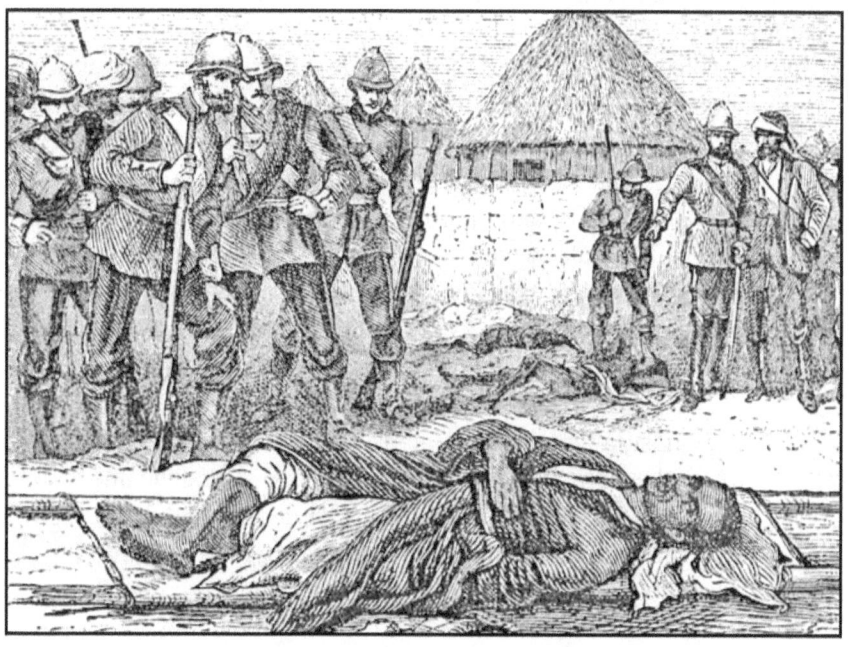

The corpse of Emperor Tewodros exhibited in front of the victors.

struck particularly by the finely-drawn, boldly aquiline nose. Naturally, we were unable to determine whether Tewodros had been stripped at the last moment by his fleeing companions, or had intentionally dressed to make himself as inconspicuous as possible.[27]

According to Count von Seckendorff, Tewodros's features expressed "intelligence and strength of will,"[28] whereas Stanley thought he discerned in them resolution and savagery.[29] Stanley also spoke of a curious and partly disrespectful treatment of the body on the part of the soldiers, officers, and other onlookers, who tore off bits of his clothing until he lay there almost naked. Only when Napier heard of it was an end put to this disgraceful behavior.[30]

The casualties in the "Battle for Magdala" were comparatively small: the British artillery's bombardment killed about twenty Ethiopian warriors and civilians and wounded about 120, whereas a further forty-five Ethiopians were killed by rifle fire during the infantry assault. Altogether, the British troops' casualties included only ten seriously wounded and five lightly wounded.[31]

In the wake of the storming of the Magdala fortress there was widespread looting of Ethiopian art treasures and cultural artifacts. According to Stanley, fifteen elephants and almost 200 mules were required to carry away the booty.[32] This kind of looting was a very common practice in the British army at this time, and was therefore tolerated by Commander-in-Chief Napier in Magdala as well.

In addition to Stanley's extensive description,[33] a few of the German observers and other participants in the assault on Magdala also provided eyewitness accounts of the looting. For example, Lieutenant Stumm:

> Almost in the center of the plateau was a church from which the alarm was now diligently sounded, and the numerous priests hurried in fear from their outlying huts to their shrine. In addition, we saw several large, round huts carefully roofed with black blankets and animal hides. A multitude of soldiers were already busy removing from these treasure houses belonging to the emperor valuables

and objects of all kinds, which their former owner had in part appropriated in his own country, and in part received as gifts from foreigners. There were piles of weapons from all countries and ages, richly decorated shields, ancient sabers with ornamented handles, English rifles, and poor-quality target pistols. Here one soldier was dragging strangely formed jugs and silver vessels, there another was carrying crosses richly set with precious stones and large, shapeless bishops' caps with delicate filigree work. Colossal parasols of red velvet, silk fabrics, rifle cases, travel kits, ecclesiastical objects, powder flasks, photographs, and even a homeopathist's pharmacy and a case of champagne—all this lay in a chaotic heap; part of it was carried off by the soldiers, and another part was sold for a pittance to late-comers.[34]

And Gerhard Rohlfs reported:

Going on, we came to the king's own apartments and here the soldiers had torn everything apart and piles of objects of all kinds lay in confusion. Here one saw monstrances, silver and copper crosses and incense burners from churches, there crowns of gold and copper, flints, precious sabers, carpets, clothes, cases full of soap, with needles, cottage pianos, books, door keys, piano keys, chairs, tools—in short, there was nothing that could not be found there. It was a regular junk shop on a large scale. Everyone was busy taking something, and we also took several objects, crosses and incense burners, in order to take them home with us as souvenirs. At the time, we did not know that when an English army takes a city all the goods that fall into the hands of the troops are their property and are sold for the common benefit. As soon as we learned this, we returned all the objects, even though we had already bought most of them from British soldiers.[35]

Rohlfs also referred to the "royal insignia, the real gold throne, saber, sword, etc." of which "Sir Robert took possession for the British government with the fullest right."[36]

The storming of Magdala was followed by a day-long, woe-begone exodus of Tewodros's defeated army and his entourage from the fortress, which Lieutenant Stumm described vividly:

> Over 50,000 men, including feeble old men, moaning old women who could hardly drag themselves away, and countless children, all loaded with their meager possessions and followed by famished asses and mules dolefully swaying from side to side, moved hurriedly past our camp. Mute desperation, or something even worse, a complete apathy, was expressed on the miserable faces of the unfortunate people. . . . Soon dying people were lying on our right and left, too old or too weak to keep up with the frantic stream. A few of them were vainly trying to make litters in order to take a moaning old person with them. Perhaps the younger ones, having gone for days without eating, no longer had enough strength, while the poorest of them was shoved under a bush, where he might be already dead this evening and in the morning eaten by hyenas and vultures. Here a mother bends with heart-rending cries over her child dying of thirst after she has sought in vain to give him nourishment from her dried-out breast. Gloomy-looking priests trudge on with their big parchment books and fortunately rescued ecclesiastical objects; there, a group of old women, emaciated, skeletal, literally reduced to skin and bones; soldiers from Tewodros's former army, heavily burdened horses, teeming children vainly seeking their relatives in the mass of people, who, trampling the languishing under their feet, constantly stream by us.[37]

Gerhard Rohlfs was also an eye-witness to this cortege of the defeated and the wretched, and he was also present when the former hostages arrived:

The exit of Emperor Tewodros's defeated army and civilians after the British conquest.

From the camp we had gone only a few miles as far as the river, but this road was already dreadful enough: the exodus of Tewodros's disarmed forces had now been going on for three days, with dying people here, children abandoned by their parents there, here a corpse beginning to decay, there a skeleton, and at every step the carcass of a horse, ass, or mule. The road to the Beshilo River was as heavily traveled as one of the most frequented roads into a European capital city; here came elephants, pulling the huge Armstrong cannons and mortars . . . , there a unit of English soldiers, here emigrants from Magdala, there the former prisoners, the Syrian Rassam and Mr. Cameron, weakened by his long privations, there the other Europeans who had lived with King Tewodros: Dr. Schimper in his red silk ceremonial garb, riding on a mule (the latter a gift of the deceased king), with his pointed hat and long white beard in the manner of Tilly, would have looked more like a wizard from the Giant Mountains than a German scholar had not the long pipe, which our plant collector always had by him, even on the mule, immediately betrayed the German; then Herr Zander, resembling a patriarch with his long gray beard, followed by an English lady, no longer dressed in the latest Leipzig fashion, missionaries who in Abyssinia concerned themselves little with religion . . . — all of them were streaming north, happy to say farewell to Magdala forever.[38]

The "arrival of the numerous prisoners with their families and their servants, each of which was also accompanied by his family, made our camp no more comfortable," as Lieutenant Stumm noted. "With the hindrances presented by the cortege following us there could, of course, be no excess of food supplies, and a few of the English hostages complained, oddly enough, that they had actually been better off in Tewodros's camp."[39]

The departure of the freed hostages with their relatives and servants.

All in all, the physical and psychological condition of the European hostages and their native (Ethiopian) wives, children, and servants seemed far better than their liberators had expected after the numerous reports of whipping, shackling, and acts of cruelty. For example, Stanley was surprised by how healthy and well-clothed the hostages were.[40] Through discussions with released German prisoners, Stumm also gained a more nuanced impression of their treatment while in captivity: "They could certainly not complain about the emperor's behavior toward them, and a few of them, like the painter Zander, who was born in Dessau, had held important posts. They were always well paid, and although Tewodros had constantly kept them in his camp, with the exception of the most recent period, they absolutely could not consider themselves prisoners. . . . Things were, of course, different for the English envoys and missionaries; they had been almost always kept in chains day and night and were exposed to the moody emperor's harassments and cruelty."[41] When on April 14, 1868, shortly after the hostages were released, a photo of England's diplomatic representatives—including Cameron and Rassam—was made, the "carefully arranged ankle shackles" were probably intentionally included in the picture.[42]

All the European ex-hostages, and especially the "prominent" ones, were treated with great courtesy not only by the English but also by the German members of the expedition. The German hostages were looked after, in particular by their countrymen, who distributed, in the name of the King of Prussia, a certain amount of money to help them get through the following weeks. For example, in his autobiography, the botanist Georg Wilhelm Schimper acknowledged the courteous treatment he received: "Sir Robert Napier and his superior officers, as well as Count von Seckendorff and Herr G. Rohlfs, treated me with great attention, kindness, and friendliness, and provided me with all the comfort I could ask for."[43]

Thus ended the bombardment and conquest of the fortress that gave its name to "the Battle of Magdala," whose most notable elements were not so much the brief and insignificant combat actions as the preceding liberation of the European hostages, the emperor's suicide, the widespread looting, and the exodus of the defeated Ethiopians.

ROLL OF THE PRINCIPAL CHIEFS LIBERATED FROM MAGDÁLA, SHOWING THE LENGTH OF THEIR IMPRISONMENT, AND WHERE THEY WENT TO AFTER RELEASE.*

No.	NAMES	Length of Imprisonment (Years)	Position and Country	Where Gone To
1	Faris Aleo	11	Chief of Edjoo	Rebelled temporarily, but probably submitted to Gobaze
2	Wagshum Tiferri	4	Chief of Wag, cousin of Wagshum Gobaze	Went to Gobaze to submit
3	Dejaz Sahelo	5	Chief of Haramat	Joined Kassai, and submitted to him at Senafe
4	Ajaj Negussy	6	Chief of Haramat, son of Sahelo	Remained at Haramat
5	Balgeda Muro	5	Chief of Tera	Remained at Dongolo
6	Shum Agame Aragavi	7	Chief of Agame	Joined Kassai of Tigre, and submitted to him
7	Lij Sahaja	5	Chief of Id	
8	Shum Salova Ezekias	5	Chief of Salowa	Went to Samnil
9	Dejaj Iman	15	Brother of Ras Ali	Left Magdála, without paying his respects
10	Burreo Gosh, and two brothers	15	Chiefs of Godjam	Joined Gobaze, and submitted to him
11	Cassa, son of Dobey	14	Chief of Semien	Brothers of the Empress; went to Semien
12	Gwangul, son of Id	14	Chief of Id	
13	Hugh Dereso	3	Chief of Selemh	Left Argeo sick; destination unknown
14	Goshu Woudia	4	Chief of Belessa	Went to his country
15	Ras Walda Mariam	1	Chief of Begemder	Ditto
16	Ras Gebrie	1	Chief of Id	Ditto
17	Ras Waheda Tadla	1	Ditto	Ditto
18	Betwaded Tadla, and two brothers	1	Ditto	Ditto
19	Engeda	Unknown	Chief of Dembea	Ditto
20	Mauresse	2	Chief of Shoa	Went to his country under safe-conduct of Masteeat, Queen of the Gallas
21	Ubié	2	Ditto	Ditto
22	Aregi, son of Sewale Sellassie	2	Ditto	Ditto
23	Ajah Wondie	1	Chief of Begemder	Went to his country
24	Ajaj Geret	3	Ditto	Ditto
25	Ajaj Gebra Selassie	1	Ditto	Ditto
26	Belala Gobazye	1	Ditto	Ditto
27	Sergie Deresso	1	Ditto	Ditto
28	Lej Meshasho	Unknown	Ditto	Ditto
29	Wossen Illma	1	Chief of Kwara	Ditto
30	Wossen Dareya	1	Chief of Id	Ditto
31	Pasha Haylo	10	Chief of Meja	Unknown
32	Talef Engela	1	Chief of Tigre	Joined Kassai of Tigre, and submitted to him
33	Ras Lebie	3	Chief of Maga	Went to Shoa
34	Balgeda Area	13	Chief of Enderta	Joined Kassai of Tigre, and submitted to him

List of the principal chiefs liberated from Magdala, showing the length of their imprisonment, and where they went after their release.

CHAPTER 10

The Looting of Ethiopian Cultural Treasures

After the Magdala expedition ended, many stolen objects, cultural artifacts, and art objects found their way, often by indirect paths, into state and private collections, family possessions, and the hands of ordinary soldiers. Most of the books and manuscripts went to the British Museum (or, subsequently, the British Library) or the Bodleian Library in Oxford, while a few went to the Royal Library in Windsor Castle and to smaller British collections. Other stolen objects, some of which had probably been among Emperor Tewodros's personal possessions, such as two crowns and a royal cap, the imperial seal, a gold chalice, ten altarpieces, and various crosses for processions, ended up in the South Kensington Museum (later the Victoria and Albert Museum), two richly ornamented tents belonging to the emperor in the present Museum of Mankind, and a few of the emperor's hairpieces in the National Army Museum. For the internationally known Ethiopia expert Richard Pankhurst, who has for many years been trying to get the art treasures from Magdala returned to Ethiopia, the looting, especially of ecclesiastical furnishings (the church of Medhane Alem), were a kind of "original immorality" and "acts of desecration," while the theft of Tewodros's great library amounted to depriving Ethiopia of its "national library" and "national archive."[1]

What happened in Magdala was completely common in other contemporary and earlier wars. The chronicle of the thefts of enemy's art works and cultural artifacts (for example, in Antiquity, the early Middle Ages, the Thirty Years' War, and in the wars of Napoleon and Hitler) is just as extensive as the chronicle of the wars themselves.[2] Art theft "was always con-

The cross of Emperor Tewodros II of Ethiopia, among the spoils taken by General Napier.

sidered part of the compensation owed to the victor and his armies."³ Thus the theft of art "for the sake of the state" is one of the oldest forms of organized criminality; but elements of psychological warfare obviously also play a role in it: "The splendor of the plundered treasures increased the victor's self-esteem, and the loss of the cultural heritage humiliated the defeated."⁴ Not until 1899 did article 28 of the Hague Convention on the Laws and Customs of War on Land prohibit any expropriation or willful destruction of cultural artifacts: "The pillage of a town or place, even when taken by assault, is prohibited." Finally, in 1954, under the impact of the destruction and cultural barbarities of the Second World War, the UNESCO convention regarding the protection of cultural artifacts during armed conflicts was adopted.

Many exhibitions and collections in ethnological museums in Western countries were established chiefly during the period between 1870 and the First World War, that is, during the era of colonialism. A significant part of this "colonial art booty" was carried off violently in the wake of military interventions. Toward the end of the 1980s, there emerged—at first in

Africa, then in other parts of the Third World—a movement that sought the return of stolen cultural artifacts and triggered a debate in the United Nations that is still continuing today. In essence, this debate involves the "recognition of the principle of repatriation" as "part of a process whose aim is the inevitable recognition of a moral and historical responsibility."[5] But these efforts—particularly those proceeding from the Third World—have been repeatedly frustrated by the delaying resistance of the great museums in the West. In December 2002, nineteen directors of the most important museums in the world (including the British Museum, the Louvre, the Metropolitan Museum of Art in New York, the Prado, the Rijksmuseum, and the Hermitage) signed a "Declaration on the Importance and Value of Universal Museums." Noting that museums "serve not just the citizens of one nation but the people of every nation," they defended their resistance to repatriation on the ground that "objects and monumental works that were installed decades and even centuries ago in museums throughout Europe and America were acquired under conditions that are not comparable with current ones," and argued that "Over time, objects so acquired—whether by purchase, gift, or partage—have become part of the museums that have cared for them, and by extension part of the heritage of the nations which house them. Today we are especially sensitive to the subject of a work's original context, but we should not lose sight of the fact that museums too provide a valid and valuable context for objects that were long ago displaced from their original source."[6] Nonetheless, although difficult legal questions were raised, a few voluntary repatriations of cultural artifacts to former colonial countries in Africa and Asia took place, for example, on the part of France and England. But on the whole, after thirty years of international debate in the United Nations, "the attempt to claim the developing countries' right to the repatriation of cultural artifacts that they had lost during the era of colonialism or other forms of foreign political domination can only be said to have failed. . . . Despite a few praiseworthy examples of voluntary restitution, from the point of view of many developing countries the problem continues to exist."[7]

This also holds for Ethiopia and its supporters in England and throughout the world who are demanding the return of the cultural artifacts and art objects stolen from Magdala. Today, "many Ethiopians take the view that the plundering of Magdala was not in accord with international law, and that the booty should be given back."[8] In any case, for reasons of state, England had from time to time voluntarily returned this or that valuable piece to Ethiopia.[9] On August 10, 1872, the former Prince Kassai of Tigray and Tewodros II's successor, Emperor Yohannes IV, wrote to Queen Victoria and British Foreign Secretary Earl Granville to demand the return of an edition of the manuscript of extreme importance for the Ethiopian state's self-conception, "Kebra Nagast" ("The Fame of Kings"), along with an icon with the picture of Christ wearing the crown of thorns, which was also of special importance for Ethiopia. Since during this time, England was interested in having good relationships with Ethiopia and wanted to acknowledge the importance the then Prince Kassai of Tigray's cooperation with Napier, a copy of the desired manuscript was returned to Yohannes IV and Ethiopia, though it was the less valuable edition. On the other hand, the icon that Yohannes asked for could not at first be found, and only years later was it discovered that it was in the private possession of Sir Richard Holmes, who had accompanied the Magdala Expedition on behalf of the British Museum.[10] When on the occasion of the coronation of King Edward VII in 1902, the Ethiopian Prince Tafari Makonnen was visiting England as Emperor Menelik II's envoy and saw what was probably the most famous private collection of Magdala manuscripts, that of Lady Valorie Meux, he announced that his emperor and his country wished to buy back these manuscripts. But Lady Meux's last will and testament—which granted this wish—raised such strong resistance among the English public that these manuscripts were ultimately not returned to Ethiopia. However, in 1924, on the occasion of the visit of Makonnen, later Emperor Haile Selassie of Ethiopia, the Empress Zawditu was given one of the two stolen crowns of Tewodros, the silver one, whereas the Victoria & Albert Museum received the other, more valuable, crown of gold. About forty years later, when Queen Elizabeth II was in Ethiopia on a state visit, she gave Tewodros's royal cap and seal to Emperor Haile Selassie.

In 1999, a series of prominent figures from Ethiopia, England, and the whole world, including Professor Richard Pankhurst of the Institute of Ethiopian Studies in Addis Ababa, established AFROMET, the Association for the Return of the Magdala Ethiopian Treasures, which from that time on pursued an information and lobbying campaign that at least succeeded in persuading a committee of the House of Commons to discuss the issue of repatriation.[11] AFROMET acknowledged that many of the stolen objects had been more securely preserved in British libraries and museums than they could have been in Ethiopia during the civil war after Tewodros's death and during later conflicts there.[12] It also recognized that the stolen manuscripts had been the object of valuable scholarly work. On the other hand, it argued, Ethiopia now had its own libraries and scholarly institutions, and the Ethiopian capital of Addis Ababa was now the center of international Ethiopian studies.[13]

We owe it to AFROMET's activity that in the interim, a few further looted treasures have been returned to Ethiopia (to the Institute of Ethiopian Studies Museum and the Ethiopian National Museum). In 2002 came the spectacular discovery of an amulet that had been taken off Tewodros's corpse by a British soldier more than 130 years earlier. According to an accompanying article in the *Times* for July 10, 1868, the soldier was sapper Henry Bailey of the Tenth Regiment of the Royal Engineers, who was one of the first to break into the fortress in Magdala. Bailey later gave the amulet to his uncle, Mr. C. W. Dunford, who lived in London's West End. The valuable amulet then remained out of sight until a private collector contacted Richard Pankhurst, who arranged for it to be returned to Ethiopia, with an insured value of about one million pounds, 134 years after it was stolen. But the majority of the objects stolen from Magdala are still in foreign hands, including the excavated fragments from Adulus, the manuscripts in the British Library and in Windsor Castle, various military trophies (e.g., in the King's Own Royal Regiment Museum), and last but not least, Henry Morton Stanley's personal plunder (shield, cap, a piece of Tewodros's tent, a saddle set with jewels). Thus there still remains much for AFROMET to do.

Afromet

AFROMET—the Association for the Return of the Maqdala Ethiopian Treasures—is an international organisation dedicated to retrieving priceless treasures looted during the British invasion of the country in 1867-8.

Its main aims are to track down the missing loot and then campaign for its return to Ethiopia. The bulk of the plunder has ended up in institutions like the UK's British and Victoria & Albert Museums. Hundreds of other items were taken back to the UK by individual soldiers and remain in private homes and collections.

Members—who include many prominent academics, politicians and church leaders—see the looting of Maqdala as a major loss. They believe the return of the treasure would be a huge boost not only to students of the country's history and culture, but to Ethiopia's tourism industry (vital to the country's development).

Membership is free and open to all friends of Ethiopia.

AFROMET is also keen to hear from anyone who thinks they may have inherited or acquired anything taken from Maqdala. All returned items are received in a spirit of gratitude and friendship. They will also be given a place of honour in one of Ethiopia's churches or museums, including the widely respected Institute of Ethiopian Studies in Addis Ababa.

The Association calls upon people of goodwill everywhere—particularly in Ethiopia and the UK—to support this pursuit of justice.

(Source: AFROMET website.)

CHAPTER 11

Orderly Withdrawal

After Magdala was taken, various difficult and sensitive problems had to be resolved before the withdrawal to the coast could begin.[1] Ten thousand Ethiopian civilians and former soldiers in Tewodros's army were living in wretched conditions near the British camp on the Aroge plain, and had not only to be provided with food and water but also protected from the attacks of the Galla warriors. Furthermore, the death of the Ethiopian emperor had to be re-examined carefully and his body appropriately buried. And finally, it had to be decided what should happen to the conquered mountain fortress of Magdala.

In order to have a professional and unchallengeable confirmation of Tewodros's suicide, Napier had the latter's body subjected to a thorough medical examination. The medical professionals' unanimous opinion was that death resulted from the firing of a pistol into the mouth.[2] After this examination, the body was dressed and laid out in a hut. The emperor's widow, who along with her son Alamayou had been put under Napier's special protection, was then given a letter from the latter "in which Sir Robert Napier offered to accomplish her desires with regard to the disposal of the body. By her request, on the 14th, it was buried with all decency, but without military honours, in the Church of Magdala."[3]

Magdala was in the territory of the Muslim Gallas, who had long ago taken it from the Amharas; however, Emperor Tewodros had won it back from them some years before. The two rival Galla queens Werkait and Mostiat, who had allied themselves with the English expeditionary army for the purpose of storming Magdala and overthrowing Tewodros, and who had surrounded the fortress with their soldiers and blocked all possible escape routes, now claimed control over the conquered fortress as their re-

Thatched church at Magdala where Tewodros was buried after his suicide on April 13, 1868.

ward. Napier himself apparently preferred to hand Magdala over to the Christian ruler, Wagshum Gobaze of Lasta, because if he were in control of the fortress, Gobaze would probably be able to halt the Muslim Gallas' advance and assume responsibility for taking care of the approximately 30,000 Christian Amharan refugees, his countrymen and co-religionists. This solution would also have relieved the British troops and their resources of a significant burden and have made the difficult withdrawal somewhat easier. However, Gobaze seemed primarily interested in Tewodros's cannons, which Napier could hardly have handed over to him without annoying Kassai of Tigray, through whose territory his retreating troops had to pass and on whose cooperation he continued to depend. So Gobaze finally rejected Napier's offer on the ground that he did not have enough troops or weapons to maintain a military outpost in the hostile Galla lands. Since the two Galla queens could not come to an agreement, but instead displayed their irreconcilable conflict before Napier, the latter ultimately decided that it would be best to destroy the Magdala fortress and consign it to the flames.[4]

Magdala in flames.

On the afternoon of April 17, 1868, the destruction of the Magdala fortress began. First, its weapons arsenal was destroyed, thirty-seven cannons and mortars in all, including the giant mortar, along with all the accompanying munitions. Then the fortifications were blown up and the huts set on fire. Since there were hardly any stone buildings, the flames quickly spread and also consumed the church, which was actually supposed to be saved.[5] According to Captain Hozier, a command issued on April 17 had ordered everyone to leave the Magdala fortress by 4 p.m.: "At that hour working-parties commenced the demolition of the captured ordnance, and the destruction of the fortress. The former were burst into atoms. The defences and gates of the AMBA were mined and sprung, and fire was applied to the palace and other houses, which spread quickly from habitation to habitation; these, burning slowly in the strong flame, sent up a heavy cloud of dense smoke, which could be seen for many miles."[6]

After this work of destruction, the last part of the British army crossed the Bashilo on April 18 and camped that night with the main force on the

British troops retreat to Zula, the starting point of the campaign.

Talanta plain. Here, further provisions for the retreat were made during the following days, the booty from Magdala was auctioned off, and the successful campaign celebrated with a large parade. The auction, which lasted two days, was described by Count von Seckendorff:

> The auction, which was very well organized by the English soldiers, brought in not insignificant sums, especially because a large portion of the real valuables were acquired by the British Museum. Among the things put up for sale were several gold and gilt crowns, vessels, weapons, carpets, crosses, and other ecclesiastical items that Tewodros had stolen from churches during his raids. A large number of books found few buyers, because no one knew their true worth, but interesting manuscripts must have been among them, some of which give particularly valuable information about the country's history. The greater part remained

in Abyssinia, since General Napier gave them to the church of Chelikot. –The proceeds from such auctions were called "prize money," and they were divided according to certain principles to officers and soldiers.[7]

The best bidder at the auction was Richard Holmes of the British Museum, who had 1,000 pounds available for this purpose, and made his choices after consulting with the expert Werner Munzinger. In all, Holmes bought, in this way, about 350 of the most precious and beautiful books and manuscripts from Tewodros's library.[8] In the end, the auction raised a sum of more than 5,000 pounds. Although the officers forewent their share, this brought the individual soldier hardly more than 25 shillings.[9]

Gerhard Rohlfs reported on an event during the auction that particularly enraged the Germans. Eduard Zander, one of the former German hostages, was deprived of nine crosses that Emperor Tewodros had given him earlier. Although he was compensated for the value of these crosses, Sir Robert Napier personally decided "that the aforementioned crosses of Zander's were to be considered Tewodros's property, and thus belong to the army, and they were sold the same day. Maintaining that the decorations were Zander's property, we three Germans, Stumm, Count Seckendorff, and I, abstained from the bidding."[10]

In an order of the day issued to his troops on April 20, 1868, Commander-in-Chief Napier acknowledged his soldier's achievements and declared the end of the Magdala campaign:

> *Adjutant-General's Office, Head-Quarters Camp, Dalanta Plain,*
> *20th April, 1868.*
> Soldiers and Sailors of the Army of Abyssinia! The Queen and the people of England entrusted to you a very arduous and difficult expedition—to release our countrymen from a long and painful captivity, and to vindicate the honour of our country, which had been outraged by Theodore, King of Abyssinia.
> I congratulate you, with all my heart, on the noble way in which you have fulfilled the commands of our Sovereign!

You have traversed, often under a tropical sun, or amidst storms of rain and sleet, four hundred miles of mountainous and rugged country.

You have crossed ranges of mountains (many steep and precipitous), more than ten thousand feet in altitude, where your supplies could not keep pace with you.

In four days you passed the formidable chasm of the Bashilo, and, when within reach of your enemy, though with scanty food, and some of you even for many hours without either food or water, you defeated the army of Thedore, which poured down upon you from its lofty fortress in full confidence of victory.

A host of many thousands have laid down their arms at your feet.

You have captured and destroyed upwards of thirty pieces of artillery, many of great weight and efficiency, with ample stores of ammunition.

You have stormed the almost inaccessible fortress of Magdala, defended by Theodore and a desperate remnant of his chiefs and followers.

After you forced the entrance to his fortress, Theodore, who himself never showed mercy, distrusted the offer of it held out to him by me, and died by his own hand.

You have released not only the British captives, but those of other friendly nations.

You have unloosed the chains of more than ninety of the principal chiefs of Abyssinia.

Magdala, on which so many victims have been slaughtered, has been committed to the flames, and now remains only a scorched rock.

Our complete and rapid success is due—firstly, to the mercy of God, whose Hand, I feel assured, has been over us in a just cause; secondly, to the high spirit with which you have been inspired!

Indian soldiers have forgotten the prejudices of race and creed to keep pace with their European comrades.

Never did an army enter on a war with more honourable feelings than yours. This it is that has carried you through so many fatigues and difficulties; your sole anxiety has been for the moment to arrive when you could close with your enemy.

The remembrance of your privations will pass away quickly; your gallant exploit will live in history.

The Queen and the people of England will appreciate and acknowledge your services; on my part, as your Commander, I thank you for your devotion to your duty, and the good discipline you have maintained throughout.

Not a single complaint has been made against a soldier, of fields injured, or villages willfully molested, either in person or property.

We must not, however, forget what we owe to our comrades who have been labouring for us in the sultriness of Zoulla, the Pass of Koomaylee, or in the monotony of the posts which maintained our communications. One and all would have given everything they possessed to be with us; they deserve our gratitude.

I shall watch over your safety to the moment of your reembarkation, and shall, to the end of my life, remember with pride that I have commanded you.[11]

On April 21, the actual retreat to Zula began. At first, the march was still greatly hindered by the tens of thousands of former followers of Tewodros (former soldiers, elderly people, the sick and wounded, women and children) with their baggage and animals, all of which had to be protected from the violent attacks of the Galla warriors swarming around them. This also held for some Ethiopians whom Tewodros had forcibly transported to Magdala and held prisoner there, and who had been freed by the English after the conquest of the fortress. This difficult initial phase of the withdrawal was described by Kodolitsch: "For military reasons, the march away from Magdala . . . was made in only 3 columns, in order to give each of them a certain strength at least half-way corresponding to the enormous number of baggage animals and to what was required for protection and defense.

As a result, these columns, with their enormous baggage trains, were quite long, and a certain military caution had, to that extent, to be kept in mind."[12] Only when more secure areas were reached could the Ethiopians being protected by the British army—including some high-ranking former hostages of Tewodros's whom the English were escorting for their safety—return to their homelands.[13]

On May 9, the troops reached Antalo: "Here the Queen, who had been ever treated with universal courtesy, and who had been attended by Dr. Lumsdaine, the medical officer attached to the personal staff of the Commander-in-Chief, was reported to be seriously unwell."[14] A few days later, on May 15, Terunash (1841-1868), Tewodros's second wife, died in the British camp: "She had received every comfort that it was possible to afford her. Her body was attended out of camp by a guard of honour and was buried by the priests of the Abyssinian creed in the church of Chelikut."[15] She was laid in her last resting place with great mourning on the part of her entourage and to the sounds of the "Dead March" from Handel's "Saul" played by the "King's Own" military band.[16]

On May 24, the expeditionary corps reached Senafe. The following day, in honor of Queen Victoria's birthday, the commander-in-chief held an inspection of the troops, attended by Prince Kassai of Tigray and several hundred mounted warriors. Kassai lavishly congratulated Napier on his great victory and accepted several gifts of weapons from him, as a well-earned reward for his loyalty to the English.[17] According to various sources, these weapons included a few mortars and field howitzers along with hundreds of muskets and large supplies of munitions and gunpowder.[18] In addition, Kassai was assigned a significant number of dispensable articles of gear and food supplies. According to Gerhard Rohlfs, Kassai received "the old rifles from the third and twenty-fifth native regiments, six mortars, six howitzers, 725 muskets, 130 shotguns, a large quantity of munitions, horse harnesses, and artillery equipment."[19] However, Napier did not yield to Kassai's pressure for the "official" assignment of a few British military advisors. But Kassai succeeded in recruiting, "unofficially," as it were, a kind of military advisor in the person of a certain J. C. Kirkham, who had served in China as a subordinate officer under General Gordon and had participated in the Magdala expedition as a provisioner.[20]

Napier wished Kassai to use the weapons given him only for defensive purposes, that is, to defend his country. However, this proved to be a "pious" wish, because the weapons transferred to him by the British made Kassai the most powerful warlord in Ethiopia, provided him with a good starting position in the subsequent intra-Ethiopian battles for hegemony, and were ultimately to bring him to the imperial throne.[21] On May 29, the last English troops marched out of Senafe. Kassai accompanied General Napier as far as the entrance to the mountain pass, where the British took their leave of him with gun salutes.

The march back to Zula, as a whole, was well planned and carried out, though it proved to be not quite so easy and fortunate as had been hoped.[22] Since the rainy season was already approaching, the march out was almost as difficult as the march in. Strong tropical storms made many roads impassable. Thus the retreat became a "race against time." But the troops succeeded in making the 400-mile march in only six weeks. Above all, natural forces—rain, floods, thunderstorms, and gales—made life hard for the soldiers and also for the baggage animals, especially because inadequate sanitary and hygienic conditions relating to clothing, cleanliness, and nutrition seriously affected their state of health. On this problem determined by the rigors of nature, Lieutenant Stumm wrote:

> Conditions became still more unfavorable when, starting at the Lat station, we entered into a period of strong thunderstorms; the roads were partly destroyed, so that the mules bearing heavy, soaked baggage could hardly struggle on any further and collapsed in large numbers. Thus we very soon had a lack of baggage animals again, and we were forced to leave supplies behind, and indeed even to destroy some of our munitions, tents, and luggage. From then on the camps were like big swamps or ankle-deep ponds from which the soiled tents, men, and animals sadly emerged. Sitting with our legs pulled up on a crate or a field cot in the tent, we saw the flood waters, against which no ditches or rain-flies sheltered us, rising higher and higher, penetrating everywhere, and the weight of the blankets, tents, etc., doubled.[23]

One day, between Senafe and Zula, Lieutenant Stumm experienced the elemental power of a mountain flood triggered by a strong downpour:

> When shortly after noon we tried to start out again, a dispatch suddenly arrived with the order for all marching columns to halt, and get out of the valley floor because of the water descending toward us. With a completely clear sky, and without being able to perceive even the distant thunder of a storm, we all thought it was a misunderstanding, when suddenly a peculiar roaring that came nearer and nearer with torrential speed convinced us of the opposite. A dirty yellow mass of water came tumultuously toward us like a foaming wall and spread over the whole breadth of the valley floor, carrying with it tree trunks, blocks of stone, dead animals, and pieces baggage, and a few tardy camel drivers who barely had time to make way for the furious element. Where a moment earlier, a bleak, stony desert had glowed in the hot sun, cool mountain water now raged, booming and roaring, striking against the rock walls on the right and left. Woe to those whom the flood takes by surprise in the narrow valley, where in many places, no escape is possible; before they have had time to look around, the flood has reached them and swept them away, leaving behind it only devastation and mutilated corpses.[24]

Moreover, in the areas increasingly traversed, attacks and looting had to be reckoned with on the part of the local tribes, who after the death of the feared Tewodros abandoned their restraint and attacked primarily stragglers and camp followers, as Captain Hozier reported:

> The wild border-tribes of Abyssinians and Gallas, through whose territory the route lay from the Takkazie to Antalo, being very little under the control of their distant and almost nominal rulers, were perfectly well behaved in the advance, but finding by degrees the vulnerable points of the army, had been for some time making attacks upon the

muleteers and camp-followers when they ventured far from their escorts, and on some occasions even on the armed soldiers. In the first instances, some camp-followers were killed, and in the latter, the soldiers being driven to use their weapons, several Abyssinians and Gallas were killed and wounded. Considerable numbers of armed men, principally Gallas, watched the march from the hills, and, although restrained by the presence of the columns, made attempts on the line of baggage, but met with little success. ... This was a clear indication of what a force returning in difficulties would have experienced.[25]

But despite all these difficulties, by June 2, the English troops had already arrived in their base camp at Zula, on the Red Sea. On June 1, Napier had crossed the Suru pass with the last column and reached Kumayli, and on the following day he was in Zula. The English troops were accompanied by Tewodros's former hostages. Their spectacular arrival in a railway car that had been festively decorated in their honor was described by the military doctor Bechtinger: "A nice railway car decorated with flowers and wreaths for the prisoners had been made ready. Many curious people gathered at the landing place for the arrival of the prisoners in order to get the closest possible look at these unfortunates who had become a subject of daily conversation throughout the world. They all ran alongside when the longed-for train decorated with branches rumbled in."[26]

However, many of the former hostages did not accept the fate envisaged for them. Commander-in-chief Napier had commanded that they must leave Ethiopia with the English troops. They argued that they had long since become alienated from their old homeland in Europe and would no longer have any chance of building a new life for their families there. As Lieutenant Stumm wrote:

> The former prisoners, with the exception of Dr. Schimper, who had returned to Adua in order to live out his life there, had also arrived here, and were not happy with the Commander-in-Chief's demand that they leave the country. Zander succeeded in staying behind, but, for better or for

worse, the rest probably had to go at least as far as Suez, and probably later returned to their second homeland. These people had adapted too much to Abyssinian customs and ways of life to be able to live in another country with their numerous families and their native wives and servants; moreover, by and large they had no property worth speaking of, and therefore had to give up any thought of returning to Europe. Thus these people's dissatisfaction was naturally very great, and did not allow them to recognize their great obligations to the English.[27]

Bechtinger also reported on the resentment of many former hostages against the British army's order to leave Ethiopia:

When I traveled to Suez, there were on our . . . steamer thirty of these unfortunates, including: Rassam, Dr. Blanc, Stern, Rosenthal, Mr. Kerans, and others, along with their European wives and children. But most of them . . . , instead of thanking Providence for their final rescue—were not at all happy with the new turn of events. They were indignant, upset, at having to leave Abyssinia. "What," they said, "are we supposed to do in Europe now, after we have spent the best years of our youth and our manhood here? What are we supposed to do now with our wives and children back in our homeland—which has become alien to us? How are we supposed to live now among people who have become alien to us and whom we no longer like? What are we supposed to live on? What prospects do our colored daughters have for the future?" I heard that most of them later returned to their adopted country by way of Massawa.[28]

Eduard Zander opposed the orders of the British command and decided to remain in Ethiopia, along with his old friend Schimper. But he died shortly afterward, on September 25, 1868, in Massawa. Zander's eldest daughter Katharina Hall traveled with her family to Jaffa, where Magdalena Hall, who was born in the British field camp on the day the Magdala fortress was stormed, married on January 12, 1889, Plato von Ustinov—"the grandfather of Sir Peter Ustinov—a 'story' the 'entertainer' always liked to tell."[29]

In the meantime, the embarkation of troops, materiel, supplies, and animals was proceeding. Of the forty-four elephants brought from India, five had died.[30] By the end of the expedition, the original 17,940 mules and ponies had dwindled to 4,126.[31] Likewise, the dismantling of the camp installations as well as the railway and telegraph systems was completed. In addition, even before his arrival in Zula, General Napier had assigned Captain Goodfellow, on behalf of the British Museum and under the supervision of Richard Holmes, to carry out a few excavations in nearby Adulis, the harbor of the ancient kingdom of Aksum. According to the ethnologist and historian Walter Raunig, in antiquity Adulis was "a hub for trade between the countries of the Hellenistic-Roman world on the Mediterranean and Arabia, Persia, and Africa, as well as India on the Erythraean Sea, that is, on the Indian Ocean and the Red Sea."[32]

Under the heavy pressure of time, Goodfellow began his work, at first with 25 men, and later with 80. Between May 28 and June 9, the remains of a building and stone columns were found, along with fragments of marble and alabaster on which crude drawings had been made, some pottery, and a coin. The archeological value of these discoveries made in great haste, which were then sent to the British Museum in two crates, is rather slender. Count von Seckendorff, who observed the excavations, expressed this disparaging judgment: "Not much that was interesting was revealed. A couple of blocks of marble, a few coins, small vessels made of clay or iron, and a few other objects that cannot be more precisely described—that was all that we could discover."[33] The contemporary museum professionals in London arrived at a similar assessment.[34] Nevertheless, modern scientists pay tribute to the fact that research was undertaken there at all. For example, Steffen Wenig, an archeologist who specializes in the Horn of Africa, points to the importance of the excavations undertaken by members of the British expedition in Adulis in 1868 and at the same time laments the lack of present-day research on the ancient ruins in the modern state of Eritrea: "Unfortunately up to now there have been no systematic excavations in Adulis, but the few things that were excavated here in 1868, 1906, and 1960-61 suggest the importance of this trade metropolis. Once they have been lain bare, our historical picture of this region and epoch will be completely transformed."[35]

Alongside the embarkation of equipment, the troops bound for England were taken by ship first to Suez, then from there by train to Alexandria, and finally to England on troop transport ships. The Indian troops and the European officers whose term of service was not yet over returned to India by sea. On June 10, 1868, the withdrawal and re-embarkation were finally completed. Only a small unit remained on shore for a few days in order to attend to the installations left behind. On the same day, Sir Robert Napier embarked on the "Feroze," after "having entrusted the Egyptian governor Abdul Kadir Pasha (who had volunteered for the task) with supervising few cultivated areas and buildings along the railway that could be dismantled only after the monsoon and with watching over the English churchyard in Zula."[36] Thus ended the Magdala campaign at precisely the place on the African coast of the Red Sea where it had begun the year before.

CHAPTER 12

The Victors' Triumphal Return to England

The first reports of the successful and victorious outcome of the Magdala campaign reached London at the end of April 1868. They came from the pen of the American correspondent Henry Morton Stanley, whose article on the storming of Magdala and the liberated European hostages arrived in London a week before those of his British colleagues and before General Napier's official report. Stanley's report had a sensational impact on the English capital, but also aroused irritation, and at first the accusation of having filed a false report. The wily and unscrupulous Stanley had carried his text 400 miles through Ethiopia to Zula, without the protection of the British army, and then by ship to Suez. An epidemic of cholera there prevented him from traveling by land, but he succeeded in smuggling his report on board a ship and getting the telegraph officer, whom he had bribed, to send the report before the cable connection broke down. Thereby Stanley achieved a journalistic scoop: he was the first on the news market with his report of the victory in Magdala, from which his subsequent career as a successful journalist surely benefited.[1]

When his report was finally confirmed, great enthusiasm and relieved joy prevailed in British public opinion and politics.[2] A triumphal reception was prepared for the day in July when the troops and their commander returned home. There were congratulations from the queen and commendations from Parliament, which awarded Napier an annual pension of 2,000 pounds. In addition, he was given the title of "Lord of Magdala." Many streets and public buildings were named after Napier. In Calcutta, an equestrian statue was erected in Napier's honor, a copy of which was also placed

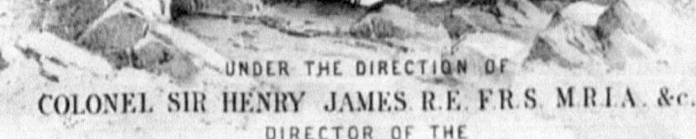

Frontispiece of the *Record of the Expedition to Abyssinia*.

THE VICTORS' TRIUMPHAL RETURN TO ENGLAND   157

on Waterloo Place in London. He himself went back to his post in India, and later served for a few years as governor of Gibraltar. In 1883, he was made a Field Marshal. After his death in 1890, Napier was given a state funeral and was buried in St. Paul's cathedral.

The national victory euphoria lasted all summer, with numerous receptions and celebratory speeches. Prime Minister Disraeli compared the Magdala expedition with the spectacular progress of the Spanish conquistador Cortez through Mexico, though he noted that while Cortez sought only to exploit and conquer, Napier's goals were justice, humanity, and the spread of civilization.[3] For the citizens of London, there were various popular amusements and entertainments, such as the song "The Abyssinian Gallop" or daily diorama shows on "The Death of Theodore" in the Royal Polytechnic Institution.

The world of science emphasized particularly the expedition's importance for research on northeast Africa. The significant scientific benefits of the Magdala campaign were listed in the official report on the expedition:[4] the geographer C. Markham made various measurements, prepared three maps of the areas through which the expedition passed, and published a geographical report in the *Journal of the Royal Geographical Society* (in 1869, he also published his book *A History of the Abyssinian Expedition*); Richard R. Holmes of the British Museum inspected the archeological excavations in the ruins of Adulis and published articles on churches in Ethiopia in the *Proceedings of the Society of Antiquaries*; the zoologist W. Jesse made an excursion into Bogosland (which had, however, already been well investigated by the German natural scientists Theodor von Heuglin and Alfred Brehm), and assembled a collection for the London Zoological Society; the meteorologist Dr. Cook wrote a "Report on the Meteorology of Abyssinia"; the geologist and natural historian William T. Blanford prepared wide-ranging natural history collections and published *Observations on the Geology and Zoology of Abyssinia made during the Progress of the British Expedition to that Country in 1867-68.*

Not the least of the expedition's scientific achievements were its contributions to geography and cartography through its preparatory work and subsequent photographs. Shortly after the beginning of the Magdala campaign, the anglophile German cartographer August H. Petermann expressed his enthusiasm about the scientific benefits connected with this expedition:

"English operations in Abyssinia have only begun and yet they have already borne rich fruits for geography and cartography by not merely relying on previous travels and research, but allowing the results of their own photographic activity already to be presented."[5] After the conclusion of the campaign, he praised the governmental publication with the title *Routes in Abyssinia*, which was laid before both the lower and the upper houses of Parliament in November 1867, as the "most important geographical and cartographical work on Abyssinia compiled up to this point," and added:

> Alongside V. Heuglin's travel book about Abyssinia, we would like to recommend this report written in the topographical and statistical department of the British War Ministry by Lieutenant-Colonel A. C. Cooke as the best guide to the theater of the English campaign. It contains, in particular, a large number of road descriptions taken from the reports of European travelers from Alonzo Mendes in 1625 to Merewether and Munzinger in 1867. For knowledge of roads, these very extensive extracts take the place of a small library.... As an agreeable bonus we find on the first sheet notes on Abyssinia of a more general, comprehensive kind, regarding nature and climate, government, religion, currency, the military, and Emperor Tewodros, and finally a translation of the report on the most interesting Portuguese campaign in Abyssinia in 1541 and 1542. In addition, there is E. G. Ravenstein's large, very useful map of the eastern and northeastern part of Abyssinia from Massawa in the north to beyond Magdala in the south and Gondar in the west.[6]

Summing up, Petermann highly praised the British army's cartographic achievements during the campaign: "The English expedition represents a new and important period in our geographical knowledge of Abyssinia and will fill many a gap."[7] As the Abyssinian highlands are among the most beautiful and magnificent regions of our earth, these photographs and research results are among the most meritorious and glorious in the field of geography. The current English campaign in Abyssinia is unquestionably the most memorable enterprise carried out by Europeans in this remarkable country of the African interior in centuries.[8]

The pictures taken by the photographic unit of the Royal Engineers are a collection of special importance for cultural history, even if they are controversial. After the first attempts in the Crimean War, the Magdala expedition was the second military enterprise in which the British army made use of photography for military purposes. According to the official report on the expedition, the war ministry decided, in September 1867, to send along a unit of trained photographers imbedded in the tenth company of the Royal Engineers. This unit consisted of six men and Sergeant John Harrold, and was led by Lieutenant Anderson.[9] Its chief task was to photograph the sketches and plans (especially the march routes) worked out by the staff officers, and then to reproduce and copy them in order to make them available as quickly as possible for further elaboration and use. Thus the photographic work functioned essentially as a field printing press. This military use of photography was obviously a lesson learned from the preceding United States Civil War.[10] The unit's enormously heavy equipment consisted of cameras, lenses, paper, chemicals, and a darkroom tent. It was packed in crates to be transported by mules and cost the significant sum of 447 pounds, 6 shillings, and 9 pence. For security reasons, two complete sets of photographic equipment were taken along. After the day's march, the unit's men were busy all night with their technical preparations for their work, and in the early morning and in the evening they produced negatives of sketches, plans, and views, numbering 15,200 in all.[11] Considering the difficult terrain and the climatic conditions as well as the current technical possibilities, the photographic unit of the Royal Engineers delivered an astonishing and admirable performance. The wet plate collodion process used for the production of the negative "was very time-consuming to prepare and demanded, especially in such a remote country, planning down to the smallest detail."[12] Sergeant Harrold was obviously "the right man in the right place," as we read in a contemporary source.[13]

The photos made by the unit during the Magdala expedition—which were also based to a lesser extent on models sketched by various members of the expedition (among others, Holmes and Simpson)—concentrated, in line with the central military tasks, on pictures of the troops and officers, the camp sites, the Magdala fortress, and the liberated hostages, and especially the difficult-to-cross terrain of the Ethiopian mountain landscape. In view of these priorities, the historian of photography James Ryan remarked critically that from a photographic point of view the Magdala expedition was almost a kind of "war against nature," since the natural obstacles and demands of the march route—such as steep passes, narrow defiles, and sharp ridges were presented as predominant.[14] In contrast, there were comparatively few pictures of objects of historical, cultural, or ethnographic significance. Such photos were apparently made incidentally, "as souvenir photographs."[15]

The lack of pictures relating to cultural history, which is understandably criticized by present-day scholars, was thus essentially due to the fact that the photographic work was done to serve military goals.[16] It was not supposed to produce, as well, scientific reports on Ethiopia's land and people, its history, and its culture. Moreover, the troops' march route did not lead through urban cultural centers such as Massawa, Adwa, Aksum, or Lalibela, where the relevant artifacts would have been found.[17] Gerhard Rohlfs, an eyewitness to the storming of Magdala, lamented in particular the lack of a photo of Emperor Tewodros's corpse. "Moreover, it is much to be deplored that no photo of Tewodros's body was made, because his face, like his whole body, remained intact, the bullet shot into the mouth having come out the back of the head, so that death must have been instantaneous. An outstanding drawing made by Mr. Holmes, who was sent by the British Museum, is by itself no substitute for a good photograph."[18] Despite these critical remarks made by contemporary observers and by posterity, at least a few of the photographs taken by the Royal Engineers are definitely of value for the cultural history of Ethiopia, as the internationally renowned expert of Ethiopia, Richard Pankhurst, acknowledges.[19] Among these are pictures of landscapes and localities with buildings and churches (Annesley Bay, Zula, Senafe, Antalo, Adigrat, and Magdala), various portraits of prominent native figures—e.g., Tewodros's son, Prince Alamayou, and Masteeat, the Galla queen of Wollo, with her eldest son and a courtier—pictures of Sir Robert Napier and his staff, and photos of the freed hostages.

Many photos taken by the Royal Engineers were later included as illustrations (sometimes in the form of engravings) in reports and books written by participants in the expedition, former hostages, or writers and scholarly authors; in the periodical the *Illustrated London News*; and in Stern's *The*

Captive Missionary, Acton's *March to Magdala*, Bates's *The Abyssinian Difficulty*, and Gräber's *Unterwegs in Abessinien*.[20] A few photo albums from the Magdala expedition are still extant. According to Gerd Gräber, an expert on Ethiopia, there are at least four series in Ethiopia and Great Britain.[21] An album with 65 pictures is in the Institute of Ethiopian Studies in Addis Ababa, the Ethiopian capital. Probably the most extensive album, with 78 pictures and the title "Views of the Abyssinian Campaign—presented by Lord Napier of Magdala," was bought in September 1980 by the German collector Robert Lebeck and is today in the archive of the Agfa-Foto-Historama in the Wallraf-Richartz Museum in Cologne (some of the photos in these albums are also in the Harvard and Princeton University Libraries; several are reproduced in this book).

Despite the clearly military orientation of the photographs made during the Magdala campaign, their value for cultural history is acknowledged by experts on the region. For example, Richard Pankhurst emphasizes that these photos were the first taken by trained photographers in Ethiopia.[22] And Gerd Gräber writes that these photos are, "alongside the previously almost uninvestigated photographs of Abyssinia taken in 1860-1862 by Henry Aaron Stern, a missionary born in Frankfurt, among the earliest pictorial documents of this country and East Africa in general,"[23] and that combined with the official report on the expedition, they represent unique sources for research on Ethiopia in the nineteenth century.[24]

The numerous pictures and drawings made by the draftsmen and painters participating in the expedition—the "artists on campaign," as they were called—can also be counted among its scientifically relevant contributions in the wider sense. These artists include in particular Major Baigrie, who drew primarily landscape scenes for military ends, and William Simpson, who concentrated on drawings of people and scenes of everyday life, as well as on subjects in ethnography and cultural history. Simpson was not only a famous artist and war illustrator, but he was also a scientifically trained archeologist and ethnographer, as his diary of the Magdala campaign clearly shows.[25] The one hundred illustrations of the expedition that appeared in the *Illustrated London News* for September 21, 1867, and September 5, 1868, which were later reprinted in part in other publications and put a lasting stamp on the contemporary image of Ethiopia, stemmed, for the most part, from originals made by Baigrie and Simpson.

In addition to these scientific collections, studies, photographs, and illustrations, in the wake of the plundering and theft of Ethiopian cultural artifacts in Magdala, numerous art objects and especially hundreds of Ethiopian manuscripts were taken to England to be evaluated scientifically, where they were to be made available to European researchers.[26] These manuscripts were examined by Werner Munzinger, who was well-acquainted with the country and the language, a title was written on each of them, and then they were transferred to the British Library, where Dr. Wright paid tribute, not without a certain pride, to the acquisition of this valuable cultural treasure as probably the "most extensive and finest collection of Ethiopian literature in the world." With its 359 volumes it surpassed even the collection of the French Ethiopian expert Antoine d'Abbadie, which included 234 manuscripts.[27]

All these scientific acquisitions and expropriated articles from the Magdala expedition stimulated and promoted an increased interest in the history and culture of Ethiopia among European researchers and the educated public: "The arrival of this booty . . . was followed by the translation of many works written in Ge'ez into English and other European languages," particularly by Ernest Budge.[28] This laid the foundations for modern Ethiopian studies, and also for research on the ancient kingdom of Aksum, primarily by the German scholar August Dillmann, who did path-breaking scientific work in this field.[29] We must not forget that the origin of all these achievements bore the stain of the violent and larcenous expropriation of Ethiopian cultural artifacts by the British army and the deaths of thousands of Ethiopians caused by British guns. After the first euphoria over the successful outcome of the Magdala campaign had settled, more critical voices were heard, pointing primarily to the astronomically high cost of the enterprise.[30] Finally, a parliamentary investigative committee was established that discovered that the overall cost of the Magdala expedition ran to nearly nine million pounds. In addition, various miscalculations, inefficiencies, and instances of sloppiness in dealing with these monies were identified. Above all, it was said that apparently public enterprises, such as the British India Steam Company and the Peninsular and Oriental Steamship Company, had been guilty of profiteering by charging inflated freight rates for transportation by ship. But since both the great political parties had been involved in the preparation and execution of the Magdala expedition, and there had been only a few British casualties, the whole affair had no further serious political consequences.

On the other hand, a few of the British diplomats and envoys involved in the hostage affair had to justify their conduct.[31] Because of his clumsy and imprudent diplomatic and political behavior before the hostage drama, Cameron was sharply criticized and treated quite harshly, receiving only a small pension. Ill, disappointed, and embittered about his poor treatment by the government, he died not long afterward. Hormuzd Rassam also had to justify his behavior during the hostage affair: he was accused of having been too indulgent with Tewodros. But he was cleared of this charge and even ultimately rewarded: he received 5,000 pounds as a special token of appreciation, and his two companions, Blanc and Prideaux, each received 2,000 pounds. Until his death in 1910, Rassam devoted himself to his archeological interests and undertook important excavations in the area of Assyrian-Babylonian culture (among other things, he discovered the clay tablet with the text of the epic *Gilgamesh*, the world's oldest extant literary work).

Tristram Speedy was also honored, receiving the "Abyssinian War Medal" for his contribution to the campaign. Shortly afterward, he went to India, where he held a leading position in the police for two years, starting in 1869; then he held various police posts in British Malaya and from 1874 to 1877 served as the deputy British resident in the Malaysian mining district of Larut. Captain Speedy returned to Ethiopia twice (1883 and 1885-1897), in each case as a member of British diplomatic missions conducting negotiations at the Ethiopian imperial court. Speedy died in 1911.[32]

Another important figure, Werner Munzinger, was disappointed because the English government did not grant him the recognition and reward that he had hoped his great contributions to the success of the Magdala expedition would win him. He was given a medal, but he was dismissed without compensation as the British vice-consul, because after the successful conclusion of the expedition, these posts were considered superfluous. At first, Munzinger served as French vice-consul in the region, but in April 1871 he entered the service of Egypt as the governor of Massawa, and supported Egypt's expansionary efforts in northeast Africa and against Ethiopia. In 1873, he even became the governor-general of the newly-formed Egyptian province of "East Sudan and the Red Sea Coast." Munzinger died during an attack while leading an Egyptian diplomatic and military expedition in the kingdom of Shoa in Ethiopia.

The German Gerhard Rohlfs traveled once again into the area of the Magdala expedition. In the winter of 1880-1881, he went to Ethiopia as an envoy of the German emperor, in order to deliver a message to Emperor Yohannes IV, who had turned to the European powers for help in a conflict with Egypt. In 1884, Rohlfs went to Zanzibar as a German imperial commissioner, but he returned to Germany for good in 1885, where he died on June 2, 1896, in Rüngsdorf bei Godesberg.

The Ethiopian Emperor Johannes IV, the former Prince Kassai of Tigray and an ally of the British.

The American correspondent Henry Morton Stanley was certainly among those for whom participating in the campaign paid rich benefits. After he took part in the Magdala expedition on behalf of the *New York Herald*, the latter's owner, James Gordon Bennet, sent him back to Africa to find out what had happened to the lost African missionary and explorer David Livingstone. In a spectacular encounter on November 10, 1971, Stanley found Livingstone unharmed near Lake Tanganyika. Stanley's success in finding Livingstone laid the foundation of his fame as an important African traveler. After serving as a war reporter during the British campaign against the Ashanti in modern-day Ghana, in November 1874 he set out for a further expedition to Central Africa, with the strong support of his newspaper and of the London *Daily Telegraph*. He played a significant part in later research on the Congo basin and its subsequent colonial subjection and exploitation. In later years, Stanley moved to England, where he resumed his original British citizenship in 1892. From 1895 to 1901, Stanley served as a member of the House of Commons, and in 1899, he was knighted. He died in London on May 10, 1904. Present-day assessments of Stanley emphasize the "shadow side" of his character, his "scientific inadequacies," and his lust for power and profit.³³ The travel historian Walter Krämer made a completely justified if harsh judgment with which most experts now agree: "Stanley pursued his goals with ruthless energy and even with brutality, caring little for human life.... Thus his voyages of discovery are comparable to military campaigns.... His undeniable achievement, on three expeditions that he was able to conduct with ample means, of revealing a previously unknown Africa is thus heavily burdened with the odium of having been a pioneer of colonialism."³⁴

Prince Alemayehu, son and heir of Emperor Tewodros II of Ethiopia.

Tewodros's son, Alamayou, whom the English had found with his mother, the Empress Terunesh, during the assault on Magdala, was met with a tragic fate. Tewodros is supposed to have been very close to his son and successor and to have asked his wife, in the event of his death, to put his son under the protection of the English and to accompany him either to India (Bombay) or to England.³⁵ According to the German Lieutenant Stumm, after the empress's death on the retreat from Magdala, "people first talked about sending little Tewodros to India; whether they really believed that the English climate would suit the little brown rascal or whether they simply wanted to bring a little homecoming gift to their dear countrymen, who were displaying such unrestrained joy at the fall of Magdala, I do not know; in any event, he was later taken along to England."³⁶

Security concerns were obviously behind Tewodros's initially surprising wish to consign his children to his European opponents. As his eldest son,

Alamayou was Tewodros II's legitimate successor. Therefore, according at least to Captain Hozier, the widow's two brothers, who had been Tewodros's prisoners for years and now wanted to return to their native region of Semien, "feared to take with them her child, Alamayou, in case that his life might be taken by any aspirant for the empire of Abyssinia."[37]

Alamayou, who was born in 1860 and whose name literally and almost prophetically means "he who has seen the world," was thereupon taken to London and entrusted for a time to the protection of Captain Speedy, in whose household (in England and temporarily also in India) he probably lived happily.[38] But this was only an interlude. Against the wishes of the little prince and also Queen Victoria, who had obviously taken a liking to the boy after their first meeting, the Exchequer, which was responsible for the prince's maintenance, finally transferred him to the tutelage of the headmaster of Cheltenham College, in order to provide him with a good education. With his new mentor, Alamayou moved to Rugby in order to complete his schooling there. Both the queen and Napier, along with other high-ranking persons, were concerned about the subsequent development of the young prince, who became increasingly lonely, unhappy, and depressed. Obviously he missed the company of Captain Speedy, who spoke Amharan and knew his way around Ethiopia.

Letter of Laqiyaye, Grandmother of Alamayou, to Queen Victoria (Jan. 1870)

In the name of the Father, and of the Son, and of the Holy Ghost, one God.

May [the letter] sent by WEYZERO Laqiyaye, the mother of ITEGE Tiru Werq, the grandmother of DEJJAZMACH Alemayyehu, reach the English queen. [You] reader, bow on my behalf.

May the Saviour of the world give [you] health. May He extend your kingdom. May He destroy your enemies. I have lost by death three DEJJAZMACHES, the fourth [loss being] the ITEGE.

Only DEJJAZMACH Alemayyehu is left to me. Please look after him for me. Although God deprived him of his father [and] his mother, He gave him you [instead]. As long as I do not see him, I count myself, too, among the dead. He calls you his mother, but he does not call me his mother, since I did not raise him. Please bring him up for the sake of God.

(Quoted in Sven Rubenson, ed., *Internal Rivalries and Foreign Threats, 1869-1979*, Addis Ababa, 2000, *Acta Aethiopica* 3, p. 40, Document no. 29.)

In the name of the Father, and of the Son, and of the Holy Ghost, one God.

May [the letter] sent by *Weyzero* Laqīyayĕ, the mother of *Itēgē* Ṭiru Werq, the grandmother of *Dejjazmach* Alemayyehu, reach the English queen. [You] reader, bow on my behalf.

May the Saviour of the world give [you] health. May He extend your kingdom. May He destroy your enemies. I have lost by death three *dejjazmaches*, the fourth [loss being] the *itēgē*.

Only *Dejjazmach* Alemayyehu is left to me. Please look after him for me. Although God deprived him of his father [and] his mother, He gave him you [instead]. As long as I do not see him, I count myself, too, among the dead. He calls you his mother, but he does not call me his mother, since I did not raise him. Please bring him up for the sake of God.

Letter from Laqiyaye to Victoria, Jan. 1870.

In 1879, Alamayou was sent to the Royal Military Academy in Sandhurst, so that after undergoing military training, he could be sent to India. The queen, worried, insisted that he be treated well by everyone at the military academy and not teased because of the color of his skin. In October 1879, Alamayou fell seriously ill, and the doctors decided that he had pleurisy. He himself was firmly convinced that he had been poisoned, and he refused to eat or take any medicine. He died on November 14, 1879, at the age of nineteen, without ever having seen his old homeland of Ethiopia again. On the evening of the day he died, the queen, who had been informed of his death by telegram, wrote in her diary that Alamayou had probably not had a happy life all alone in a foreign land. In accord with Queen Victoria's express wish, a verse from the Bible was added to the inscription on the funeral plaque in the royal chapel in Windsor. The inscription read:

> Near this spot lies buried ALAMAYU the son of Theodore King of Abyssinia born 23 April 1861 dies 14 November 1879. This tablet is placed to his memory by QUEEN VICTORIA
> I was a stranger and ye took me in

After the withdrawal of the English, fighting for the succession to Tewodros's throne raged in Ethiopia from 1868 to 1872. Modern European firearms played an even greater role in these conflicts. The British victory in April 1868 can be seen as a crucial turning point in Ethiopia's military history.[39] Afterward, all the princes and warlords sought even more eagerly than before to acquire modern weapons and training for their troops. Kassai of Tigray, not least because of the British weapons that had been handed over to him by the withdrawing Magdala expedition, was able to expand his power and to prevail over his intra-Ethiopian rivals.[40] In July 1871, he won the battle of Assam near Adwa, even though he had far fewer troops, defeating his old rival Wagsum Gobaze of Lasta, who, as Emperor Tekla-Giorgis, had ruled over Ethiopia from 1868 to 1871. In January 1872, Kassai had himself crowned Emperor of Ethiopia, taking the name Yohannes IV. Both Yohannes and his successor, Emperor Menelik II, ultimately continued Tewodros II's policies, making serious and successful efforts to unite, strengthen, and modernize the Ethiopian state and to defend it against external enemies and threats.

CHAPTER 13

Balance Sheet: Military Intervention without Colonial Occupation

The precise planning and professional execution of the Magdala expedition, the easily won British victory over Tewodros, and the successful liberation of the hostages impressed and astonished participants as well as contemporary observers and later historians: "A military campaign has probably seldom been undertaken against such resistance, planned so precisely, and so quickly and completely carried out as the English expedition against Abyssinia. Sir Robert Napier could write, like Caesar, *Veni, vidi, vici!* The king dead, Magdala taken by storm, the hostages free!"[1] In retrospect, the Austrian military observer Theodor von Kodolitsch also praised the excellent planning and preparation of the expedition: "And this is certainly one of the most useful lessons that can be drawn from this expedition, that proper preparation for war, down to the smallest detail, makes success fall like a ripe fruit into the lap of those who have foreseen and anticipated it."[2] In view of the outcome of the Magdala campaign, the myth of a glorious military victory over the Ethiopians quickly emerged, though doubt was cast upon it by both contemporaries and later historians.[3] For example, several participants, such as Gerhard Rohlfs and the military physician Josef Bechtinger, pointed to the "fortunate circumstances" that made an important contribution to the success of the march on Magdala and demanded only a few losses on the English side.[4] Among these circumstances was the asymmetry of the military power relationships acknowledged by many contemporary observers: "We should hardly be surprised by the rapidity and decisiveness of the success, the complete annihilation of Tewodros and his power. From the outset, the battle between an English army with English weapons and a force consisting of ill-trained though brave Abyssinians was hopeless for the latter."[5] Today, if we compare from the point of view of military history and technology the Magdala expedition with Napoleon's Egyptian campaign seventy years earlier, it becomes clear that in the meantime, important changes had occurred in the art of waging war.[6] Great strides had been made in professionalizing military forces. Science and technology had been put in the service of military goals. The planning, leadership, and logistics of military actions came to resemble the management of a large industrial organization. During the Magdala campaign, the visible signs of this "industrialization of war" were, above all, the use of steamships and railways for transportation, the improved supply for the soldiers and care for the sick and wounded, including the use of hospital ships and also technical innovations such as the field telegraph, the field signaling system, and filtering machinery for producing drinking water. In addition, there were elements of what would now be called the "privatization of war": the army rented shipping space for its troop transport fleet from private companies and had private firms provide materiel and supplies as well as perform services. On the other hand, the expedition was also characterized by more traditional ways of waging war, such as the predominant use of sailing ships (in addition to steamships) for transporting troops as well as the massive use of baggage animals (ten thousand mules, horses, asses, oxen, camels) and more than forty elephants brought from India to transport the heavy cannons. Whereas the Magdala expedition's (white) British troops were armed with modern breech-loading rifles, the Indian troops had only obsolete muzzle-loaders. A few units already wore the newfangled khaki uniforms, while others still wore the traditional red coats from the time of the Battle of Waterloo and the Crimean War. Thus taken as a whole, the Magdala army was a complex, hybrid force consisting of both old and new elements.[7]

A Modern Military View of the Abyssinian Expedition of 1868: "Do We Have Anything to Learn from the Victorians?"

This article argues that there is something to be gained from a study of past experience. It examines the expeditionary experience of the Victorians and offers insights into the reasons for their success that could have relevance for today. . . .

The Abyssinian expedition of 1868 was an enormous undertaking, in size, in duration, and in financial cost. Essentially a hostage rescue operation, it is one of the classic examples of combined expeditionary warfare. The Royal Navy transported a force . . . from Bombay to Zulla bay. . . . The troops then marched 400 miles into the heart of Abyssinia, defeated an enemy equipped with modern rifles and artillery, rescued the hostages and returned safely to the coast. The expedition was a conspicuous success: casualties were miraculously light, not a single hostage was lost and the expeditionary force left the country without becoming embroiled in a protracted confrontation. The contrast of the Abyssinian expedition with the American attempt to rescue their hostages from Iran in 1980 could not be more striking. The 1868 expedition is thus of considerable interest.

(Source: Lieutenant Commander A. C. Ashcroft RN, "As Britain Returns to an Expeditionary Strategy, Do We Have Anything to Learn from the Victorians?" *Defence Studies* 1, no. 1, 2001, p. 77.)

Despite the Britons' massive superiority in military technology, the expedition was not without risks. There were definitely strategic options available to Tewodros that might have caused the English serious difficulties or even led to their defeat. For example, he could have conducted a moving guerilla war on a territory familiar to him and his warriors, lying in ambush and making raids, just as the Afghans had done against the English or Abd-el-Kader had done against the French in Algeria. He could have done this all the more effectively because the English communication and supply lines were so long and susceptible to disruptions, and they were also threatened now and again by armed bands.[8] Today such a mode of fighting would be called an "asymmetrical war" with the following typical elements: "Military weakness relies on its familiarity with the land and the people, has a defensive war goal, avoids open conflict, and instead attacks supply lines and the morale of the stronger power."[9] It was also never entirely out of the question that the Ethiopian princes might still make common cause with Tewodros, since their loyalty to the English was never completely certain: "As an enemy, what damage the prince of Tigray could have wrought on the English troops! It is not an exaggeration to say that he could have caused the British expedition to fail. Tewodros allied with Kassai!"[10] But Tewodros entrenched himself with his heavy cannons in the mountain fortress of Magdala, whereas he had earlier been famed and feared as a wily Shifta leader and a brilliant general for his mobile way of waging war with sudden attacks and raids.[11] For Lieutenant Stumm, this mistaken strategy was the true reason for Tewodros's defeat: "The inertia to which this aping of European means of waging war condemned him was to lead to his death and made him incapable of pursuing the mode of fighting he had earlier used, which was demanded by the nature of the territory and consisted in forced marches, detours, and raids."[12] And finally, by prematurely releasing the European hostages, the emperor had given away his greatest trump card, as Gerhard Rohlfs noted: "Tewodros was literally struck blind to give away without conditions his only weapon, the prisoners."[13]

Considering these "fortunate circumstances," the true achievement of the British army consisted not in glorious military feats, but rather in nonmilitary acts: the professional planning and execution of the expedition, the construction and maintenance of supply lines and logistics, overcoming the hardships of the march, and confronting natural forces.[14] In this vein, Richard Andree wrote: "The true achievement of the English consisted not in conquering the Abyssinians, but rather in conquering the land. Nature fought against them, but science and organization overcame this most dangerous of opponents."[15] Seckendorff's judgment was the same: "The climatic conditions and illnesses were more dangerous opponents."[16]

According to Lieutenant Stumm, the English army "could look back with justified pride on those days of hardship and renunciation that immediately preceded the taking of Magdala."[17] These assessments were later qualified by the historian of Ethiopia, Sven Rubenson, who rightly pointed out that on his march to Magdala, Tewodros had to overcome problems similar to those confronting the English, and with far fewer modern technological aids.[18]

If we now leave the point of view of military history and examine the political dimensions of this conflict, we find a similarly ambivalent picture. This becomes clear as soon as we inquire into the rationale of the whole enterprise. Participants in the campaign and contemporary observers already noted that England shared the blame for the conflict with Tewodros. For example, Gerhard Rohlfs thought it "certain that the English themselves were also largely to blame for the war."[19] More skilful and tactful behavior on the part of England with respect to the Ethiopian emperor could have avoided the whole war and spared human lives, effort, and expense. For Richard Andree, the contemporary German author of a book on Ethiopia, the expedition was in itself a great success "for which England had, however, to pay dearly. Had the letter Tewodros wrote to Queen Victoria at the end of 1862 not been forgotten in the Foreign Office and remained unanswered, there would have been no reason to undertake the expedition at all, to sacrifice six million pounds sterling, and to cut down a few thousand poorly-armed Abyssinians with Armstrong cannons and breech-loading rifles."[20] At the beginning of the twentieth century, the German historian Gustav Adolf Rein offered this criticism of the Magdala expedition: "England had to expose thousands of its sons to incalculable risks by sending them on a precarious enterprise, merely because a letter from a sensitive half-barbarian to the queen got lost in the Foreign Office as a result of negligence."[21] However, the fact that Tewodros's letter "got lost" or "was forgotten" probably did not result from mere bureaucratic negligence. Instead, what we see in the behavior of England and the English military leadership is the expression of arrogance on the part of European colonial and world powers with regard to Emperor Tewodros: first, the underestimation of the pride, honor, and dignity of an African potentate who was apparently politically unimportant; second, the interpretation of the hostage-taking solely in terms of the European conception of legality; and third, the ambivalent and ultimately treacherous treatment of Tewodros's peace offering (the herd of livestock) shortly before the assault on Magdala.

In contrast to its behavior in the run-up to the military conflict, after the decision was made to embark upon a punitive expedition, the British showed diplomatic and political skill by successfully exploiting intra-Ethiopian quarrels and pursuing a policy on the basis of the principle of "divide and rule." Without the more or less active support of local strongmen, especially Kassai of Tigray, they would hardly have been able to achieve such an unambiguous success. For the Austrian military observer Kodolitsch, this was "great diplomatic and military masterpiece.... The skilled handling of the chieftains therefore represents, in my opinion, one of the highpoints of the Abyssinian expedition."[22] The journalist Stanley summed up the unequal relationship between the minor military achievements and the major logistic and diplomatic achievements in the curt but apt formula: "Although it was a small war it was a splendid campaign."[23]

Contrary to this British and Eurocentric way of seeing things, it must constantly be pointed out that it was not the British who sealed Tewodros's fate, but chiefly the preceding political developments and relationships in Ethiopia itself. From this point of view, the English invasion was instead the proximate cause of the emperor's defeat, and not its true, profound cause.[24] The British expedition had no decisive influence on power relationships in Ethiopia. Even before their invasion, Tewodros's plans for unification and modernization had already been brought to nothing by internal opponents and quarrels. Thus the Ethiopian historian Bahru Zewde argues that Tewodros's fate was already sealed before the British invasion: "The war was won by the English before a shot was fired."[25] As in many later colonial wars in Ethiopia as well, the Europeans were ultimately only one of the parties, albeit an important one, engaged in a conflict involving several native parties who, from their own point of view, were waging a very ordinary local war and thus cooperated with the interventionary power and entered into tactical alliances only on a temporary basis.[26]

Nonetheless, it was widely recognized that in dealing with the civilian population of the country, Napier's army had acted with astounding restraint. It was the first army in Ethiopian military history that paid for its food and forage and did not simply expropriate them by force.[27] Lieutenant Stumm expressed himself on this point quite enthusiastically: "The expedition's leadership may be assessed favorably or unfavorably, but it will always have to be honestly acknowledged that Napier dealt with his enemies with a humanity whose parallel would not be easy to find. He was able to prevent a war against barbarians from becoming barbarian itself, and none of his rules and commands contradicts the laws of the gallant and humane way of waging war that our century demands."[28] In fact, in comparison to many earlier, contemporary, and later colonial wars (e.g., the crushing of the Sepoy Rebellion in India, Great Britain's intervention in China, or the Abyssinian war waged by Fascist Italy), which with their brutal and ruthless actions against the civilian population and their cruelties tend to display the traits of genocidal or total war, the Magdala expedition seems markedly "humane."[29] A significant exception is represented by the looting after the storming of the Magdala fortress. It is true that at that time, such looting was absolutely normal in wars, and for contemporaries required no particular justification. But for the defeated, it meant an incalculable loss of the national cultural assets and thus an enduring injury to their national identity.

Ultimately, participants, contemporaries, and later historians all repeatedly challenged the British government's justification in terms of its "humanitarian" goals and raised the central question as to why the British carried out the expedition at all and why after their great victory they withdrew from Ethiopia without occupying the country over the long term and exploiting it economically. Did England in fact act exclusively out of humanitarian motives, as the author of the official report, Captain Henry Hozier, claimed: "The British Expedition to Abyssinia was prompted by no thirst for glory, by no lust of conquest." According to Lieutenant Stumm, everyone thought the opposite, "that the sole objective was the occupation of what was assumed to be the fertile and mineral-rich land of Abyssinia."[30] Didn't England have ulterior motives, then, and wasn't it pursuing secret interests of its own? It was obviously difficult to understand why the English would have set in motion such a massive expedition only in order to liberate a few hostages:

> No one ... had ever imagined that such a large campaign would be undertaken and millions of pounds willingly expended just to liberate an English consul and a few pris-

oners unless in addition other, more relevant ... grounds had served as the basis for this strategic operation. Even in the army, from the most superior general to the most ordinary soldier, the men were firmly convinced that after Tewodros was subjugated and the Europeans were freed, a golden profit would somehow have to be drawn from the presence of the troops in this African mountain world.[31]

It was not only in Great Britain that people speculated about the real grounds for the enterprise. In France in particular, great mistrust prevailed with regard to British goals. It was feared that England was using the Magdala expedition simply as a pretext for apermanent occupation of the coast of the Red Sea, to better control communication by sea through the Suez Canal and the route to India.[32] A few missionaries and former hostages of Tewodros's, including Wilhelm Schimper, lamented the English withdrawal from Ethiopia and argued for a European "tutelage" for the country or a kind of English protectorate.[33]

But all these wishful ideas, hypotheses, and speculations and alleged interests, motives, and goals regarding the British punitive expedition proved to be groundless and untenable. After the liberation of the hostages, England withdrew its troops, in accord with its previous public announcements.[34] One reason for this is that the Magdala campaign took place at a time when Great Britain and other European powers still made no claims to have vital interests in Ethiopia and northeast Africa.[35] The colonial and imperial "race" for spheres of influence in (northeast) Africa was to begin only two decades later.

Yet, the Magdala expedition was not solely a military intervention undertaken on humanitarian grounds, but it was also intended to restore or strengthen England's national prestige; it was thought that no injury to the latter could be accepted, if only to prevent giving other peoples occasion to challenge England's claim to supremacy.[36] Lieutenant Stumm expressed this intention somewhat bombastically: "The fame of the greatness and power of a nation that spent millions and mobilized a legion of men and animals in order to erase a stain on its honor and help a few of its citizens will penetrate the remotest areas of Africa and Asia."[37] In addition, from a military point of view, the Magdala campaign also had a desirable secondary effect in England and the British empire: the British army, whose reputation had been damaged in the eyes of Europeans by its not particularly glorious acts during the Crimean War and the Sepoy Rebellion in India, had now proven once again its professionalism and fighting ability.[38] Thus Captain Hozier emphasized precisely this aspect: "Its success was great. England acquired from it no territorial aggrandizement. Yet it did not pass unrewarded, for its result was greatly to raise the British Army in European estimation."[39]

In the years after the Magdala expedition, the impression that this was an easily won and glorious victory by a modern European army over the undisciplined and poorly-armed "warrior hordes" of an African country became firmly established. This myth and the underestimation of the Ethiopians' fighting power and the will to resist associated with it was later to lead to devastating defeats during Egyptian and Italian attempts to invade Ethiopia.[40] The Ethiopians learned from the defeat at Magdala, which was the first military conflict between their country and a European power and its regular army.[41] Therefore Magdala became a turning point in the military history of Ethiopia.[42] Ethiopian princes and warlords subsequently upgraded their weapons technology and adjusted to new threats on the part of external enemies (chiefly Egyptian and Italian). But above all, they increasingly used modern European weapons in their intra-Ethiopian wars for hegemony. As Wolbert Smidt has explained with some plausibility, in this respect, the Magdala expedition must definitely be assigned a significant importance for the history of Ethiopia, which probably would have developed differently without this intervention—without it, Kassai would presumably not have established himself as the later emperor; without it, Egypt would not have been tempted into making its own recklessly carried out invasion in 1875; and without it, the relationship of the Ethiopian generals to the Europeans as potential partners and opponents would also have been different—in any case, in 1868, Menelik learned a great deal about European weapons potential and afterward transformed what he had learned into an extremely effective policy.[43]

In 1875-1876, Kassai of Tigray, who became emperor Yohannes IV of Ethiopia with the help of British weapons, inflicted several devastating defeats on the Egyptian invasion troops trained and led by European and American officers.[44] Two decades later, Emperor Menelik II soundly defeated the invading Italian army in the famous Battle of Adwa (1896).[45] The defeat at Magdala thus resulted in a very successful collective learning process among the ruling elites of Ethiopia.

If in conclusion we try to sum up the Magdala expedition in its historical context, it can most aptly be described, following the historian of Ethiopia Sven Rubenson, as an operation of liberation and punishment.[46] This apparently offensive military intervention also amounted more to a withdrawal from and a turning away from Ethiopia, since for years after the campaign, England no longer showed any interest in the country.[47] From the British point of view, the Magdala expedition was surely seen at first as a complete success: Tewodros and the Ethiopians—as representatives for other African and Asian peoples—had been "taught a lesson," namely that the European powers had to be respected, and British claims to be a world power had been strengthened with regard to other European colonial powers as well. At the same time, by engaging in a punitive action, the British unintentionally made Tewodros a national martyr. By committing suicide, the Ethiopian emperor, who had long been controversial in his own country, became a symbol of the Ethiopian will to independence with regard to external enemies.[48] The emperor's conduct did not fail to have an effect on some members of the expedition as well: for the German Count Seckendorff, Tewodros was the true "hero of Magdala" who was "worthy of standing beside Abd-el-Kader, and can be counted among the most outstanding figures in the history of Africa."[49] In the same vein, Josef Bechtinger wrote: "Tewodros is a towering figure for his country. He will unquestionably long mark the memories and history of the Abyssinians, and indeed be unforgettable."[50] And Bechtinger was right: in Ethiopia, Tewodros is still considered a national hero, and his battle against the British in Magdala is still considered a heroic act of anti-colonial resistance.

Notes

Introduction
A Curious Campaign

1. Moorehead: *The Blue Nile*, p. 230.
2. Gräber: "Unterwegs in Abessinien," p. 241.
3. Smidt: "Teilnehmer und Beobachter bei der britischen Intervention in Abessinien," p. 225.
4. Pankhurst: *Mäqdäla*, p. 763.
5. Smidt: "Teilnehmer und Beobachter," p. 226.
6. Strebel: "Leben auf dem Missionsfeld," p. 121.
7. Farwell, *Queen Victoria's Little Wars*.
8. For example, in Kohn: *Dictionary of Wars*, p. 155; Dupuy/Dupuy: *The Encyclopedia of Military History*, p. 848 f.; Laffin: *Brassey's Battles*, p. 259.
9. The contemporary understanding of the phrase "small wars" is explained in Colonel Charles Callwell's book *Small Wars*, published in 1896 and at the time widely read.
10. Caulk: Review of Darrell Bates, *The Abyssinian Difficulty*, p. 102; Chandler: "The Expedition to Abyssinia," p. 109.
11. Chandler: "The Expedition to Abyssinia," p. 108.
12. Cf. Debiel: "Souveränität verpflichtet: Spielregeln für den neuen Interventionismus"; Cholet: "Dilemmata der humanitären Intervention," p. 66.
13. Gräber: "Unterwegs in Abessinien," p. 241.
14. Ibid.
15. Cf. Bartnicki/Mantel-Niecko: *Geschichte Äthiopiens*, vol. 1, p. 254 ff., 266 ff.; Guadalupi: *Der Nil. Die Geschichte seiner Entdeckung und Eroberung*, p. 212–233; Volker-Saad/Greve, eds.: *Äthiopien und Deutschland*, p. 284; Smidt: *Äthiopien und Deutschland: 100 Jahre diplomatische Beziehungen*, p. 10 f., 16 f.
16. Cf. Gräber: "Unterwegs in Abessinien"; Strebel: "Leben auf dem Missionsfeld"; Smidt: "Teilnehmer und Beobachter."
17. Gräber: "Unterwegs in Abessinien," p. 242.
18. Cf. Henty: *The March to Magdala*; Kodolitsch: *Die englische Armee in Abyssinien im -Feldzuge 1867–1868*; Markham: *A History of the Abyssinian Expedition*; Rassam: *Narrative of the British Mission to Theodore, King of Abyssinia*; Rohlfs: *Im Auftrage Sr. Majestät des Königs von Preussen mit dem*

Englischen Expeditionscorps in Abessinien; Seckendorff: *Meine Erlebnisse mit dem englischen Expeditionscorps in Abessinien 1867–1868*; Simpson: *Diary of a Journey to Abyssinia, 1868*; Stanley: *Coomassie and Magdala*; Stumm: *Meine Erlebnisse bei der Englischen Expedition in Abyssinien*.
19. Acton: *The Abyssinian Expedition and the Life and Reign of King Theodore*.
20. Holland/Hozier: *Record of the Expedition to Abyssinia*; for a more critical summary, see Hozier: *The British Expedition to Abyssinia*.
21. E.g., Arnold: *Prelude to Magdala*; Myatt: *The March to Magdala*; Bates: *The Abyssinian Difficulty*; Moorehead: *The Blue Nile*.
22. One of the best studies on Ethiopia, which discusses the long-prevailing Eurocentric perspective, is Sven Rubenson's *The Survival of Ethiopian Independence*, published in 1976.
23. Smidt: "Teilnehmer und Beobachter," p. 224.

Chapter 1
Mysterious Ethiopia

1. Matthies: *Kriege am Horn von Afrika*, p. 30.
2. Pankhurst: *The Ethiopians*, p. 143.
3. Loth: "Asien und Afrika im Spiegel der Reiseberichte des 18. und 19. Jahrhunderts," p. 179 f.
4. Dufton: *Narrative of a Journey through Abyssinia in 1862–3*; Krapf: *Travels, Researches and Missionary Labours*; Lefebvre: *Voyage en Abyssinie*; Parkyns: *Life in Abyssinia*; Rochet d'Hericourt: *Reise in das Königreich Schoa*.
5. Henze: *Enzyklopädie der Entdecker und Forscher der Erde*, vol. 3, p. 586.

Chapter 2
Tewodros II Defies Queen Victoria

1. Bahru Zewde: *A History of Modern Ethiopia*, p. 40.
2. Cf. Pankhurst: "Introduction: The British Expedition to Magdala," p. 22–25.
3. Gräber: "Unterwegs in Abessinien," p. 243.
4. Ibid.
5. Hozier: *The British Expedition to Abyssinia*, p. 28-29.
6. Bates: *The Abyssinian Difficulty*, p. 56 f.; Pankhurst: *The Abyssinian Expedition*, p. 24.
7. On the way the British government dealt with Tewodros's letter, cf. Bates: *The Abyssinian Difficulty*, p. 51–66.
8. Northrup: "Ethiopia's Openings to the West, 1306–1974," p. 20.
9. Pankhurst: *The Ethiopians*, p. 151.
10. Gräber: "Unterwegs in Abessinien," p. 245.
11. Ibid., p. 247.

NOTES   181

12. On the details of Tewodros's technological demands, see Bates: *The Abyssinian Difficulty*, p. 76 f.
13. Gräber: "Unterwegs in Abessinien," p. 248.
14. On the prolonged negotiations between England and the Ethiopian emperor, cf. details in Arnold: *Prelude to Magdala: Emperor Theodore of Ethiopia and British Diplomacy*.
15. Cf. Pankhurst: "The Abyssinian Expedition," p. 25.

Chapter 3
The European Hostages

1. Stanley: *Coomassie and Magdala*, p. 136 f.
2. Gräber: "Die befreiten Geiseln Kaiser Tewodros' II," p. 162.
3. Ibid., p. 161 ff.
4. Strebel: "Leben auf dem Missionsfeld," p. 121.
5. Ibid., p. 143, 157.
6. Ibid., p. 133.
7. Schimper: *Meine Gefangenschaft in Abessinien*, p. 295.
8. Gräber: "Die befreiten Geiseln Kaiser Tewodros' II," p. 161.
9. On Schimper's biography, see: *Enzyklopädie der Entdecker und Forscher der Erde*, vol. 4, p. 36 f.; Schimper: *Meine Gefangenschaft in Abessinien*, p. 295 f.
10. Schimper: *Meine Gefangenschaft in Abessinien*, p. 296.
11. Gräber: "Eduard Zander. Abenteurer, Naturforscher, Maler, Architekt und Handwerker in Äthiopien."
12. Andree: *Abessinien, das Alpenland unter den Tropen und seine Grenzländer*, p. 139–157.
13. Pankhurst: "Introduction: The British Expedition to Magdala," p. 164, n. ii-33; Maggs Bros. Ltd.: *From the Abyssinian Expedition to the Mau Mau Insurrection*, p. 10 f.
14. Bates: *The Abyssinian Difficulty*, p. 70 f.; Moorehead: *The Blue Nile*, p. 221.
15. Gräber: "Die befreiten Geiseln Kaiser Tewodros' II," p. 162.
16. Bates: *The Abyssinian Difficulty*, p. 113; Moorehead: *The Blue Nile*, p. 227.
17. Ibid., p. 114.

Chapter 4
The British Empire Prepares for War

1. Bates: *The Abyssinian Difficulty*, p. 86 f.
2. Gräber: "Unterwegs in Abessinien," p. 249.
3. Müller/Pankhurst: *Napier Expedition*, p. 1139.
4. On these debates, cf. Arnold: *Prelude to Magdala*, p. 3 ff., and Pankhurst: "Popular Opposition in Britain to British Intervention against Emperor

Tewodros of Ethiopia," p. 141–203.
5. Bates: *The Abyssinian Difficulty*, p. 81.
6. Pankhurst: "Introduction: The British Expedition to Magdala," p. 14.
7. Hoover: *Victorian War Correspondents G. A. Henty and H. M. Stanley*, p. 39 ff.
8. Bates: *The Abyssinian Difficulty*, p. 79.
9. Hoover: *Victorian War Correspondents G. A. Henty and H. M. Stanley*, p. 127.
10. Kodolitsch: *Die englische Armee in Abyssinien im Feldzuge 1867–1868*, p. 6 f.
11. Rubenson: *The Survival of Ethiopian Independence*, p. 254.
12. Stanley: *Coomassie and Magdala*, p. 16.
13. Chandler: "The Expedition to Abyssinia," p. 115 f.
14. Hozier: *The British Expedition to Abyssinia*, p. 62.
15. Ibid., p. 46-48.
16. Pankhurst: *The Ethiopians*, p. 157.
17. Chandler: "The Expedition to Abyssinia," p. 110; Gräber: "Unterwegs in Abessinien," p. 249.
18. Bartnicki/Mantel-Niecko: *Geschichte Äthiopiens*, Part 1, p. 267.
19. Cf. Harcourt: "Disraeli's Imperialism, 1866–1868: A Question of Timing," p. 87–109, and Rogers: "The Abyssinian Expedition of 1867–1868: Disraeli's Imperialism or James Murray's War?" p. 129–149.
20. Chandler: "The Expedition to Abyssinia,"p. 116.
21. On his biography, see Chandler: "The Expedition to Abyssinia 1867–68," p. 118 f.; Bates: *The Abyssinian Difficulty*, p. 96 f.; Hozier: *Der Britische Feldzug nach Abessinien*, p. 47 ff.; Kodolitsch: *Die englische Armee in Abyssinien im Feldzuge 1867–1868*, p. 4 ff.; Seckendorff: *Meine Erlebnisse*, p. 48 ff.
22. Seckendorff: *Meine Erlebnisse*, p. 48.
23. Hozier: *The British Expedition to Abyssinia*, p. 57.
24. Bates: *The Abyssinian Difficulty*, p. 97.
25. Chandler: "The Expedition to Abyssinia 1867–68," p. 119.
26. Alan Moorehead: *The Blue Nile*, p. 233.
27. Chandler: "The Expedition to Abyssinia 1867–68," p. 118.
28. Hozier: *Der Britische Feldzug nach Abessinien*, p. 52 f.
29. Walter: "Warum Kolonialkrieg?" p. 28 f.
30. Smidt: "Teilnehmer und Beobachter," p. 226.
31. Chandler: "The Expedition to Abyssinia," p. 117.
32. Pankhurst: "The Abyssinian Expedition," p. 25.
33. Pankhurst: "Introduction: The British Expedition to Magdala," p. 15; Pankhurst: "The Abyssinian Expedition," p. 26.
34. Matthies: *Kriegsschauplatz Dritte Welt*, p. 40 f.; cf. Koller: "Von Wilden aller Rassen niedergemetzelt"; Morlang: *Askari und Fitafita."Farbige" Söldner in den deutschen Kolonien.*
35. Pankhurst: "The Abyssinian Expedition," p. 26.

36. Chandler: "The Expedition to Abyssinia," p. 119 f.
37. Ibid., p. 121.
38. Rubenson: *The Survival of Ethiopian Independence*, p. 257 f.; Bates: *The Abyssinian Difficulty*, p. 99 f.
39. Smidt: "Teilnehmer und Beobachter," p. 226.
40. Rubenson: *The Survival of Ethiopian Independence*, p. 257 f.
41. Smidt: "Teilnehmer und Beobachter," p. 226 f.
42. Kodolitsch: *Die englische Armee in Abyssinien im Feldzuge 1867–1868*, p. 20.
43. Stanley: *Coomassie and Magdala*, p. 75.
44. See Stanley: *Coomassie and Magdala*, p. 8 ff.
45. Kodolitsch: *Die englische Armee in Abyssinien im Feldzuge 1867–1868*, p. 28.
46. Hozier: *The British Expedition to Abyssinia*, p. 1.
47. Holland/Hozier: *Record of the Expedition to Abyssinia*, vol. 2, p. 370.
48. Maggs Bros. Ltd.: *From the Abyssinian Expedition to the Mau Mau Insurrection*, p. 9.
49. Beck: *Große Reisende. Entdecker und Erforscher unserer Welt*, p. 209.
50. Ibid., p. 10.
51. Cf. Gräber/Smidt: "Krapf, Johann Ludwig," p. 438.
52. Rohlfs: *Im Auftrage Sr. Majestät des Königs von Preussen*, p. 50, 67.
53. Seckendorff: *Meine Erlebnisse*, p. 116.
54. Bohlander: *World Explorers and Discoverers*, p. 205 f.
55. Moorehead: *The Blue Nile*, p. 233 f.
56. Hozier: *The British Expedition to Abyssinia*, p. 52.
57. Ibid., p. 55.
58. Petermann: "Die neuesten Aufnahmen und Karten von Abessinien," p. 432.
59. Rohlfs: *Im Auftrage Sr. Majestät des Königs von Preussen*, p. vi (Foreword).
60. Rubenson: *The Survival of Ethiopian Independence*, p. 282.
61. Cf. Matthies: *Historische Reisen nach Aksum*, p. 65 f.
62. Kodolitsch: *Die englische Armee in Abyssinien im Feldzuge 1867–1868*, p. 30. Similarly positive remarks are also found in Bechtinger: *Ost-Afrika. Erinnerungen und Miscellen aus dem Abessinischen Feldzuge*, p. 214; Stumm: *Meine Erlebnisse*, p. 20.
63. Müller/Smidt: *Napier Expedition*, p. 1072; on the controversial debate about Munzinger, cf. also Müller/Smidt: "Munzinger, Werner," p. 1070–1073; Henze: *Enzyklopädie der Entdecker und Forscher der Erde*, p. 551–553.
64. Caulk: Review of Darrell Bates: *The Abyssinian Difficulty*, p. 102.
65. Hozier: *The British Expedition to Abyssinia*, p. 59-61.

Chapter 5
A Harbor City Built Overnight

1. Hozier, *The British Expedition to Abyssinia*, p. 65 f.
2. Seckendorff: *Meine Erlebnisse*, p. 22 f.
3. Bechtinger: *Ost-Afrika. Erinnerungen und Miscellen*, p. 19 ff.; cf. also Stumm: *Meine Erlebnisse*, p. 8; Hozier: *Der Britische Feldzug nach Abessinien*, p. 75.
4. Seckendorff: *Meine Erlebnisse*, p. 103 f.
5. Hozier: *The British Expedition to Abyssinia*, p. 100.
6. Seckendorff: *Meine Erlebnisse*, p. 103 f.
7. See Raunig: "Die erste Eisenbahn in Nordostafrika," p. 174.
8. Stumm: *Meine Erlebnisse*, p. 19.
9. Bates: *The Abyssinian Difficulty*, p. 212, n. 1.
10. Seckendorff: *Meine Erlebnisse*, p. 90 f.
11. Hozier: *The British Expedition to Abyssinia*, p. 96.
12. Kodolitsch: *Die englische Armee in Abyssinien im Feldzuge 1867–1868*, p. 149.
13. Bechtinger: *Ost-Afrika. Erinnerungen und Miscellen*, p. 25 f.
14. Kodolitsch: *Die englische Armee in Abyssinien im Feldzuge 1867–1868*, p. 215 f.
15. Stumm: *Meine Erlebnisse bei der Englischen Expedition in Abyssinien*, p. 18.
16. Bechtinger: *Ost-Afrika. Erinnerungen und Miscellen*, p. 25 ff.
17. Stumm: *Meine Erlebnisse*, p. 17.

Chapter 6
Embedded Journalists

1. The only study on this previously neglected aspect of the Magdala expedition is Hoover's dissertation: *Victorian War Correspondents G. A. Henty and H. M. Stanley: The "Abyssinian" Campaign 1867–1868*. On the history of war reporting in general, cf., for example, Daniel, ed.: *Augenzeugen. Kriegsberichterstattung vom 18. bis zum 21. Jahrhundert*; Beham: *Kriegstrommeln. Medien, Krieg und Politik*; Bremm: "Der moderne Krieg und die Anfänge der Kriegsberichterstattung," p. 10–13; Schwarte: *Embedded Journalists. Kriegsberichterstattung im Wandel*; Löffelholz: "Kriegsberichterstattung in der Mediengesellschaft," p. 25–31.
2. Cf. Simpson: *Diary of a Journey to Abyssinia, 1868. With the Expedition under Sir Robert Napier.*
3. Gellen: "Das Auge der Geschichte. Was uns die ersten Kriegsfotografien erzählen," p. 19.
4. On his reporting during the Crimean War and in other wars, see Russell: *Meine sieben Kriege. Die ersten Reportagen von den Schlachtfeldern des neunzehnten Jahrhunderts.*

5. Cf. Rid: "Revolution in Reporting Affairs," p. 295–304.
6. Matthies: *Kriegsschauplatz Dritte Welt*, p. 23 ff.
7. Rohlfs: *Im Auftrage Sr. Majestät des Königs von Preussen*, p. 52.
8. Bechtinger: *Ost-Afrika. Erinnerungen und Miscellen*, p. 112.
9. Ibid., p. 109.
10. Stumm: *Meine Erlebnisse*, p. 69 f.
11. On this and the following, see Hoover: *Victorian War Correspondents G. A. Henty and H. M. Stanley*, p. 2, 4, 135 f.
12. Ibid., p. 104.
13. Stumm: *Meine Erlebnisse*, p. 106.
14. According to Hoover: *Victorian War Correspondents G. A. Henty and H. M. Stanley*, p. 11, 126, 134.
15. Stanley: *Coomassie and Magdala*.
16. Hoover: *Victorian War Correspondents G. A. Henty and H. M. Stanley*, p. 100 ff.

Chapter 7
The Long March to Magdala

1. Kodolitsch: *Die englische Armee in Abyssinien im Feldzuge 1867–1868*, p. 216.
2. Ibid., p. 219.
3. Hoover: *Victorian War Correspondents G. A. Henty and H. M. Stanley*, p. 105.
4. Kodolitsch: *Die englische Armee in Abyssinian im Feldzuge 1867–1868*, p. 205.
5. Ibid., p. 206.
6. Ibid., p. 210.
7. Hozier: *The British Expedition to Abyssinia*, p. 97.
8. Kodolitsch: *Die englische Armee in Abyssinien im Feldzuge 1867–1868*, p. 124.
9. Hozier: *The British Expedition to Abyssinia*, p. 92.
10. Seckendorff: *Meine Erlebnisse*, p. 95.
11. Stumm: *Meine Erlebnisse*, p. 15.
12. Ibid., p. 47.
13. *Kodolitsch: Die englische Armee in Abyssinien im Feldzuge 1867–1868*, p. 164.
14. Seckendorff: *Meine Erlebnisse*, p. 96.
15. Ibid., p. 97.
16. Stumm: *Meine Erlebnisse*, p. 61.
17. Rubenson: *The Survival of Ethiopian Independence*, p. 261.
18. Moorehead: *The Blue Nile*, p. 220.
19. Kodolitsch: *Die englische Armee in Abyssinien im Feldzuge 1867–1868*, p. 98.

20. Chandler: "The Expedition to Abyssinia," p. 134 f.
21. Bates: *The Abyssinian Difficulty*, p. 139 f.
22. Hozier: *The British Expedition to Abyssinia*, p. 86.
23. Stumm: *Meine Erlebnisse*, p. 71.
24. Rohlfs: *Im Auftrage Sr. Majestät des Königs von Preussen*, p. 55.
25. Ibid., p. 106.
26. Ibid., p. 115.
27. Schiffers: *Gerhard Rohlfs*, p. 112.
28. Embacher: *Lexikon der Reisen und Entdeckungen*, p. 250.
29. Rohlfs: *Im Auftrage Sr. Majestät des Königs von Preussen*, p. 53 f.
30. Rohlfs: *Von Magdala nach Lalibela, Sokota und Antalo*, p. 313–324.
31. Henze: *Enzyklopädie der Entdecker und Forscher der Erde*, vol. 4, p. 653.
32. Stumm: *Meine Erlebnisse*, p. 72 f.
33. Rohlfs: *Im Auftrage Sr. Majestät des Königs von Preussen*, p. 78.
34. Stumm: *Meine Erlebnisse*, p. 59.
35. Ibid., p. 58.
36. Hozier: *The British Expedition to Abyssinia*, p. 76-77.
37. Rubenson: *The Survival of Ethiopian Independence*, p. 259 f.; Stanley spoke of "skillfull diplomacy" (*Coomassie and Magdala*, p. 85).
38. The title "Dajazmach" was synonymous with "Prince" and meant literally "Warror at the Gate"; cf. Pankhurst: "Introduction: The British Expedition to Magdala," p. 163, n. ii-18.
39. Bates: *The Abyssinian Difficulty*, p. 168 f.
40. Pankhurst: "Introduction: The British Expedition to Magdala," p. 16.
41. See Matthies: *Kriege am Horn von Afrika. Historischer Befund und friedenswissenschaftliche Analyse*, p. 255 ff.
42. Hozier: *The British Expedition to Abyssinia*, p. 121.
43. Stumm: *Meine Erlebnisse*, p. 34.
44. Hozier: *The British Expedition to Abyssinia*, p.108, 121. On the thoroughly good discipline of the troops, see also Chandler: "The Expedition to Abyssinia," p. 132.
45. Hozier: *The British Expedition to Abyssinia*, p. 108.
46. Stumm: *Meine Erlebnisse*, p. 61.
47. Seckendorff: *Meine Erlebnisse*, p. 99, 118.
48. Stumm: *Meine Erlebnisse*, p. 52, 67 f.
49. Hozier: *The British Expedition to Abyssinia*, p. 121.
50. Ibid., p. 110-119.
51. Ibid., p. 180.
52. Bates: *The Abyssinian Difficulty*, p. 175; Gräber: "Unterwegs in Abessinien," p. 253.

Chapter 8
The Aroge Massacre

1. Chandler: "The Expedition to Abyssinia," p. 136; Bates: *The Abyssinian Difficulty*, p. 170.
2. Bates: *The Abyssinian Difficulty*, p. 174 f.
3. Ibid., p. 177.
4. Chandler: "The Expedition to Abyssinia," p. 137; Bates: *The Abyssinian Difficulty*, p. 172.
5. Bates: *The Abyssinian Difficulty*, p. 167.
6. Ibid., p. 180.
7. Ibid., p. 177.
8. Rohlfs: Im Auftrage Sr. Majestät des Königs von Preussen, p. 157 f.
9. Chandler: "The Expedition to Abyssinia," p. 138 f.; Bates: *The Abyssinian Difficulty*, p. 181.
10. Hozier: *The British Expedition to Abyssinia*, p. 194-195.
11. Bates: *The Abyssinian Difficulty*, p. 184.
12. Stumm: *Meine Erlebnisse*, S. 110 ff.
13. Hozier: *The British Expedition to Abyssinia*, p. 195-196.
14. Bates: *The Abyssinian Difficulty*, p. 184 f.
15. Pankhurst: "Introduction: The British Expedition to Magdala," p. 172, n. 5-2.
16. Rubenson: *The Survival of Ethiopian Independence*, p. 264 and n. 434.
17. Ibid., p. 264.
18. Hozier: *The British Expedition to Abyssinia*, p. 197.
19. Bates: *The Abyssinian Difficulty*, p. 185.
20. Hozier: *The British Expedition to Abyssinia*, p. 199-200.
21. Ibid., p. 200.
22. Stanley: *Coomassie and Magdala*, p. 131; cf. Bates: *The Abyssinian Difficulty*, p. 185.
23. Rubenson: *The Survival of Ethiopian Independence*, p. 264.
24. Hozier: *The British Expedition to Abyssinia*, p. 197-198.
25. On this and the following, see Kodolitsch: *Die englische Armee in Abyssinien im Feldzuge 1867–1868*, p. 77 ff.
26. Bates: *The Abyssinian Difficulty*, p. 182, n. 2.
27. Chandler: "The Expedition to Abyssinia," p. 122.
28. Kodolitsch: *Die englische Armee in Abyssinien im Feldzuge 1867–1868*, p. 80.
29. Chandler: "The Expedition to Abyssinia," p. 122.
30. Bates: *The Abyssinian Difficulty*, p. 183.
31. Kodolitsch: *Die englische Armee in Abyssinien im Feldzuge 1867–1868*, p. 117 ff.
32. Ibid., p. 119.
33. Hozier: *The British Expedition to Abyssinia*, p. 200.

34. Bechtinger: *Ost-Afrika. Erinnerungen und Miscellen*, p. 227. There is a similar observation in Rohlfs: *Im Auftrage Sr. Majestät des Königs von Preussen*, p. 159.
35. Seckendorff: *Meine Erlebnisse*, p. 198.

Chapter 9
The Assault on the Fortress

1. Arnold: *Prelude to Magdala*, p. 319.
2. Pankhurst: "Introduction: The British Expedition to Magdala," p. 17; Arnold: *Prelude to Magdala*, p. 319; Bates: *The Abyssinian Difficulty*, p. 169.
3. Hozier: *The British Expedition to Abyssinia*, p. 203-204.
4. Arnold: *Prelude to Magdala*, p. 322.
5. Ibid., p. 320; Pankhurst: *The Ethiopians*, p. 158.
6. Hozier: *The British Expedition to Abyssinia*, p. 175 f.
7. Pankhurst: *The Ethiopians*, p. 158.
8. Rubenson: *The Survival of Ethiopian Independence*, p. 266.
9. Pankhurst: "The Abyssinian Expedition," p. 27.
10. Hozier: *The British Expedition to Abyssinia*, p. 212-213.
11. On this and the following, see Arnold: *Prelude to Magdala*, p. 323 ff.; Rubenson: *The Survival of Ethiopian Independence*, p. 266 f.; Rubenson: "Meqdela Revisited," p. 16 ff.
12. For instance, according to Arnold: *Prelude to Magdala*, p. 324.
13. Rubenson: "Meqdela Revisited," p. 16.
14. For example, according to Rubenson: *The Survival of Ethiopian Independence*, p. 267, n. 437; Rubenson: "Meqdela Revisited," p. 16.
15. D. Bates: *The Abyssinian Difficulty*, p. 189-191.
16. Rubenson: *The Survival of Ethiopian Independence*, p. 266-67, with all the relevant sources in n. 437, p. 267.
17. Appleyard/Pankhurst: "The Last Two Letters of Emperor Tewodros II of Ethiopia," p. 23-42.
18. Ibid., p. 33.
19. Rubenson: *The Survival of Ethiopian Independence*, p. 267.
20. Chandler: "The Expedition to Abyssinia," p. 144 ff.
21. Stumm: *Meine Erlebnisse*, p. 121.
22. Ibid., p. 122 f.
23. Ibid., p. 124 f.
24. Hozier: *The British Expedition to Abyssinia*, p. 235-236.
25. Pankhurst: "The Abyssinian Expedition: Causes and Consequences," p. 27.
26. Rubenson: *The Survival of Ethiopian Independence*, p. 268.
27. Stumm: *Meine Erlebnisse*, p. 126.
28. Seckendorff: *Meine Erlebnisse*, p. 165.

29. Stanley: *Coomassie and Magdala*, p. 149.
30. Ibid., p. 150, 156.
31. Bates: *The Abyssinian Difficulty*, p. 202; Chandler: "The Expedition to Abyssinia," p. 149.
32. Stanley: *Coomassie and Magdala*, p. 164.
33. Ibid., p. 153 ff., 164, 168 f.
34. Stumm: *Meine Erlebnisse*, p. 127.
35. Rohlfs: *Im Auftrage Sr. Majestät des Königs von Preussen*, p. 171 f.
36. Ibid., p. 177.
37. Stumm: *Meine Erlebnisse*, p. 132.
38. Rohlfs: *Von Magdala nach Lalibela, Sokota und Antalo*, p. 314.
39. Stumm: *Meine Erlebnisse*, p. 119.
40. Stanley: *Coomassie and Magdala*, p. 136.
41. Stumm: *Meine Erlebnisse*, p. 119 f.
42. Gräber: "Die befreiten Geiseln Kaiser Tewodros' II," p. 168.
43. Schimper: *Meine Gefangenschaft in Abessinien*, p. 297.

Chapter 10
The Looting of Ethiopian Cultural Treasures

1. Pankhurst: "Ethiopia, the Aksum Obelisk, and the Return of Africa's Cultural Heritage," p. 230 f.
2. Such actions were recently seen in the context of the latest Gulf War. Cf. Baque: *Räuber und Sammler*, p. 20.
3. Warnke: "Die höhere Moral der Diebe."
4. Frankfurter Rundschau, Nr. 197 vom 25.8.2004: "Hintergrund: Raub von Staats wegen."
5. Müller: *Koloniale Beutekunst*, p. 18 f.
6. "Declaration on the Importance and Value of Universal Museums, December 2002." In *The International Council of Museums (ICOM), ICOM News*, no. 1, 2004, p. 4.
7. Fitschen: "30 Jahre 'Rückführung von Kulturgut'," p. 51.
8. Pankhurst: "Äthiopiens Verbindung zu den Nachbarn in Afrika, Asien und Europa," p. 36.
9. On the following, see Pankhurst: "Ethiopia, the Aksum Obelisk, and the Return of Africa's Cultural Heritage," p. 232 ff.; Pankhurst: "The Napier Expedition and the Loot from Maqdala," p. 233–240; and Pankhurst: "The Removal and Restitution of the Third World's Historical and Culture Objects. The Case of Ethiopia," p. 134–140.
10. Cf. Pankhurst: "The History of an Ethiopian Icon," p. 117–125.
11. House of Commons: *Memorandum Submitted by the Association for the Return of Magdala Ethiopian Treasures (AFROMET), Culture, Media and Sport Committee*, p. 354–358.

12. It is interesting in this connection that the official report on the Magdala expedition states that in taking along valuable Ethiopian (Christian) writings from Magdala, the goal was to save them from the destructive rage of the [Muslim] "Galla"; cf. Holland/Hozier: *Record of the Expedition to Abyssinia*, p. 396.
13. See AFROMET's website for the press conference announcing its foundation on April 13, 1999.

Chapter 11
Orderly Withdrawal

1. Cf. Chandler: "The Expedition to Abyssinia," p. 149.
2. Stanley: *Coomassie and Magdala*, p. 149 f.; Bates: *The Abyssinian Difficulty*, p. 205 f.
3. Hozier: *The British Expedition to Abyssinia*, p. 244.
4. Bates: *The Abyssinian Difficulty*, p. 207 f.
5. Ibid., p. 209.
6. Hozier: *The British Expedition to Abyssinia*, p. 249.
7. Seckendorff: *Meine Erlebnisse*, p. 177 f.
8. Bates: *The Abyssinian Difficulty*, p. 204, n. 1.
9. Ibid., p. 204.
10. Rohlfs: *Im Auftrage Sr. Majestät des Königs von Preussen*, p. 176.
11. Hozier: *The British Expedition to Abyssinia*, p. 251-253.
12. Kodolitsch: *Die englische Armee in Abyssinien im Feldzuge 1867–1868*, p. 207.
13. Bates: *The Abyssinian Difficulty*, p. 210.
14. Hozier: *The British Expedition to Abyssinia*, p. 255.
15. Ibid., p. 258-259.
16. Stanley: *Coomassie and Magdala*, p. 178; Bates: *The Abyssinian Difficulty*, p. 210.
17. Stanley: *Coomassie and Magdala*, p. 178 f.
18. Bates: *The Abyssinian Difficulty*, p. 212; Pankhurst: "Introduction: The British Expedition to Magdala," p. 182 f., n. 9-1; Rubenson: *The Survival of Ethiopian Independence*, p. 275 f.
19. Rohlfs: *Meine Mission in Abessinien*, p. 45.
20. Bahru Zewde: *A History of Modern Ethiopia*, p. 49.
21. Chandler: "The Expedition to Abyssinia," p. 150.
22. Bates: *The Abyssinian Difficulty*, p. 210 f.; Pankhurst: "The Abyssinian Expedition," p. 28.
23. Stumm: *Meine Erlebnisse*, p. 137 f.
24. Ibid., p. 157.
25. Hozier: *The British Expedition to Abyssinia*, p. 256-257.
26. Bechtinger: *Ost-Afrika: Erinnerungen und Miscellen*, p. 234 f.

27. Stumm: *Meine Erlebnisse*, p. 154 f.
28. Bechtinger: *Ost-Afrika. Erinnerungen und Miscellen*, p. 225 f.
29. Gräber: "Eduard Zander. Abenteurer, Naturforscher, Maler, Architekt und Handwerker in Äthiopien," p. 28.
30. Pankhurst: "Introduction: The British Expedition to Magdala," p. 175, n. 6-10; on the Indian elephants that may have been left in Ethiopia, see Smidt: "Teilnehmer und Beobachter," p. 227.
31. Pankhurst: "Introduction: The British Expedition to Magdala," p. 170, n. 2-23.
32. Raunig: "Die erste Eisenbahn in Nordostafrika," p. 177.
33. Seckendorff: *Meine Erlebnisse*, p. 198.
34. Cf. Holland/Hozier: *Record of the Expedition to Abyssinia*, vol. 2, p. 399.
35. Wenig: "Archäologie und Tourismus. Eritrea—ein unerkanntes Eldorado," p. 44.
36. Hozier: *Der Britische Feldzug nach Abessinien*, p. 224.

Chapter 12
The Victors' Triumphal Return to England

1. Hoover: *Victorian War Correspondents G. A. Henty and H. M. Stanley*, p. 34 f., 126.
2. Bates: *The Abyssinian Difficulty*, p. 214 f.; Müller/Pankhurst: "Napier Expedition," p. 1139.
3. Bates: *The Abyssinian Difficulty*, p. 213.
4. Holland/Hozier: *Record of the Expedition to Abyssinia*, vol. 2, p. 370 ff.
5. Petermann: "Die ersten Aufnahmen der Englischen Armee in Abessinien," p. 66.
6. Petermann: "Der Englische Feldzug in Abessinien," p. 184 f.
7. Petermann: "Die ersten Aufnahmen der Englischen Armee in Abessinien," p. 68.
8. Petermann: "Der Englische Feldzug in Abessinien," p. 180.
9. Holland/Hozier: *Record of the Expedition to Abyssinia*, vol. 2, p. 357 ff.
10. Ibid., p. 360.
11. Ibid., p. 359.
12. Gräber: "Unterwegs in Abessinien," p. 242.
13. *The Photographic Journal*, no.193, May 1868, p. 58.
14. James R. Ryan: *Picturing Empire*, p. 92 f.; cited in Maggs Bros. Ltd.: *From the Abyssinian Expedition to the Mau Mau Insurrection*, p. 7.
15. Gräber: "Die befreiten Geiseln Kaiser Tewodros' II," p. 161.
16. Pankhurst/Gerard: *Ethiopia Photographed*, p. 20 f.
17. Ibid., p. 20.
18. Rohlfs: *Im Auftrage Sr. Majestät des Königs von Preussen*, p. 174 f.

19. Pankhurst/Gerard: *Ethiopia Photographed*, p. 21.
20. Ibid., p. 21.
21. Gräber: "Unterwegs in Abessinien," p. 241.
22. Pankhurst/Gerard: *Ethiopia Photographed*, p. 20.
23. Gräber: "Unterwegs in Abessinien," p. 241.
24. Gräber: "Die befreiten Geiseln Kaiser Tewodros' II," p. 160.
25. Simpson: *Diary of a Journey to Abyssinia, 1868. With the expedition under Sir Robert Napier.*
26. Cf. Pankhurst: "The Library of Emperor Tewodros II at Maqdala (Magdala)," p. 14–42, and Pankhurst: "The Mäqdäla Library of Tewodros," p. 223–243.
27. Holland/Hozier: *Record of the Expedition to Abyssinia*, vol. 1, p. 397 f.
28. Pankhurst: "Äthiopiens Verbindung zu den Nachbarn in Afrika, Asien und Europa," p. 36; cf. Pankhurst: "Mäqdäla," p. 764, and Müller/Pankhurst: "Napier Expedition," p. 1139.
29. Phillipson: *Ancient Ethiopia. Aksum: Its Antecedents and Successors*, p. 28 f.
30. Bates: *The Abyssinian Difficulty*, p. 215 ff.
31. Ibid., p. 217.
32. On Speedy's biography, see Southon/Harder: *The Rise and Fall of Basha Felika*.
33. Henze: *Enzyklopädie der Entdecker und Forscher der Erde*, vol. 5, p. 214.
34. Krämer: *Die Entdeckung und Erforschung der Erde*, p. 351 f.
35. Ibid., p. 205, 210.
36. Stumm: *Meine Erlebnisse*, p. 155.
37. Hozier: *The British Expedition to Abyssinia*, p. 256.
38. On the relation between Alamayou and Speedy, see Southon: "Prince Alamayehu and Captain Speedy," p. 251–263.
39. Pankhurst: *A Social History of Ethiopia*, p. 287 f.; Matthies: *Kriege am Horn von Afrika*, p. 215.
40. Pankhurst: *The Ethiopians*, p. 161; Bahru Zewde: *A History of Modern Ethiopia*, p. 49 f.; Chandler: "The Expedition to Abyssinia," p. 150.

Chapter 13
Balance Sheet: Military Intervention without Colonial Occupation

1. Andree: *Abessinien, das Alpenland unter den Tropen und seine Grenzländer*, p. 299.
2. Kodolitsch: *Die englische Armee in Abyssinien im Feldzuge 1867–1868*, p. 111.
3. Cf., for example, Chandler: "The Expedition to Abyssinia," p. 153.
4. Rohlfs: *Im Auftrage Sr. Majestät des Königs von Preussen*, Foreword, p. v; Bechtinger: *Ost-Afrika. Erinnerungen und Miscellen*, p. 236.

5. Andree: *Abessinien, das Alpenland unter den Tropen und seine Grenzländer*, p. 299; similar observations can be found in Kodolitsch: *Die englische Armee in Abyssinien im Feldzuge 1867–1868*, p. 2, and Stumm: *Meine Erlebnisse*, p. 100.
6. On this comparison, see Moorehead: *The Blue Nile*, p. 233 f.
7. Chandler: "The Expedition to Abyssinia," p. 108.
8. Chandler: "The Expedition to Abyssinia," p. 153; Hozier: *Der Britische Feldzug nach Abessinien*, p. 84 f., 109 f., 204 ff.; Stanley: *Coomassie and Magdala*, p. 117.
9. Walter: "Warum Kolonialkrieg?" p. 34 f.
10. Rohlfs: *Im Auftrage Sr. Majestät des Königs von Preussen*, p. 45.
11. Rubenson: *The Survival of Ethiopian Independence*, p. 261.
12. Stumm: *Meine Erlebnisse*, p. 64.
13. Rohlfs: *Im Auftrage Sr. Majestät des Königs von Preussen*, p. 163.
14. Cf. Chandler: "The Expedition to Abyssinia," p. 153; Seckendorff: *Meine Erlebnisse mit dem englischen Expeditionscorps in Abessinien*, p. 202 f.; Kodolitsch: *Die englische Armee in Abyssinien im Feldzuge 1867–1868*, p. 2.
15. Andree: *Abessinien, das Alpenland unter den Tropen und seine Grenzländer*, p. 299.
16. Seckendorff: *Meine Erlebnisse mit dem englischen Expeditionscorps in Abessinien*, p. 82.
17. Stumm: *Meine Erlebnisse bei der Englischen Expedition in Abyssinien*, p. 100.
18. Rubenson: *The Survival of Ethiopian Independence*, p. 261.
19. Rohlfs: *Im Auftrage Sr. Majestät des Königs von Preussen mit dem Englischen Expeditionscorps in Abessinien*, p. 92.
20. Andree: *Abessinien, das Alpenland unter den Tropen und seine Grenzländer*, p. 299.
21. Rein: *Abessinien. Eine Landeskunde nach Reisen und Studien in den Jahren 1907–1913*, p. 190.
22. Kodolitsch: *Die englische Armee in Abyssinien im Feldzuge 1867–1868*, p. 27.
23. Stanley: *Coomassie and Magdala*, p. 177.
24. Bartnicki/Mantel-Niecko: *Geschichte Äthiopiens*, Teil 1, p. 269 f.
25. Bahru Zewde: *A History of Modern Ethiopia*, p. 40.
26. Walter: "Warum Kolonialkrieg?" p. 25 f.
27. Cf., for example, Bahru Zewde: *A History of Modern Ethiopia*, p. 41; Pankhurst: *The Ethiopians*, p. 157; Hozier: *Der Britische Feldzug nach Abessinien*, p. 108; and Rohlfs: *Im Auftrage Sr. Majestät des Königs von Preussen*, Foreword, p. vi.
28. Stumm: *Meine Erlebnisse*, p. 129.
29. See Walter: "Warum Kolonialkrieg?" p. 36 ff.; Neitzel/Hohrath: *Kriegsgreuel. Die Entgrenzung der Gewalt in kriegerischen Konflikten vom Mittelalter bis ins 20. Jahrhundert.*

30. Stumm: *Meine Erlebnisse*, p. 159 f.
31. Bechtinger: *Ost-Afrika: Erinnerungen und Miscellen*, p. 211 f.
32. Bates: *The Abyssinian Difficulty*, p. 213; Seckendorff: *Meine Erlebnisse*, p. 46 f.
33. Strebel: "Leben auf dem Missionsfeld," p. 148 f.; Schimper: "Meine Gefangenschaft in Abessinien," p. 297.
34. Pankhurst: *The Ethiopians*, p. 160 f.
35. Bahru Zewde: *A History of Modern Ethiopia*, p. 41; Pankhurst: *The Ethiopians*, p. 161; "Chandler: "The Expedition to Abyssinia," p. 151; Newell: "A Resounding Defeat?" p. 371; Arnold: *Prelude to Magdala*, p. 326; Rubenson: "Meqdela Revisited," p. 12.
36. This is Seckendorff's assessment: *Meine Erlebnisse*, p. 46; Stumm: *Meine Erlebnisse*, p. 160; Moorehead: *The Blue Nile*, p. 262; Chandler: "The Expedition to Abyssinia," p. 151, 153.
37. Stumm: *Meine Erlebnisse*, p. 160.
38. Chandler: "The Expedition to Abyssinia," p. 153.
39. Hozier: *The British Expedition to Abyssinia*, p.1.
40. Rubenson: *The Survival of Ethiopian Independence*, p. 287; Rubenson: "Meqdela Revisited," p. 14; Chandler: "The Expedition to Abyssinia," p. 153.
41. Tsypkin: *Ethiopia in Anti-Colonial Wars*, p. 310.
42. Matthies: *Kriege am Horn von Afrika*, p. 215.
43. Smidt: "Teilnehmer und Beobachter," p. 225.
44. Matthies: *Kriege am Horn von Afrika*, p. 37 ff.
45. Ibid., p. 62 ff.
46. Rubenson: *The Survival of Ethiopian Independence*, p. 284.
47. Ibid.
48. Pankhurst: *The Ethiopians*, p. 160, n. 36.
49. Seckendorff: *Meine Erlebnisse*, p. 165.
50. Bechtinger: Ost-Afrika. Erinnerungen und Miscellen, p. 189.

Bibliography

Acton, Roger: *The Abyssinian Expedition and the Life and Reign of King Theodore, with Engravings from the Illustrated London News.* London 1868.

Andree, Richard: *Abessinien, das Alpenland unter den Tropen und seine Grenzländer. Schilderungen von Land und Volk vornehmlich unter König Theodoros (1855–1868).* Leipzig 1869.

Arnold, Percy: *Prelude to Magdala. Emperor Theodore of Ethiopia and British Diplomacy.* London 1992.

Ashcroft, A. C.: "As Britain Returns to an Expeditionary Strategy, Do We Have Anything to Learn from the Victorians?" *Defence Studies* 1, 2001.

Baque, Philippe: "Räuber und Sammler." *Le Monde diplomatique*, January 2005, p. 20.

Bartnicki, Andrzej/ Joanna Mantel-Niecko: *Geschichte Äthiopiens*, 2 vols. Berlin 1978.

Bates, Darrell: *The Abyssinian Difficulty: The Emperor Theodorus and the Magdala Campaign 1867–68.* Oxford 1979.

Bechtinger, Josef: *Ost-Afrika. Erinnerungen und Miscellen aus dem Abessinischen Feldzuge.* Vienna 1870.

Beck, Hanno: *Große Reisende. Entdecker und Erforscher unserer Welt.* Munich 1971.

Beham, Mira: Kriegstrommeln. *Medien, Krieg und Politik.* Munich 2006.

Blanc, Henry: *A Narrative of Captivity in Abyssinia.* London 1868.

Bohlander, Richard E. (ed.): *World Explorers and Discoverers.* New York 1998.

Bremm, Klaus-Jürgen: "Der moderne Krieg und die Anfänge der Kriegsberichterstattung." *Militärgeschichte—Zeitschrift für historische Bildung* 3, 2006, pp. 10–13.

Brunold, Georg: "Das Erdenrund und ein Gottesstaat." *Le Monde diplomatique*, May 2008, pp. 12–13.

Campbell, Charles E.: *Small Wars. Their Principles and Practice.* London 1896.

Caulk, Richard A.: "Review of Darrell Bates, *The Abyssinian Difficulty*." *The International Journal of African Historical Studies*, 15, 1982, 1, pp. 101–104.

Chandler, David G.: "The Expedition to Abyssinia 1867–8." In Brian Bond (ed.): *Victorian Military Campaigns.* London 1967, pp. 109–159.

Cholet, Jerome: "Dilemmata der humanitären Intervention." *Entwicklungspolitik* 8–9, 2003.

Crummey, Donald: "The Violence of Tewodros." *Journal of Ethiopian Studies* 9, no. 2, July 1971, pp. 107–125.

Daniel, Ute (ed.): *Augenzeugen. Kriegsberichterstattung vom 18. bis zum 21. Jahrhundert.* Göttingen 2006.

Debiel, Tobias: "Souveränität verpflichtet: Spielregeln für den neuen Interventionismus." *Internationale Politik und Gesellschaft*, 3, 2004, pp. 61– 81.

Dufton, Henry: *Narrative of a Journey through Abyssinia in 1862–3.* London 1867.

Dupuy, R. Ernest/Trevor N. Dupuy: *The Encyclopedia of Military History.* New York/Evanston 1970.

Embacher, Friedrich: *Lexikon der Reisen und Entdeckungen.* Leipzig 1882.

Farwell, Byron: *Queen Victoria's Little Wars.* London 1972.

Fisseha, Girma (ed.): *Äthiopien. Christentum zwischen Orient und Afrika* (Catalog of the Staatlichen Museums für Völkerkunde in Munich). Munich 2002.

Fitschen, Thomas: "30 Jahre 'Rückführung von Kulturgut.'" *Vereinte Nationen*, 2, 2004, pp. 46–51.

Flad, Johann Martin: *Zwölf Jahre in Abessinien oder Geschichte des Königs Theodoros II. und der Mission unter seiner Regierung.* Basel 1869.

Gellen, Adam: "Das Auge der Geschichte. Was uns die ersten Kriegsfotografien erzählen." *Frankfurter Rundschau*, November 5, 2002.

Gräber, Gerd: "Die befreiten Geiseln Kaiser Tewodros II. Aus dem Photoalbum der Royal Engineers 1867/68." *Aethiopica*, 2, 1999, pp. 159–182.

_____: "Eduard Zander. Abenteurer, Naturforscher, Maler, Architekt und Handwerker in Äthiopien—Eine Biographie." *Aethiopica* 8, 2005, pp. 10–28.

_____: "Unterwegs in Abessinien. Das Photoalbum der Royal Engineers und die britische Magdala-Expedition im Jahre 1867/68." In *Alles Wahrheit! Alles Lüge! Photographie und Wirklichkeit im 19. Jahrhundert* (catalog of an exhibit at the Agfa Foto-Historama). Köln 1997, pp. 241–255.

Gräber, Gerd/Wolbert Smidt: "Krapf, Johann Ludwig." In *Encyclopedia Aethiopica*, vol. 3. Wiesbaden 2007, pp. 436–438.

Guadalupi, Gianni: *Der Nil. Die Geschichte seiner Entdeckung und Eroberung.* Erlangen 2001.

Harcourt, Freda: "Disraeli's Imperialism, 1867–68: A Question of Timing." *The Historical Journal* 23, no. 1, 1980, pp. 87–109.

Harrington, Peter: "Introduction: William Simpson (1823–1899)." In *William Simpson: Diary of a Journey to Abyssinia, 1868. With the Expedition under Sir Robert Napier, K.C.p.I. The Diary and Observations of William Simpson of the Illustrated London News.* Ed. with commentary by Richard Pankhurst. Hollywood, CA, 2002, pp. 26–37.

Hassert, Kurt: *Die Erforschung Afrikas.* Leipzig 1941.

Hein, Ewald/Brigitte Kleidt: *Äthiopien—christliches Afrika: Kunst, Kirchen und Kultur.* Ratingen 1999.

Henty, George Alfred: *The March to Magdala.* London 1869.

Henze, Dietmar: *Enzyklopädie der Entdecker und Forscher der Erde.* 5 vols. Graz 1978–2004.

Holland, Thomas/Henry Montague Hozier: *Record of the Expedition to Abyssinia, compiled by order of the Secretary of State for War*, 2 vols. London 1870.
Hoover, Nora K.: "Victorian War Correspondents G. A. Henty and H. M. Stanley: The 'Abyssinian' Campaign 1867–1868" (dissertation). Florida 2005.
House of Commons: *Memorandum Submitted by the Association for the Return of Magdala Ethiopian Treasures (AFROMET), Culture, Media and Sport Committee* (Seventh Report on Cultural Property: Return and Illicit Trade) 3, London 2000, pp. 354–358.
Hozier, Henry M.: *Der Britische Feldzug nach Abessinien. Aus officiellen Aktenstücken.* Berlin 1870.
_____: *The British Expedition to Abyssinia.* London 1869.
Junge, Peter/Silke Sybold: *Bilder aus Äthiopien. Malerei und Fotografie 1900– 1935* (Übersee-Museum Bremen). Bremen 2002.
Kayser, Kurt (ed.): *Die berühmten Entdecker und Erforscher der Erde.* Köln s.d.
Klein, Thoralf/Frank Schumacher (eds.): *Kolonialkriege. Militärische Gewalt im Zeichen des Imperialismus.* Hamburg 2006.
Kodolitsch, Theodor von: *Die englische Armee in Abyssinien im Feldzuge 1867– 1868.* Vienna 1869.
Kohn, George C.: *Dictionary of Wars.* New York/Oxford 1986.
Koller, Christian: "Von Wilden aller Rassen niedergemetzelt." Stuttgart 2001.
Krämer, Walter (ed.): *Die Entdeckung und Erforschung der Erde.* 8th ed. Leipzig 1976.
Krapf, Johann Ludwig: *Travels, Researches and Missionary Labours during an Eighteen Year Residence in Eastern Africa.* London 1860 (German trans.: *Reisen in Ostafrika ausgeführt in den Jahren, 1837–1855.* Stuttgart 1858).
Laffin, John: *Brassey's Battles.* London 1986.
Lefebvre, Theophile: *Voyage en Abyssinie*, 6 vols. Paris 1845–1848.
Löffelholz, Martin: "Kriegsberichterstattung in der Mediengesellschaft." *Aus Politik und Zeitgeschichte* 16–17/2007, pp. 25–31.
Loth, Heinrich: "Asien und Afrika im Spiegel der Reiseberichte des 18. und 19. Jahrhunderts." In Wolfgang Griep (ed.): *Sehen und Beschreiben. Europäische Reisen im 18. und frühen 19. Jahrhundert* (Eutiner Forschungen, vol. 1). Heide 1991, pp. 179–184.
Maggs Bros. Ltd.: *From the Abyssinian Expedition to the Mau Mau Insurrection. 100 Years of Military and Naval Operations in Eastern and North-Eastern Africa (1860s–1960s). Books, Maps, Artifacts, Artwork, Photographs, Manuscripts, Articles, Pamphlets and Ephemera from the Africana Library of Humphrey Winterton, Catalog 1343.* London 2003.
Markham, Clements Robert: *A History of the Abyssinian Expedition.* London 1869.
Matthies, Volker: *Historische Reisen nach Aksum. Europäische Entdecker und Forscher beschreiben das antike Zentrum der äthiopischen Kultur.* Berlin 2003.
_____: *Kriege am Horn von Afrika. Historischer Befund und friedenswis-*

senschaftliche Analyse. Berlin 2005.

_____: *Kriegsschauplatz Dritte Welt*. Munich 1998.

Moorehead, Alan: *The Blue Nile*. Harmondsworth 1983.

Morlang, Thomas: *Askari und Fitafita. "Farbige" Söldner in den deutschen Kolonien*. Berlin 2008.

Mountfield, David: *A History of African Exploration*. London 1976.

Müller, Bernard: "Koloniale Beutekunst." *Le Monde diplomatique* July 2007, pp. 18–19.

Müller, C. Detlef G./Richard Pankhurst: "Napier Expedition." In *Encyclopedia Aethiopica*, vol. 3. Wiesbaden 2007, pp. 1137–1139.

Müller, C. Detlef G./Wolbert Smidt: "Munzinger, Werner." In *Encyclopedia Aethiopica*, vol. 3. Wiesbaden 2007, pp. 1070–1073.

Myatt, Frederick: *The March to Magdala: The Abyssinian War of 1868*. London 1970.

Napier, Henry Dundas: *Field Marshal Lord Napier of Magdala*. London 1927.

Neitzel, Sönke/Hohrath, Daniel (eds.): *Kriegsgreuel. Die Entgrenzung der Gewalt in kriegerischen Konflikten vom Mittelalter bis ins 20. Jahrhundert*. Paderborn 2008.

Newell, Jonathan: "A Resounding Defeat? The Shangant and Mbemb Engagements of the Anglo-Ndebele War and the Adwa Campaign: A Comparative Study." In Ahmad, Abdussamad H./Richard Pankhurst (eds.): *Adwa. Victory Centenary Conference 26 February–2 March 1996*. Institute of Ethiopian Studies. Addis Ababa 1998.

Nomachi, Kazuyoshi: *Äthiopien: geheimnisvolles Land zwischen Blauem Nil und Rotem Meer*. Munich 1998.

Northrup, David: "Ethiopia's Openings to the West, 1306–1974." In Frederic A. Sharf, (ed.): *Abyssinia, 1867–1868: Artists on Campaign. Ethiopia through the Eyes of a British Military Expedition*. Hollywood, CA, 2003, pp. 16–21.

Pankhurst, Richard: *A Social History of Ethiopia*. Addis Ababa 1990.

_____: "Äthiopiens Verbindung zu den Nachbarn in Afrika, Asien und Europa." In Girma Fisseha (ed.): *Äthiopien. Christentum zwischen Orient und Afrika* (catalog of the Staatlichen Museums für Völkerkunde in Munich). Munich 2002, pp. 26–39.

_____: "Detached Ethiopian Illustrated Manuscripts Folios from Maqdala." In Walter Raunig/Asfa Wossen Asferate (eds.): *Orbis Aethiopicus* (*Beiträge zu Geschichte, Religion und Kunst Äthiopiens*, vol 10). Lublin 2007, pp. 185–191.

_____: "Ethiopia, the Aksum Obelisk, and the Return of Africa's Cultural Heritage." *African Affairs* 98, 1999, pp. 229–239.

_____: "Introduction: The British Expedition to Magdala: Its Causes and Consequences." In *William Simpson: Diary of a Journey to Abyssinia, 1868. With the Expedition under Sir Robert Napier, K.C.p.I. The Diary and Observations of William Simpson of the Illustrated London News*. Ed. with commentary by

Richard Pankhurst. Hollywood, CA, 2002, pp. 5–25.

———: "Mäqdäla." In *Encyclopedia Aethiopica*, vol. 3. Wiesbaden 2007, pp. 763– 765.

———: "Popular Opposition in Britain to British Intervention against Emperor Tewodros of Ethiopia (1867–1868)." *Ethiopia Observer* 16, 1973, pp. 141– 203.

———: "The Abyssinian Expedition: Causes and Consequences." In Frederic A. Sharf (ed.): *Abyssinia, 1867–1868: Artists on Campaign. Ethiopia through the Eyes of a British Military Expedition*. Hollywood, CA, 2003, pp. 22–29.

———: *The Ethiopians. A History*. Oxford 2001.

———: "The Napier Expedition and the Loot from Magdala." *Présence Africaine* 133–134, 1985, pp. 233–240.

———: "The Removal and Restitution of the Third World's Historical and Cultural Objects. The Case of Ethiopia." *Development Dialogue* 1–2, 1982, pp. 134–140.

———: "Two Unpublished 19th Century Ethiopian Letters: From Emperor Tewodros to Sir Robert Napier, and from Däggazmao to Naib Hasan Bey." *Aethiopica* 11, 2008, pp. 61-67.

Pankhurst, Richard/Denis Gerard: *Ethiopia Photographed. Historic Photographs of the Country and Its People Taken between 1867 and 1935*. London/New York 1996.

Pankhurst, Rita: "The Library of Emperor Tewodros II. at Mäqdäla." *Bulletin of the School of Oriental and African Studies* 36, no. 1, 1973, pp. 14–42.

———: "The Mäqdäla Library of Tewodros." In Taddesse Beyene/Richard Pankhurst/Shiferaw Bekele (eds.): *Kasa and Kasa: Papers on the Lives, Times and Images of Tewodros II and Yohannes IV (1855–1889)*. Addis Ababa 1990, pp. 223–243.

Parkyns, Mansfield: *Life in Abyssinia: Being Notes Collected during Three Years' Residence and Travels in That Country*. London 1853.

Petermann, August: "Der Englische Feldzug in Abessinien." *Petermann's Geographische Mitteilungen* 14, no. 5, 1868, pp. 180–181.

———: "Die ersten Aufnahmen der Englischen Armee in Abessinien, November 1867 bis Januar 1868." *Petermann's Geographische Mitteilungen* 14, no. 1, 1868, pp. 66–68.

———: "Die neuesten Aufnahmen und Karten von Abessinien." *Petermann's Geographische Mitteilungen* 13, no. 11, 1867, pp. 432–433.

Phillipson, David W.: *Ancient Ethiopia. Aksum: Its Antecedents and Successors*. London 1998.

Pöppinghege, Rainer (ed.): *Tiere im Krieg. Von der Antike bis zur Gegenwart*. Paderborn 2009.

Rassam, Hormuzd: *Narrative of the British Mission to Theodore, King of Abyssinia*. 2 vols. London 1869.

Raunig, Walter: "Die erste Eisenbahn in Nordostafrika." In Stefan Brüne/Heinrich Scholler (eds.): *Auf dem Weg zum modernen Äthiopien* (Festschrift for Bairu Tafla). Münster/Berlin 2005, pp. 173–179.

Raunig, Walter (ed.): *Das christliche Äthiopien. Geschichte—Architektur—Kunst*. Regensburg 2005.

Raupp, Werner (ed.): *Johann Ludwig Krapf. Reisen in Ostafrika, ausgeführt in den Jahren 1837–1855* (unrevised reprinting of the book that originally appeared in 1858). Münster/Hamburg 1994.

Rein, Gustav K.: *Abessinien. Eine Landeskunde nach Reisen und Studien in den Jahren 1907–1913*, vol. 1. Berlin 1918.

Rid, Thomas: "Revolution in Reporting Affairs. Der Krimkrieg und seine Bedeutung für die Geschichte der Kriegsberichterstattung." *Österreichische Militärische Zeitschrift* 3, 2003, pp. 295–304.

Rochet d'Hericourt, Charles E. Xavier: *Reise in das Königreich Schoa im mittäglichen Abyssinien während der Jahre 1842, 1843 und 1844*. Stuttgart 1847.

Rogers, Nini: "The Abyssinian Expedition of 1867–1868: Disraeli's Imperialism or James Murray's War?" *The Historical Journal* 27, no. 1, 1984, pp. 129–149.

Rohlfs, Gerhard: *Im Auftrage Sr. Majestät des Königs von Preussen mit dem Englischen Expeditionscorps in Abessinien*. Bremen 1869.

———: *Meine Mission nach Abessinien*. Leipzig 1883.

———: "Von Magdala nach Lalibela, Sokota und Antalo, April/Mai 1868." *Petermann's Geographische Mitteilungen* 14, no. 9, 1868, pp. 313–324.

Rubenson, Sven: "Alämayyähu Tewodros." In *Encyclopedia Aethiopica*, vol. 1. Wiesbaden 2003, pp. 189–190.

———: "Meqdela Revisited." In Taddese Beyene/Richard Pankhurst/Shiferaw Bekele (eds.): *Kasa and Kasa: Papers on the Lives, Times and Images of Tewodros II and Yohannes IV (1855-1889)*. Addis Ababa 1990, pp. 11–21.

———: *The Survival of Ethiopian Independence* (Lund Studies in International History 7). London 1976.

Rubenson, Sven (ed.): "Internal Rivalries and Foreign Threats, 1869-79." *Acta Aethiopica* 3, Addis Ababa-Lund-New Brunswick, NJ, 2000.

Rubenson, Sven (ed.): "Tewodros and His Contemporaries, 1855-1868." *Acta Aethiopica* 2, Lund-Addis Ababa 1994.

Russell, William Howard: *Meine sieben Kriege. Die ersten Reportagen von den Schlachtfeldern des neunzehnten Jahrhunderts*. Frankfurt a. M. 2000.

Schiffers, Heinrich: "Gerhard Rohlfs, 1831–1896." In Kurt Kayser (ed.): *Die berühmten Entdecker und Erforscher der Erde*. Köln s.d., pp. 112–113.

Schimper, G. H. Wilhelm: "Meine Gefangenschaft in Abessinien." *Petermann's Geographische Mittheilungen* 14, no. 8, 1868, pp. 294–298.

Schwarte, Kristina Isabel: *Embedded Journalists. Kriegsberichterstattung im Wandel*. Münster 2007.

Seckendorff, G. Graf von: *Meine Erlebnisse mit dem englischen Expeditionscorps*

in Abessinien 1867–1868. Potsdam 1869.
Sharf, Frederic A.: *Abyssinia, 1867–1868: Artists on Campaign. Ethiopia through the Eyes of a British Military Expedition*. Hollywood, CA, 2003.
Simons, Peter: *Entdeckungsreisen in Afrika*. Braunschweig 1984.
Simpson, William: *Diary of a Journey to Abyssinia, 1868. With the Expedition under Sir Robert Napier, K.C.p.I. The Diary and Observations of William Simpson of the Illustrated London News.* Ed. and commentary by Richard Pankhurst. Hollywood, CA, 2002.
Smidt, Wolbert: *Äthiopien und Deutschland. 100 Jahre Diplomatische Beziehungen*. Addis Ababa 2005.
_____: "Teilnehmer und Beobachter bei der britischen Intervention in Abessinien 1867/68 nach dem österreichischen Beobachter k.u.k. Major Kodolitsch." In Witold Witakowski/Laura Lykowska (eds.): *Wälätta Yohanna. Ethiopian Studies in Honour of Joanna Mantel-Niecko on the Occasion of the 50th Year of Her Work at the Institute of Oriental Studies*. Warschau 2006, pp. 224–254.
Southon, Jean: "Prince Alamayehu and Captain Speedy." *Proceedings of the Eleventh International Conference of Ethiopian Studies*, vol. 1. Addis Ababa 1994, pp. 251–263.
Southon, Jean/Robert Harder: *The Rise and Fall of Basha Felika: Captain Speedy. His Life and Times*. Penzance 2004.
Stanley, Henry Morton: *Coomassie and Magdala: The Story of Two British Campaigns in Africa*. London 1874.
Stern, Henry: *The Captive Missionary: Being an Account of the Country and People of Abyssinia*. London 1868.
Stern, Henry: *Wanderings among the Falashas in Abyssinia*. London 1862.
Strebel, Barbara: "Leben auf dem Missionsfeld. Chrishona-Pilgermissionare in Äthiopien (1856–1868)." *Aethiopica* 4, 2001, pp. 121–157.
Stumm, Ferdinand Freiherr von: *Meine Erlebnisse bei der Englischen Expedition in Abyssinien, Januar bis Juni 1868*. Frankfurt a. M. 1868.
Tsypkin, Georgii Viktorovich: *Ethiopia in Anti-Colonial Wars*. Moskau 1988.
Volker-Saad, Kerstin/Anna Greve (eds.): *Äthiopien und Deutschland. Sehnsucht nach der Ferne*. Munich/Berlin 2006.
Waldmeier, Theophil: *Erlebnisse in Abessinien in den Jahren 1858–1868 von Theophil Waldmeier, Pilgermissionar.* Basel 1869.
Walter, Dierk: "Warum Kolonialkrieg?" In Thoralf Klein/ Frank Schumacher (eds.): *Kolonialkriege. Militärische Gewalt im Zeichen des Imperialismus*. Hamburg 2006, pp. 14–43.
Warnke, Martin: "Die höhere Moral der Diebe." *Die Zeit* April 24, 2003.
Wenig, Steffen: "Archäologie und Tourismus. Eritrea—ein unerkanntes Eldorado." *EINS Entwicklungspolitik* 2–3, 2007, pp. 43–44.
Zewde, Bahru: *A History of Modern Ethiopia, 1855–1974*. London 1991.

Index of Geographical Names

The entries refer primarily to the regions of the Ethiopian empire in 1867-1868 in which the Magdala expedition was conducted; alternate spellings are indicated in parentheses. Because it appears so often in the text, Magdala is not included in the index.

Adabagi 93
Addis Ababa xvii, 119, 123, 138-140, 161, 167
Adigrat (Adigerat, Atigerath) 73, 78, 89, 96, 100, 160
Adulis 61, 80, 153, 157
Adwa (Adowa, Adua) 22, 23, 48, 82, 98, 151, 160, 168, 178
Aksum xvi, 2, 5, 84, 153, 160, 162
Axum 48
Ankober 45
Annesley Bay 53, 54, 57, 65, 77, 112, 160
Antalo 38, 73, 77-79, 82, 84, 85, 89, 96, 100, 148, 150, 160
Aroge (Arogi) xv, 105-109, 111-114, 118, 141
Ashangi, Lake 82

Bashilo River (Baschilo, Beschilo) 105
Begemeder 22
Bogosland 12, 47, 157

Debra Tabor 8, 9, 20, 78
Deresge 23
Diab 93, 99

Fahla (Fala) 105-107, 109, 110, 124

Gafat 20, 22, 24
Garadigdig 82
Gondar 2-5, 7, 9, 10, 14, 45, 158
Gorgora 23
Gunna-Gunna (Gunnagunna) 82

Hawzen (Hauzzein) 89, 93, 101

Keren 47
Kumayli (Komayloo) 54, 57, 73, 151
Kumayli Pass (Koomaylo Pass) 41, 54
Kwara 7

Lalibela 84, 160
Lasta 88, 100, 142, 168

Massawa (Massaua, Massowah) 9, 10, 13, 22, 38, 41, 43, 47-49, 53, 152, 158, 160, 163
Messino 82
Mulkutoo (*see* Zula) 53

Salamge (Islamgee) 105, 124
Santara 89
Selassie (Selasse, Selassieh) 5, 45, 105, 106, 110, 124, 138
Semien 166
Senafe 41, 54, 73, 77, 100, 148-150, 160
Shelikut (Tscheliku) 85
Shoa (Königreich) 45, 164
Sokota 84
Suru Pass 151

Takkazie 150
Talanta 144
Tana, Lake (Lake Tana) 7, 23, 45
Tigray (Tigre) 1, 5, 22, 48, 77, 82, 84, 88, 89, 93, 94-98, 100, 138, 142, 148, 164, 168, 172, 174, 177

Zula (Zulla, Zoulla) 48, 51, 53-58, 60, 61, 73, 78, 80, 144, 147, 149-151, 153-155, 160, 171

Index of Names of Persons

Because they appear so often in the text, Tewodros II and Robert Napier have not been included in this index.

Abd-el-Kader 172, 178
Abdul Kadir 154
Acton, Roger 161
Adare, Lord (correspondent) 63
Alamayou (Prince) 141, 160, 165, 166, 168
Alame (Prince) 115
Alexander the Great 44
Anderson (Lieutenant) 159
Andree, Richard 172, 173
Annesley, George (Lord Valentia) 5, 53
Arnold, Percy xxiii
Austin, Charles 63

Baigrie (Major) 161
Bailey, Henry 139
Baker, Samuel 44
Bardel (French adventurer) 24
Barth, Heinrich 83
Bates, Darrell xxiii
Bechtinger, Josef 54, 58, 169, 178
Beck, Hanno 45
Beke, Charles T. 44
Bell, John 9, 103
Bender, Christian Friedrich 19
Bennet, James Gordon 164
Blanc, Henry 15
Blanford, William T. 44, 157
Brehm, Alfred 157
Bruce, James 5, 46
Budge, Ernest 162

Cameron, Charles Duncan 10
Caulk, Richard xxiii, 49
Chamberlain (officer) 11, 107, 109
Clapperton (African traveler) 83
Cook, Dr. (meteorologist) 44, 157
Cooke, A. C. 158

Cortez, Hernán 157
D'Abbadie, Antoine 162
D'Héricourt, Rochet 5
Da Gama, Christopher 4
Dillmann, August 162
Disraeli, Benjamin 28, 34
Dufton, Henry 5
Dunford, C. W. 139

Edward VII 138
Elizabeth II 138

Fasilides (Emperor) 2
Flad, Martin 20, 45, 115

Gabriye, Fitawrawi (Gabri Fit-aurari) 106
Gladstone, William 28
Gobaze (Gobase), Wagshum 88, 89, 96, 142
Goodfellow (officer) 153
Gordon, Charles George 35
Gräber, Gerd xix, xxii, 19, 161
Gran, Ahmad 2
Grant, James Augustus 46
Granville (Earl) 138

Hall, Katharina 152
Hall, Magdalena 152
Hall, Moritz 105
Harris, William Cornwallis 45, 56
Harrold, John 159
Henry, George A. 63, 69
Heuglin, Theodor von 47, 157
Hitler, Adolf 135
Holland, Thomas xxiii
Holmes, Richard 44, 84, 138, 145, 153, 157
Hozier, Henry Montague 175, 177

Ingeda (Prince) 120
Jesse, W. 44, 157
Johannes IV (see Kassai, Prince of Tigray) 164

Kassai (Kassa) (Prince of Tigray) 3, 7, 23, 88, 89, 93-102, 138, 142, 148, 149, 164, 168, 172, 174, 177
Kerans (hostage) 152
Kielmannsegg, Count 43
Kienzlen, Johann Gottlieb 19
Kirkham, J. C. 148
Kitchener, Horatio Herbert 35
Kodolitsch, Theodor von xxiii, 43, 169
Krämer, Walter 165
Krapf, Johann Ludwig xxiii, 5, 42, 45

Layard, Austin 23
Lebeck, Robert 161
Lefebvre, Théophile 5
Livingstone, David 71, 164
Lumsdaine, Dr. (staff physician) 148

Makonnen, Tafari 138
Markham, Clements Robert 44
Mashesha (Gobaze's representative) 89
Masteeat (Queen) 88, 160
Maximilian (Archduke) 27
Meier (missionary craftsman) 21
Mendes, Alonzo 158
Menelik II 138, 168, 177
Merewether, William 15, 29, 41, 47
Meux, Valorie 138
Meyer, Johannes 19
Moorehead, Alan xix, xxiii, 35, 46
Munzinger, Joseph 47
Munzinger, Werner xxiii, 45, 47, 88, 145, 162, 163
Myatt, Frederick xxiii

Nachtigal, Gustav 83
Napoleon III 27
Napoleon Bonaparte xxii, 44, 135, 170

Pankhurst, Richard xv, xxiii, 31, 33, 104, 119, 123, 135, 138, 139, 160, 161
Parkyns, Mansfield 5
Petermann, August 47, 157
Phayre, Robert 37, 41, 47
Plowden, William C. 9

Prideaux, W. F. 15
Rassam, Hormuzd xxiii, 15, 23, 24, 163
Raunig, Walter 153
Ravenstein, E. G. 158
Rein, Gustav Adolf 173
Rohlfs, Gerhard xviii0, 45, 67, 82, 83, 106, 129, 130, 145, 148, 160, 164, 169, 172, 173
Rosenthal (missionary aide) 13, 152
Rowlands, John (see Stanley, Henry Morton) 69, 70
Rubenson, Sven xviii, 47, 119, 123, 167, 173, 178
Rüppel, Eduard 5
Russell, William Howard 66
Ryan, James 160

Saalmüller (missionary craftsman) 21, 107, 110
Salama, Abuna 13, 45
Salt, Henry 5, 46
Schimper, Wilhelm xviii, 19, 21, 133, 176
Seckendorff, Graf G. von xxiii, 35, 34, 46, 54-57, 77, 113-114, 128, 133, 144-145, 153, 172, 178
Selassie, Haile 138
Selassie, Sahle 5, 45
Shepherd, Alex 63
Simpson, William xviii, 63, 80, 84, 161
Smidt, Wolbert 41, 177
Speedy, Tristram Charles Sawyer (Captain Speedy) 41
Speke, John Hanning 46
Stanley, Henry Hope 69, 71
Stanley, Henry Morton 19, 41, 63, 69, 70, 139, 155, 164
Stavely, Charles 55
Stern, Henry Aaron 13, 24, 161
Stumm, Freiherr Ferdinand von 43, 57, 60, 67-68, 70, 77, 82, 84-85, 90-92, 109, 124-126, 128, 130, 132-133, 145, 149-151, 165, 172-176

Terunesh (Tewodros's second wife) 165

Ubie (Prince) 22
Ustinov, Plato von 153
Ustinov, Sir Peter 153

Victoria (Queen of England) xvi, xix, xxi,
  7, 9, 11, 13, 15-17, 23, 24, 46, 135,
  138, 140, 148, 166-168, 173
Vogel, Eduard 47
Waldmeier, Theophil 19
Walter, Dierk 37
Wenig, Steffen 153
Werkait (Queen) 88, 141
Werque, Mircha 89
Whiteside, W. Owen 63
Webe (Prince) 23
Wilkins (Lieutenant Colonel) 53
Wright, W. 162

Zander, Eduard xxiii, 21, 23, 105, 145,
  152
Zawditu Empress) 138
Zewde, Bahru xxiii, 174

About the Authors and Translator

VOLKER MATTHIES is on the faculty of the Institute of Political Science at the University of Hamburg, with a specialization in peace and conflict research. For many years, he was co-editor of the *Jahrbuch Dritte Welt (The Third World Almanac)*. He has written many books and articles on peace and conflict issues and on the region known as the Horn of Africa.

RICHARD PANKHURST (Foreword) is the leading scholar in and about Ethiopia. In 1962, Dr. Pankhurst founded the Institute of Ethiopian Studies at the University of Addis Ababa and was its first director. Pankhurst has coauthored 22 books and has edited or compiled 17 books on Ethiopia. In addition, he has written more than 400 scholarly articles about Ethiopian history, culture, and tradition that have appeared in numerous academic journals, magazines, and newspapers throughout the world.

STEVEN RENDALL (translation) is professor emeritus of Romance Languages at the University of Oregon and the author of numerous books and articles about French and European literature. He is also editor emeritus of *Comparative Literature* and has translated over 50 books and 50 articles from French and German. Rendall was awarded both the National Jewish Book Society's Sandra Brand and Arik Weintraub Award and the Modern Language Association's Scaglione Prize.

www.ingramcontent.com/pod-product-compliance
Lightning Source LLC
Chambersburg PA
CBHW020946230426
43666CB00005B/193